A Shabbat Reader
Universe of Cosmic Joy

· A ·
SHABBAT
READER

Universe
of Cosmic Joy

Edited with an Introduction by

DOV PERETZ ELKINS

UAHC PRESS ✦ NEW YORK

To Jamie and Abby,
who bring so much love and warmth
to our Shabbat table.
May the joy of the Sabbath bring ever new
depth and richness to your loving relationship
and to your tender and deep commitment
to each other.
You have given so much pride to us
and to so many others.

Copyright © 1998 by Dov Peretz Elkins

Acknowledgment of permission to reprint previously
published material may be found on pp. v-viii.

Library of Congress Cataloging–in–Publication Data

A Shabbat reader: universe of cosmic joy / edited by Dov Peretz
Elkins.
p.   cm.
Includes bibliographical references.
ISBN 0–8074–0631–7 (pbk. : alk. paper)
1. Sabbath   I. Elkins, Dov Peretz
BM685.S4186   1997
296.4 ' 1—dc21   97–13469
                                               CIP

This book is printed on acid-free paper
Manufactured in the United States of America
10 9 8 7 6 5 4 3 2 1

Acknowledgments

The author gratefully acknowledges the following for permission to reprint previously published material:

JASON ARONSON, INC.: Excerpts from *Out of the Depths I Call to You:A Book of Prayers for the Married Jewish Woman,* edited by Nina Beth Cardin (Northvale, NJ: Jason Aronson, Inc., 1992). Copyright © 1992 by Jason Aronson, Inc. Reprinted by permission of Jason Aronson, Inc.

CHANA BELL: "Shechinah" by Chana Bell. First published in *Women Speak to God:The Prayers and Poems of Jewish Women,* edited by Marcia Cohn Spiegel and Deborah Lipton Kremsdorf (San Diego, CA: Woman's Institute for Continuing Jewish Education, 1987). Reprinted by permission of Chana Bell.

B'NAI B'RITH HILLEL FOUNDATIONS: "Law as Living Discipline: The Sabbath as Paradigm" by Norman E. Frimer, from *Tradition and Contemporary Experience,* edited by Alfred Jospe (New York: Schocken Books, 1970). Reprinted by permission of the B'nai B'rith Hillel Foundations, Inc.

GEORGES BORCHARDT: "A Niggun for Shabbat" by Elie Wiesel. All rights reserved. Reprinted by permission of Georges Borchardt, Inc., for the author. Adapted from an address to the Fortieth General Assembly of the Council of Jewish Federations and Welfare Funds, Pittsburgh, PA, November 31, 1971.

CROSSROAD PUBLISHING CO.: "The Place of the Sabbath in Rabbinic Judaism" by Robert Goldenberg and "A Jewish Theology and Philosophy of the Sabbath" by Walter S. Wurzburger, from *The Sabbath in Jewish and Christian Traditions,* edited by Tamara C. Eskenazi; Daniel J. Harrington, S.J.; and William H. Shea. Copyright © 1991 by the University of Denver (Colorado Seminary). Reprinted by permission of the Crossroad Publishing Co., New York, NY.

DOUBLEDAY: Excerpts from *This Is My God* by Herman Wouk. Copyright © 1959 by the Abe Wouk Foundation, Inc. Reprinted by permission of Doubleday, a division of Bantam Doubleday Dell Publishing Group, Inc.

AMY EILBERG: "The Serenity of the Shabbat Walk" by Amy Eilberg. First published in the *Har Zion Bulletin* (February 1989). Reprinted by permission of Amy Eilberg.

MARCIA FALK: English translation of "Light a Candle" by Zelda, translated from the Hebrew by Marcia Falk. Translation copyright © 1980 by Marcia Lee Falk. First published in *Women Speak to God:The Prayers and Poems of Jewish Women,* edited by Marcia Cohn Spiegel and Deborah Lipton Kremsdorf (San Diego, CA: Woman's Institute for Continuing Jewish Education, 1987). Reprinted by permission of Marcia Falk.

GAVRIEL AND PAMELA GOLDMAN: "Shabbat on Middle Mountain" by Gavriel and Pamela Goldman. First published in *Hadassah Magazine* (October 1994). Copyright © 1994 by Gavriel and Pamela Goldman. Reprinted by permission of Gavriel and Pamela Goldman.

SYLVIA GREEN: Excerpt from *Sex, God and the Sabbath* by Alan S. Green. Reprinted by permission of Sylvia Green.

HENRY HOLT AND CO: Excerpt from *The Forgotten Language: An Introduction to the Understanding of Dreams, Fairy Tales, and Myths* by Erich Fromm. Copyright © 1951, 1979 by Erich Fromm. Reprinted by permission of Henry Holt and Company, Inc.

INTERNATIONAL UNIVERSITIES PRESS: Excerpt from *Life Is with People* by Mark Zborowski and Elizabeth Herzog. Copyright © 1952 by International Universities Press, Inc. Reprinted by permission of International Universities Press, Inc.

JEWISH CHRONICLE: "The Home Where Warmth Rules over Technology" by Jonathan Sacks. First published in the *Jewish Chronicle.* Copyright © 1986 by the *Jewish Chronicle,* London. Reprinted by permission of the *Jewish Chronicle,* London.

JEWISH LIGHTS PUBLISHING: "Praising the Work of Valiant Women" by Amy Bardack and "A Family Sabbath: Dreams and Reality" by Sue Levi Elwell from *Lifecycles,* vol. 1: *Jewish Women on Life Passages and Personal Milestones,* edited by Debra Orenstein (Woodstock, VT: Jewish Lights Publishing, 1994); "Challah" and "Seudat Mitzvah" by Ron Wolfson from *The Shabbat Seder* by Ron Wolfson. Copyright © 1985 by the Federation of Jewish Men's Clubs. Reprinted by permission of Jewish Lights Publishing.

MICHAEL S. KOGAN: "Kingdom Present" by Michael S. Kogan. Copyright © 1990 by Michael S. Kogan. Reprinted by permission of Michael Kogan.

ILANA NAVA KURSHAN: "Sleeping through Sunrise" by Ilana Nava Kurshan. Copyright © 1998 by Ilana Nava Kurshan. Used by permission of Ilana Nava Kurshan.

LAWRENCE KUSHNER: "Thinking Shabbat" by Lawrence Kushner. First published in *Reform Judaism* (Spring 1984). Reprinted by permission of Lawrence Kushner.

MIDSTREAM: "The Meaning of the Sabbath" by Jerome Braun. First published in *Midstream* (Aug./Sept. 1996), 32: 32–33. Reprinted by permission of *Midstream*.

PUTNAM PUBLISHING GROUP: Excerpt from *Jewish Renewal* by Michael Lerner. Copyright © 1994 by Michael Lerner. Reprinted by permission of the Putnam Publishing Group.

RECONSTRUCTIONIST MAGAZINE: "Shabbat" by Arthur Waskow. First published in the *Reconstructionist Magazine* (April–May 1986). Reprinted by permission of the *Reconstructionist Magazine*.

RUTGERS UNIVERSITY PRESS: Excerpt from *The Nakedness of the Fathers: Biblical Visions and Revisions* by Alicia Suskin Ostriker. Copyright © 1994 by Alicia Suskin Ostriker. Reprinted by permission of Rutgers University Press.

SANDY EISENBERG SASSO: "First a Spark" by Sandy Eisenberg Sasso. Used by permission of Sandy Eisenberg Sasso.

SCHOCKEN BOOKS: Excerpt from *On the Kabbalah and Its Symbolism* by Gershom Scholem. English translation copyright © 1965 by Schocken Books, Inc. Reprinted by permission of Schocken Books, published by Pantheon Books, a division of Random House, Inc.

ISMAR SCHORSCH: "Tending to Our Cosmic Oasis" by Ismar Schorsch. First published in the *Melton Journal* (Spring 1991). Copyright © 1991 by Ismar Schorsch. Reprinted by permission of Ismar Schorsch.

MAHLIA LYNN SCHUBERT: English translation of "Prayer for Sabbath" by Chana Katz, translated from the Yiddish by Bertha Held and Mahlia Lynn Schubert. First published in *Women Speak to God:The Prayers and Poems of Jewish Women,* edited by Marcia Cohn Spiegel and Deborah Lipton Kremsdorf (San Diego, CA: Woman's Institute for Continuing Jewish Education, 1987). Reprinted by permission of Mahlia Lynn Schubert.

HAROLD M. SCHULWEIS: "Serenity Lost" by Harold M. Schulweis. First published in *Reform Judaism* (Spring 1998). Reprinted by permission of Harold M. Schulweis.

DANNY SIEGEL: "Erev Shabbas" from *Unlocked Doors* by Danny Siegel. Reprinted by permission of Danny Siegel.

SIMON AND SCHUSTER: Excerpts from *Turning East* by Harvey Cox, copyright © 1977 by Harvey Cox, and *How to Run a Traditional Jewish Household* by Blu Greenberg, copyright © 1983 by Blu Greenberg. Reprinted by permission of Simon and Schuster, Inc.

SYRACUSE UNIVERSITY: "The Sabbath as Protest" by W. Gunther Plaut. From *Tradition and Change in Jewish Experience,* edited by A. Leland Jamison. B. G. Rudolph Lecture Series, Syracuse University, Department of Religion, 1978. Reprinted by permission of Syracuse University.

TIMES BOOKS: Excerpt from *The Search for God at Harvard* by Ari L. Goldman. Copyright © 1991 by Ari L. Goldman. Reprinted by permission of Times Books, a division of Random House, Inc.

NAHUM M. WALDMAN and THE WOMEN'S LEAGUE FOR CONSERVATIVE JUDAISM: "To Kindle the Sabbath Lights" by Nahum M. Waldman. First published in *Outlook Magazine* (Summer 1973). Copyright © 1973 by the Women's League for Conservative Judaism. Reprinted by permission of Nahum M. Waldman and the Women's League for Conservative Judaism.

ARNOLD JACOB WOLF: "Reclaiming Shabbat" by Arnold Jacob Wolf. First published in *Reform Judaism* (Fall 1983). Reprinted by permission of Arnold Jacob Wolf.

WOMAN'S INSTITUTE FOR CONTINUING JEWISH EDUCATION: Excerpts from *On Our Spiritual Journey: A Creative Shabbat Service.* Copyright © 1984 by the Woman's Institute for Continuing Jewish Education. Reprinted by permission of the Woman's Institute for Continuing Jewish Education, San Diego, CA.

Contents

II ◆ Shabbat as the Ultimate Mitzvah

III ◆ Jews Celebrate Shabbat

Preface

As one who grew up in a Jewish home that made no distinction between Shabbat and the rest of the week, I came to love Shabbat not because of demands pressed on me by tradition, family, or community but from sheer need. Once I discovered Shabbat, through youth groups and Jewish summer camp experiences, I found that my life would be bereft without it.

Observing and loving Shabbat now for four decades, I find it has become an increasingly significant part of my life. The ancient rabbis described Shabbat as a bride. In my own personal experience of Shabbat, I consider her to be a loving part of my family, an indispensable member of my small circle of intimate companions.

I cannot imagine getting through a week without looking forward to the healing balm that Shabbat brings to my soul after six days of the routine and mundane. I came to the practice and study of Judaism in the 1950s, mainly because the life my family and I were living until that time was mostly without moments of transcendence. Not only was holiness the exception in my lifestyle, I knew of no way to access holiness even after having experienced it in those rare and precious moments when it came.

My love of Shabbat developed and led me to be a constant reader on the various layers of meaning, on the subtle nuances of perspectives, on the ways in which my ancestors and my contemporaries have seen and experienced Shabbat. Out of that wide exploration emerged a desire to bring together in one place some of the major ideas that propel this holy day into its position of prominence in modern Jewish life.

The essays and articles in this anthology come from a broad spectrum of individuals, each with their own particular vision. The pieces are reprinted as they originally appeared, with the addition of occasional explanatory phrases. Styles of transliteration have generally been preserved, excluding words that have entered the English language, such as challah and mitzvah. Language that is not gender-neutral has not been changed.

I would like to express gratitude to the following people at UAHC Press who have worked with me on this project over a period of several years: David Kasakove, Ellen Nemhauser, Elyn Wollensky, and Bennett Lovett-Graff. Seymour Rossel was the first to see the value of the book and envision its usefulness as a reader for individuals as well as in adult education classes. Thanks to Dr. Ralph Simon of Cleveland, Ohio, Jewish librarian par excellence, who helped with the juvenile section of the annotated bibliography, and to Roslyn Vanderbilt, children's librarian at the Jewish Center of Princeton, who updated it. I am also grateful to the members of my congregation, The Jewish Center, Princeton, New Jersey, who have listened to my ideas about Shabbat observance and helped to reinforce my commitment to Shabbat as a gateway to Jewish living. Helen Schlaffer has been of invaluable assistance for the past five years at The Jewish Center in making my life and work reasonable enough to allow me to complete this book in the little spare time I managed to find. My beloved wife, Maxine, has been a support and companion in all things I do. The editor expresses profound humility and gratitude to the Creator, to the Torah and the Fourth Commandment, where it all began.

Dov Peretz Elkins
Princeton, NJ

Introduction:
Shabbat as Universe, as Cosmic, as Joy

Why Is Shabbat a Universe?

When Friday evening comes, the world of the Jew who observes Shabbat is transformed. This is because Shabbat is a state of being that brings a new level of consciousness. Shabbat's demands are not limited to rituals, prayers, or prohibitions against this or that activity. To fully experience Shabbat requires us to transport ourselves to a new place, yet a place we must return to week after week, as if our visit there the previous week had not happened. It is in this sense alone that Shabbat is a Universe where we have never set foot before and must go to again and again.

In the Universe of Shabbat, a person finds everything new, different, more elevated and exalted. All one's physical, emotional, and spiritual being is given over to this newly discovered Universe. We enter Shabbat, the day on which God rested from the work of creation, "with all our heart, all our soul, and all our might." Concerns of the secular workaday world are not part of this Universe and may be ignored.

Those who observe Shabbat experience something strange and unique. They feel as though they are entering a place that is forever new. For the truly pious, Shabbat is seen not as a holiday of requirements and prohibitions but rather as one of opportunities. While some of these opportunities arise from commandments in the Torah, they are never seen as demands by those who carry them out.

Shabbat is not measured by the number of things one can or cannot, should or should not do. Of course the Jew who observes Shabbat will not go into the office to catch up on unfinished work, but that decision not to go to the office is not merely because work is prohibited on Shabbat. That decision is also based on the understanding that Shabbat is our one chance to devote a full day to activities that uplift and inspire. Thoughts of how to acquire more authority, prestige, or material goods are foreign to this day. On Shabbat, we cease from our daily labor not because we do not love it but because our ancestors have taught us that there are other tried-and-true ways to exalt the spirit. These include resting our minds and bodies, enjoying time with family and friends, preparing, serving, and eating festive meals, and engaging in prayer, meditation, and study.

Shabbat is a paradox. The Universe of Shabbat seems to last forever, in part because we never want it to end. At the same time, Shabbat, which according to the ancient rabbis is a foretaste of the world-to-come, is the completion and climax of time. But Shabbat is most like the sea, ebbing and flowing through time itself. Shabbat is with us even when it is "officially" over. When the Shabbat Queen departs, we ceremonially bid her farewell and wait another six days until she visits again. But while we wait, we luxuriate in the holiness that follows in her passage. And as we enter that other, "secular" universe, her sweetness lingers, diminishing until the middle of the week when we sense her approach and feel her holy light growing as she draws nearer.

Shabbat Is Cosmic

Like the holy city of Jerusalem, Shabbat, too, has an earthly reality and a heavenly counterpart. Our ancestors who could not reach the earthly Jerusalem lived daily with the hope and dream of reaching a heavenly Jerusalem. This hope and dream was expressed in their every prayer and utterance. This dual aspect is also true of Shabbat.

Living in the Universe of Shabbat is like living in a city whose inhabitants are—each and every one—angelic and divine. On Shabbat, we recognize that while we are physically here on earth, our mind and soul occupy a different space. In the Universe of Shabbat, there is an ethereal, mystical, heavenly aura to everything that takes place.

On Shabbat we flip a special switch within our consciousness, a switch that lets us relocate ourselves in a place where we have more control over ourselves and our surroundings. In the Universe of Shabbat no outsider commands our heart or spirit. In the secular world, we are too often at the beck and call of our bosses and coworkers, clients and customers. We have busy schedules to keep; we must be careful about what we say and how we speak, how we dress and with whom we eat. But in the Universe of Shabbat, the only ones to whom we have to answer are ourself and God.

In the Universe of Shabbat we are transported to a place of dreams, to an idealized world. Our mind's eye sees people anew, people living in peace and harmony with good will toward one another, filled with love for their families, friends, and neighbors. In this protected atmosphere there is no room for strife or anxiety, for competition or overreaching. The only desire expressed is to help, to reach out, to heal, to love. On Shabbat, we live as if under a canopy stretched tight by God's love, the wings of the *Shekhinah* hovering over us with an extra measure of warmth and affection.

With no time pressures, deadlines, bills to pay, or projects to complete, we are free to turn our attention to what uplifts our spirit and opens our heart. The great ideas of the centuries become our topics of conversation and the search for truth our only intellectual pursuit. Where an argument arises, it is in the spirit of discussion that brings no animosity in its train. We debate in peace, for egotism has no place on this day of rest.

In the Universe of Shabbat, we walk only to look at the trees and the birds, to listen to the sounds of the wind or the rain, to gaze from the top of hills or the bottom of valleys, to smell the fragrance of flowers and marvel at their varied beauty. The irony of the Native American saying "The white man wears his god on his wrist" points up how Shabbat shields us from the idolatry of the working week. On Shabbat time is marked off not in minutes or hours but in periods of prayer, study, eating, and lovemaking.

Though no one has ever returned from Heaven to describe it, we all know what is meant when we characterize a symphony or a painting or a poem as "heavenly." Of all things, Shabbat is the most heavenly—it is Heaven itself, the perfected Universe of Heaven—experienced on earth.

Shabbat as a Universe of Cosmic Joy

Shabbat joy is not to be compared to frivolous enjoyment or moments of laughter. It is rather a mood of satisfaction and contentment. It is the spiritual joy of having found meaning and purpose in God's exalted world. It is the recognition on some modest level of what our Creator wants of us during our brief life on earth.

Shabbat joy is the highest kind of joy there is. It is the joy of a mother giving birth, an artist painting on the canvas, the teacher watching a pupil grasp a difficult subject. It is the joy of having achieved something different and unusual—the joy of working as God's partner in making the world better today than it was yesterday.

Cosmic joy is indescribable yet palpable. It opens the heart, it touches the nerve endings, it stirs the deepest possible emotion. Whoever experiences this kind of joy may not always be happy in the conventional sense. Sometimes this joy coexists with struggle and strain, with care and worry. But it remains joy about matters that inhabit the highest heights of the universe. For such high matters, it is a sublime joy and unparalleled privilege to be able to struggle and strive.

Because there is more time on Shabbat—for music, for poems and prayers, for being alone and being together in community—the joy of Shabbat is more evident. The structure of time and activities on Shabbat—the special meals, synagogue services, study sessions alone or with others—all contribute to a sense of inner joy, the kind of joy for which life was created.

The joy of God's love is central to the Universe of Shabbat. We know we are here on earth because a benevolent Supreme Being brought us here, a Being that constantly offers us protection and love. On Shabbat we have more time to sing of God's love, of God's unity, of the connectedness of all God's creatures—human, animal, vegetable—to one another.

It is easier on Shabbat to reach a higher consciousness because the restrictions and opportunities of Shabbat work together to make it possible. We have fewer choices on Shabbat and thus more freedom. Unlike our working week, during which our choices are dictated to us, the restriction to put aside workaday responsibilities on Shabbat allows us a freedom to choose that we do not often exercise. The beauty of Shabbat's traditions, explored and explained by the men and women whose thoughts and recollections of Shabbat have been gathered here, offers us a renewed understanding of the endless possibilities of Shabbat.

Those who welcome Shabbat, entering the Universe of Cosmic Joy that it represents, embark on a quest for greater richness and beauty, for larger responsibilities and more opportunities to change and expand, to learn and to grow, to mature in mind and soul. Those who live one day out of seven in the Universe of Cosmic Joy feel the security of being part of an everlasting covenant. In celebrating Shabbat, they imitate God who rested after creation. They also enlarge the circle of people whom they love and from whom they receive love. In such joy, God's goodness is all around them.

This most precious of days is a priceless gift that our people has treasured for over thirty centuries. By kindling lights, singing, and drinking wine to proclaim God's sanctification of this special day, we partake of the creation of our Divine Partner. We feel closer to our Torah, the written testimony of God's love for us, because on this special day we hear the Torah chanted aloud and pore over its text with a loving attention and singular devotion to each word, each letter, each moment of proximity to a new idea.

In the Universe of Shabbat it is our obligation and our privilege to search for *menuchah*, God's gift of spiritual rest. On Shabbat we have ample occasion to thank God for this blessing, both from the words of the Siddur (prayer book) and from the spontaneous expression of our hearts. God has sanctified a special segment of time, for which Israel, God's children, sanctifies God's name. Together, Israel and its Creator celebrate the treasured gift of this day.

Values Inherent in Shabbat

I have often been asked to summarize what Shabbat brings to those who are privileged to observe it. If we accept Ahad Ha'am's observation that the Shabbat has kept the Jewish people more than they have kept Shabbat, we should be able to list in clear language for the contemporary Jew the ways in which Shabbat enriches and enhances the daily life of its faithful observers.

Keeping Shabbat brings dignity to our life

Our lives too often lack humanity. How many times have we felt like robots endlessly repeating the same tasks? We listen to our boss, do our work, carpool the kids, check our computerized calendars, run from meeting to meeting, party to party, and event to event. One day stop and look at the people waiting for a commuter train and you'll see what's wrong with how we live. Peer closely and you'll notice the blank, sometimes bitter, look on their faces. Even the people I see early in the morning when I take my daily walk around the block look harried and unhappy as they drive by in their Mercedes or Cadillac to their office, talking into their cellular phone.

Shabbat reminds us that we are not slaves but free people—free to choose a life of sanctity and specialness. Our goal in life should not be that of running on a self-created treadmill, trying to catch up with those ahead and stay in front of those behind.

My colleague Rabbi Samuel Dresner has written:

> The real purpose of life is not to conquer nature but to conquer the self; not to fashion a city out of a forest but to fashion a soul out of a human being; not to build bridges but to build human kindness; not to learn to fly like a bird or swim like a fish but to walk on the earth like a man; not to erect skyscrapers but to establish mercy and justice; not to manufacture an ingenious technical civilization but to be holy in the midst of unholiness. The real tasks are to learn how to remain civilized in the midst of insanity; how to retain a share in man's dignity in the midst of the Dachaus and Buchenwalds, how to keep the mark of Cain from obscuring the image of the divine, how to fashion a home of love and peace, how to create children obedient and reverent, how to find the strength to perform the mitzvot, how to bend our will to God's will.

With Rabbi Dresner, I, too, believe life's purpose is "to learn how to remain civilized in the midst of insanity."

Shabbat offers us a way to keep Jewishness in our home, family, and personal life

In ancient times the Greeks accused Jews of being lazy because they did not work every seventh day. To the ancient Greeks such a practice was sinful. Even today, according to most sociologists, the pattern of work among Americans is the legacy of the "Protestant work ethic." Like the ancient Greeks, too many Americans still believe that taking a day off from work is a sign of laziness or lack of ambition.

But the glory of ancient Greece is gone, while the Jewish people has survived. Work by itself does not preserve a people, faith does. Ahad Ha'am was right to remind us of Shabbat's role in preserving the Jewish people. For Shabbat has been, and still is, our portable sanctuary. Shabbat is like a home that we never leave, restoring to us our own sense of ourselves as Jews, even when we are not among other Jews. Consider the case of Chaim Nachman Bialik, as described by Pinchas Peli:

> Chaim Nachman Bialik, Hebrew poet laureate of the twentieth century, tells a beautiful story of how his family when cruelly deported from its home in Tsarist Russia found itself desolately and aimlessly wandering in a forest. Suddenly, his mother realized that it was Friday afternoon and as sunset was approaching, she immediately pulled out from somewhere two little candles, lit them, covered her face to recite the blessing over the Sabbath and all at once [Bialik said] "We were back home again." Between the stars flickering above and the Sabbath candles flickering below, they no longer felt uprooted and ashamed. While probably realizing subconsciously that the Sabbath was bound inevitably to come to an end, they were, for the time being, in a peaceful, serene (and Jewish) home. (Pinchas Peli, *Shabbat Shalom*, p. 81)

Shabbat gives us a set of values and imposes a template of meaning on our life

Shabbat is special not merely because of the time it offers us to relax and reflect. It also gives our conversations a moral framework for talking deeply and without disturbance about the things that matter: honesty, truth, justice, fairness, transcendence. The opportunity to discuss these issues and others is itself framed around the weekly *sidrah* (Torah portion). By discussing the *sidrah* on Shabbat, we rediscover weekly the link between thought and ethics. On Shabbat not only are we required to think about how we should conduct ourselves, but we have the *time* to think about our conduct as well. This time to read the *sidrah* and discuss with its help what it means to be and do good is what transforms Shabbat from just another holiday to a holy day.

My late, beloved teacher, Rabbi Abraham Joshua Heschel, once asked: If God could make beautiful mountains and flowing rivers, stately trees and green meadow, the sunrise and the sunset, why did the Almighty not create for us Jews—God's chosen people—a sanctuary, a place of peace and prayer? Heschel's answer was that God did create a sanctuary. But it was a sanctuary in *time*, not in *space*. Where most other religions sanctified space, Judaism sanctified *time*. Only time and people are holy; *things* in themselves cannot be holy in the deepest sense of the word. For to make physical objects holy is to transform them into a fetish.

The Shabbat, wrote Heschel, is our sanctuary in time. The Shabbat reminds us that we are adherents to a faith that sanctifies time instead of space, that favors *being over doing,* that prefers loving people to using them. All of this is what Shabbat teaches us.

Shabbat is deeply healing to the psyche

We can reach that deep plane of true inner peace only when our mind is at ease and our ego firm. Consider the Shabbat law that forbids us from worrying on the Sabbath day. When the Bible dictated that we finish all our work in six days and rest on the seventh, the rabbis asked, How can we really finish all our work in six days? Surely there will be more work next week! But to this objection the rabbis already knew the answer. As they reasoned, of course we cannot finish all of our work within a week, but on Shabbat we must act and think as *if* all of our work had been completed. We cannot concern ourselves about what has been left unfinished, for such thoughts only disturb our Shabbat *menuchah* (Sabbath rest).

Some years ago a popular song by Bobby McFerrin called "Don't Worry, Be Happy" rose to the top of the record charts. Millions of copies of the record that included the song were sold. Why? Because McFerrin had reminded people—people who spend all their time worrying about their work, their families, their finances, and much else—to let go, to relax, to be happy. We all need a day of the week like Shabbat, a day when we can give ourself permission to smell the flowers, look at the trees, play with our children, converse quietly with our spouse, exchange stories with our neighbors, and enjoy the fruits of God's glorious creation.

So on Shabbat we are not allowed to worry. If the letter carrier brings us bills on Shabbat, we are not supposed to open them. If the lawn needs mowing or the fence needs mending, we leave them be. If we have an un-solved problem at work, we leave it there Friday afternoon, where it will no doubt be waiting for us Monday morning.

There is a story told by Herman Wouk, the author of *The Winds of War, War and Remembrance,* and other best-selling novels, about his cele-brating Shabbat. In his autobiographical *This Is My God,* he describes the magical transformation that occurs as he leaves the tense atmosphere of a Broadway production about to premiere for the Shabbat-mandated quiet comforts of home. Wouk's description of that transformation in time and feeling should serve as a reminder to us of Shabbat's true value:

> Friday afternoon, during these rehearsals, inevitably seems to come when the project is tottering on the edge of ruin. I have sometimes felt guilty of treason, holding to the Sabbath in such a desperate sit-uation. But then, experience has taught me that a theater enterprise almost always is in such a case. Sometimes it does totter to ruin, and sometimes it totters to great prosperity, but tottering is its nor-mal gait, and cries of anguish are its normal tone of voice. So I have reluctantly taken leave of my colleagues on Friday afternoon and rejoined them on Saturday night. The play has never yet collapsed in the meantime. When I return I find it tottering as before, and the anguished cries as normally despairing as ever. My plays have en-countered in the end both success and failure, but I cannot hon-estly ascribe either result to my observing the Sabbath.
>
> Leaving the gloomy theater, the littered coffee cups, the jumbled scarred-up scripts, the haggard actors, the shouting stagehands, the bedeviled director, the knuckle-gnawing producer, the clattering typewriter, and the dense tobacco smoke and backstage dust, I have come home. It has been a startling change, very like a brief re-turn from the wars. My wife and my boys, whose existence I have almost forgotten in the anxious shoring up of the tottering ruin, are waiting for me, gay, dressed in holiday clothes, and looking to be marvelously attractive. We have sat down to a splendid dinner, at a table graced with flowers and the old Sabbath symbols: the burning candles, the twisted loaves, the stuffed fish, and my grandfather's silver goblet brimming with wine. I have blessed my boys with the ancient blessing; we have sung the pleasantly syncopated Sabbath table hymns. The talk has had little to do with tottering ruins. My

wife and I have caught up with our week's conversation. The boys, knowing that the Sabbath is the occasion for asking questions, have asked them. The Bible, the encyclopedia, the atlas have piled up on the table. We talk of Judaism, and there are the usual impossible boys' queries about God, which my wife and I field clumsily but as well as we can. For me it is a retreat into restorative magic.

Saturday has passed in much the same manner. The boys are at home in the synagogue, and they like it. They like even more the assured presence of their parents. In the weekday press of schooling, household chores, and work—and especially in a play-producing time—it often happens that they see little of us. On the Sabbath we are always there, and they know it. They know too that I am not working and that my wife is at her ease. It is their day.

It is my day, too. The telephone is silent. I can think, read, study, walk, or do nothing. It is an oasis of quiet. When night falls, I go back to the wonderful nerve-racking Broadway game. Often I make my best contribution of the week then and there to the grisly literary surgery that goes on and on until opening night. My producer one Saturday night said to me, "I don't envy you your religion, but I envy you your Sabbath."

Shabbat is a time for family

We must remember that the flame of the Jewish family is easily extinguished. One moment it brings warmth, beauty, and light into our homes and our lives; the next moment, it can be gone, leaving us hollow and desolate. All it takes is a brief moment of neglect or a cold blast of indifference to snuff out the beautiful light of the flame of the Jewish family. At this crucial moment in Jewish history, when assimilation is rampant, the warming fire of the Jewish family is in our hands. It is ours to nurture, protect, and preserve. And it is our responsibility to keep it burning brightly!

Of course there are many opportunities during the six other days of the week to strengthen the bonds of family. But there is no other day on which family bonding is so ritualized, regularized, institutionalized, and thus easily carried out, as on Shabbat.

As with all worthy ideals, such as reading, exercising, losing weight, or visiting our aging uncle in a nursing home, what is less important often squeezes out of our tight schedule what is more important. Only by making our family a priority and building into the cluttered rooms of our life a space for lingering in ease and quiet with loved ones will the ideal of a strongly bonded family have a possibility to be created. Shabbat is such a time. If we avoid scheduling every minute and hour of our day, there is hope that large segments of time will be available for the most important people in our life. By celebrating Shabbat, the Jewish family finds—and will find again and again—within the island of peace that Shabbat creates, the strength that keeps the family together.

Shabbat helps to redeem society

A gentile reporter, after her first visit to Israel, published the following observation in a popular fashion magazine:

> The official beginning of the Sabbath is at sunset the previous evening, and a notice in the paper tells exactly what time it is. After you've been through a few of them you can see why. They don't just close the stores; they shut down the whole city. Now that I'm used to it, I'm all for it and think if they'd shut down the whole world one day a week, we wouldn't be in the mess we're in. (*Vogue,* July 1969, p. 11)

How right this reporter was! Just look at our modern automated society. Our lives seem crazed, our priorities confused, our days rushed, our fears and anxieties many, our families broken, our citizens addicted to alcohol, nicotine, and drugs, and our days crippled by fear of crime and violence. Even in our quiet, wealthy suburbs, murder and rape seem to intrude themselves into our living rooms through the television set and VCR, if not in reality. Sometimes I wonder what we would discover if we surveyed our modern Jewish suburbs and compared the number of burglar alarms installed on the doors of Jewish homes to the number of mezuzot attached to their doorposts.

In *The Rise and Fall of the Roman Empire,* Edward Gibbon argued that the barbarian hordes who invaded Rome were less responsible for the Roman Empire's collapse than the perversion of its citizens' values and the internal decay of its once glorious institutions. Of all the rituals and values that have guarded us, none has done so more than Shabbat.

The Jewish home and Shabbat have always been a fortress to defend us from the perverted values of the outside world. When we gave up Shabbat, we broke down the walls that separated us from that hedonistic and materialistic reality. Now, we too contribute to the scourge of juvenile delinquency, white-collar crime, divorce, alcoholism, and drug abuse. We once had a higher immunity to these societal diseases. Is it possible that the celebration of Shabbat could restore that immunity?

If we look at the rising tide of intermarriage that has inundated the modern Jewish community, that too was once stemmed by our observance of Shabbat. How did Shabbat keep the floodwaters at bay? By creating for our children a set of beautiful memories that shaped their sense of identity and Jewish self-worth. Through these memories, our children also receive the gift of courage to select a mate who shares those memories and the values that they represent.

I have been a rabbi now for over thirty years, and I have had many parents bring their son or daughter into my study and plead with me to convince their child not to date or marry a non-Jew. After a few minutes of conversation the young person turns to his or her parents and says:

"Why now? Why all of a sudden do you care about my bringing home a Jewish girl? Why, while I was growing up, was it okay to go shopping on Saturday and never make Kiddush or light Shabbat candles, to ignore all standards of Jewish observance, to promise me I could quit Hebrew school the day after my bar mitzvah? Why now do you want me to become the pious Jew that you never were and bring home a Jewish spouse? Why should I do that? What heritage did you give me that I must preserve by raising Jewish grandchildren for you?"

This summary account of what I've witnessed in my own offices is not invented. These encounters occur in the private chambers of rabbis all around this country.

And how does this story end? What happens to the parents and their child? Sometimes the ending is not a terribly happy one. Too often the child marries a non-Jew, leaving his or her Judaism behind and re-creating the secular household of his parents. Sometimes the child follows the prompting of his or her parents and rabbi and meets and marries another Jew. And sometimes the child marries a non-Jew, who not only converts but becomes a better Jew than that child's parents ever were, exposing the xenophobic parochialism that had been disguised as piety.

Shabbat brings to our lives a spiritual feeling that cannot be duplicated in the workaday world

Welcoming the Shabbat *kallah* (bride) to our home Friday evening, attending synagogue, reciting the Havdalah service as Shabbat comes to a close—these weekly Jewish experiences are the foundation stones upon which a spiritual fortress is built and an impregnable sanctuary formed that protects our children. Where our children do not find this fortress in their religion, where they find neither roots nor values, direction nor spirituality, where they find, ultimately, no Jewishness, they may look to drugs, drink, or cults for their anchor.

In following God's commandment to observe a day of rest, we Jews gave a great gift to the world. But in giving this gift to the world, have we made the mistake of giving it away? One does not have to pay a psychiatrist to learn that for over thirty centuries Shabbat has been an antidote to boredom, bitterness, stress, anxiety, and depression. One does not have to follow around a guru to realize that the relaxation literally commanded by God on Shabbat is as deep a form of meditation and reflection as that proffered by any Eastern religion.

A few years ago, a cartoon appeared in *The New Yorker* showing two yogis sitting in a cave on top of a high mountain. Suddenly their serene meditation is shattered by the deafening whoosh of a jumbo jet airliner. One yogi turns to the other and says: "Ah, they have the know-*how*, but do they have the know-*why*?"

On Shabbat, we must ask ourselves, "Do we know *why*?"

Do we know why we have drifted away from our roots and our heritage? Do we know why we are losing our children to secularism, workaholism, drugs, materialism, and hedonism? Is there any better time than that allowed us on Shabbat to ask ourselves these difficult questions? Is there any better time to answer them than on Shabbat, a day on which we have ample time to rediscover our Jewish values and, through those values, our true Jewish selves?

If we care about our remaining Jews, if we care about our grandchildren remaining Jewish, we must learn to bring Shabbat back into our homes and lives. On Shabbat, time is set aside for us to put into practice the values and goals that make us moral and spiritual human beings. On Shabbat, there is time for acts of *menschlichkeit* (decency) and *tikkun olam* (mending the world), time for us to think about how we can bring into being the world envisioned by the Hebrew prophets, a world filled with peace in our hearts, in our homes, and in our communities.

A Shabbat Reader

In the Talmud, there is a wonderful passage about the value of study:

> When Rabbi Tarfon and the sages were dining in the upper chamber in the house of Nitzah in Lydda, this question was asked of them, "Which is greater, study or practice?" Rabbi Tarfon answered, "Practice is greater." Rabbi Akiva answered, "Study is greater." Then the sages responded, "Study is greater because it leads to practice." (*Kiddushin* 40b)

Shabbat is a day of rest, and as a day of rest it is also a day of study, for in Judaism study is not considered work. Traditionally, Jews study the Torah and other books of the Bible on Shabbat. They may do this through Shabbat study groups or beginners' minyans. The homiletic portion of the synagogue experience itself is a form of study.

Jews often supplement their study of the Bible on Shabbat by exploring other texts related to the Jewish tradition. Some Jews read short stories by Jewish authors; others pore over pages of Talmud. Many study Shabbat itself: the whys and wherefores of its rules and regulations; its spiritual meaning for us as individuals and as members of our immediate community; its past, present, and future value for the Jewish people as a whole. The purpose of this reader is to offer Jews an opportunity and the resources to explore in greater depth the history and meaning of Shabbat and its observance.

The pieces collected in this reader, which are only a smattering of the many available, are divided into four larger categories: Shabbat in Classical Texts; Shabbat as the Ultimate Mitzvah; Jews Celebrate Shabbat; Shabbat in Modern Thought. Each category describes the general character of the essays, poems, letters, prayer services, opinion pieces, and other literary forms contained within it.

"Shabbat in Classical Texts" comprises essays and meditations by notable scholars about Shabbat's representation in classical sources. Michael S. Kogan uses selected quotes from the Bible and prayer book as a starting point for thinking about Shabbat's meaning to him. Essays by Robert

Goldenberg and Walter S. Wurzburger examine the sources of Shabbat's work rules and offer interpretations of their value for us today. Gershom Scholem examines the metaphorical reinterpretation of Shabbat by the Jewish mystics of sixteenth-century Safed, providing us with the background for contemporary Shabbat traditions. Rabbi Amy Bardack looks at the tradition of a husband's singing Eshet Hayil (Woman of Valor) to his wife before the Shabbat meal.

"Shabbat as the Ultimate Mitzvah" explores Shabbat's meaning in a less scholarly fashion. Rabbi Norman E. Frimer looks at how Shabbat combats the depersonalizing effects of our modern assembly-line way of life; Rabbi Alan S. Green describes the spiritual and sensual character of Shabbat celebration; Harvey Cox, a non-Jewish scholar of religion, draws important and interesting parallels between Shabbat observance and Eastern meditation; Jerome Braun looks at how Shabbat worship itself radically differs from our normal conceptions of leisure and recreation; Blu Greenberg offers a personal and pedagogical foray into the spiritually fulfilling intricacies of preparing for and celebrating Shabbat; Rabbi Harold M. Schulweis takes a close look at the seduction of work and its toll on our personal lives, positing the mitzvah of Shabbat as the antidote.

In "Jews Celebrate Shabbat," the tone of the pieces is far more personal. Alongside essays and companion pieces are poems, personal recollections, historical re-creations, and prayer services. Mark Zborowski and Elizabeth Herzog's re-creation of Shabbat celebration in the shtetls of Eastern Europe is complemented by Elie Wiesel's nostalgic recollection of singing *niggunim* (wordless melodies) as a child. Ari L. Goldman shares more recent memories of a Shabbat celebration in his home while he was studying at Harvard Divinity School, and Ilana Nava Kurshan describes Shabbat in the life of a university student. Danny Siegel and Rabbi Sandy Eisenberg Sasso turn to poetry to express their deep feelings about Shabbat. Nahum M. Waldman's scholarly overview of the candlelighting tradition on Shabbat is followed by two collections of prayers, traditional and contemporary, written for the candlelighting ceremony. A sampling of women poets in praise of Shabbat includes Chana Katz, Penina Moise, Jessie Sampter, Zelda, and Chana Bell. Other aspects of Shabbat celebration are treated by Ron Wolfson, who discusses the challah and the idea of *seudat mitzvah* (Hebrew idiom for a religiously ordained festive meal). Shabbat's meaning to us as both individuals and family members is addressed by Albert and Jeannette Kall's letter to their nephew and niece, Sue Levi Elwell's look at the reality of family celebration of Shabbat, and my description of Shabbat fantasy as a means of self-discovery. Essays by Chief Rabbi Jonathan Sacks and Gavriel and Pamela Goldman, each in its own way, support a vision of Shabbat as a time when the technological workaholism of modern life gives way to spiritual peace and communion with nature.

"Shabbat in Modern Thought" places us squarely in the present even as the pieces contained in it look to the future. For Ismar Schorsch, Michael Lerner, Arthur Waskow, and Erich Fromm, Shabbat is a holiday that is not merely about rest and worship. For Lerner and Waskow, Shabbat is also about acting justly and doing right by those who have less; for Schorsch and Fromm, Shabbat obligates us to think more about preserving our environment. Rabbi Lawrence Kushner shows us how Shabbat compels us to live in the present by preventing us from planning for the future. Rabbi Amy Eilberg looks at Shabbat as a complex holiday because of the difficulties posed to its celebration in an era of modern transportation. For Rabbi Arnold Jacob Wolf, Shabbat is a topic of great relevance to Reform Judaism as it struggles to reformulate its relationship to Shabbat observance. To Rabbi W. Gunther Plaut, Shabbat is a protest against the pervasive competition of the modern world. In Alicia Suskin Ostriker's piece, Shabbat is metaphor for the descent of God's holiness into the mundane world. This section closes with a Havdalah service, the ceremony marking the end of Shabbat, written by the Woman's Institute for Continuing Education.

A Shabbat Reader includes suggestions for further reading for those who want to learn more about Shabbat and share it with their family and friends. Books for adult study, children's books, and curricular materials are listed, allowing beginners and experts alike to explore the rich tradition of Shabbat observance.

Shabbat is a time of loving and learning, of peace and justice, goodness and spiritual awakening. Shabbat is a gift that we have been given by God and an opportunity to look deeply into ourselves and discover what good lies within our own hearts. This book's purpose is to awaken that sense of goodness, to restore to consciousness the wellsprings of Jewish spirituality, to teach us that on Shabbat there is always time to rethink and, if necessary, reinvent who we are and rearrange how we shall live. Read, study, and discuss the contents of this book, and open your mind to the universe of cosmic joy that Shabbat gives us leave to enter.

· I ·

SHABBAT
IN
CLASSICAL
TEXTS

Shabbat in the Bible and Rabbinic Sources

Moses would not recognize the Shabbat of Rabbi Akiva, nor would Akiva have understood the Shabbat observance of Rabbi Joseph Caro or, centuries later, of Chaim Nachman Bialik. The institution of Shabbat has grown over the centuries, becoming more enriched and enriching, as it was embellished with ideas and practices that enhance and expand its meaning, beauty, and personal relevance.

Below are some of the earliest sources referring to Shabbat in the classic texts of Judaism: Torah, Talmud, and Midrash. This is the foundation upon which our tradition of Shabbat observance is based and upon which it has grown.

In the selections below, see if you can find the additions to the concept of Shabbat. Which ideas add to the biblical concept of Shabbat in Genesis? Which concepts from the Talmud represent new ideas? Are there any contradictions in the various midrashic pronouncements on Shabbat, or do they supplement each other? Which view of the meaning of Shabbat is closest to your own?

Biblical Sources

The heaven and the earth were finished, and all their array. And on the seventh day God finished the work that had been done and ceased on the seventh day from all the work that had been done. God blessed the seventh day and declared it holy, because on it God ceased from all the work of creation that had been done. (Gen. 2:1–3)

The people of Israel shall keep Shabbat, observing Shabbat throughout the generations as a covenant for all time. It shall be a sign for ever between Me and the people of Israel, for in six days God made heaven and earth, and on the seventh day God rested and was refreshed. (Exod. 31:16–17)

Remember Shabbat and keep it holy. Six days you shall labor and do all your work, but the seventh day is a sabbath of Adonai your God: you shall not do any work, you, your son or daughter, your male or female slave, or your cattle, or the stranger who is within your settlements. For in six days Adonai made heaven and earth and sea, and all that is in them, and rested on the seventh day; therefore Adonai blessed Shabbat and sanctified it. (Exod. 20:8–11)

Observe Shabbat and keep it holy, as Adonai your God has commanded you. Six days you shall labor and do all your work, but the seventh day is a sabbath of Adonai your God: you shall not do any work, you, your son or your daughter, your male or female slave, your ox or your ass, or any of your cattle, or the stranger in your settlements, so that your male and female slave may rest as you do. Remember that you were a slave in the land of Egypt and Adonai your God freed you from there with a mighty hand and an outstretched arm; therefore Adonai your God has commanded you to observe Shabbat. (Deut. 5:12–15)

Rabbinic Sources

It was taught that Rabbi Jose ben Rabbi Judah said: "Two ministering angels escort a person home from the synagogue on the eve of Shabbat. One of these angels is a good one, and the other an evil one. When the person comes home and finds the Shabbat lights kindled and the table set, the good angel says, "May it be thus next Shabbat," and the evil angel, against his will, says, "Amen." But if the home is not found thus prepared, the evil angel says, "May it be thus next Shabbat," and the good angel, against his will, says "Amen." (Babylonian Talmud *Shabbat* 119b)

Rabbi Simeon ben Lakish said, "On the eve of Shabbat, the Blessed Holy One gives us an extra soul. At the conclusion of the Shabbat, this extra soul is taken away, as it is written in the Scriptures, on the seventh day, "*shavat va-yinafash*" (Exod. 31:17). Once Shabbat ceases, *vay, eyn nefesh*; "Woe, the [additional] soul is no more." (Babylonian Talmud *Bezah* 16a) [This is a pun on the word *va-yinafash*, "rested," which sounds like the expression *vay, eyn nefesh*, "woe, no soul." —Ed.]

What is the proof that danger to human life suspends the laws of Shabbat? Rabbi Jonathan ben Joseph said, "For it is holy unto you" (Exod. 31:14). Shabbat is committed to your keeping, not you to its keeping. Rabbi Simeon ben Menasia said, "The children of Israel shall keep the Sabbath" (Exod. 31:16). The Torah says: Profane one Sabbath for the sake of saving a life so that that person will be able to observe many Sabbaths. (Babylonian Talmud *Yoma* 85b)

When the world was created, Shabbat said to the Holy One, "Ruler of the Universe, every living thing created has its mate, and each day has its companion, except me, the seventh day. I am alone!" God answered, "The people of Israel will be your mate." When the Israelites arrived at Mount Sinai, the Holy One said to them, "Remember what I said to Shabbat—that the people of Israel would be her mate." It is with reference to this that My fourth commandment for you reads: "Remember the Sabbath day, to keep it holy." (Midrash *Genesis Rabbah* 11:8)

"It is a sign between Me and the children of Israel forever." This implies that the Sabbath will never disappear from Israel. And you thus find that the things for which the Israelites sacrificed their lives, such as the Sabbath, circumcision, and the study of Torah, were the things that remained with them forever. But the things for which the Israelites did not sacrifice their lives were not preserved in their midst. (Midrash *Mekhilta Shabbata*, 1)

"Six days you will labor and do all your work" (Exod. 20:9). But is it possible for us to do all our work in six days? Rather, we should rest as though all our work were finished. (Midrash *Mekhilta Yitro* 7)

"Remember Shabbat, 'to keep it holy,' " How do you make it holy? By [studying] Bible and Mishnah, with food and drink, with clean clothing and with rest. (Midrash *Tanna d'bei Eliyahu*, chap. 26)

Even though Israel is busy with their work all six days, on Shabbat they get up early, come to the synagogue, recite the Shema, pass before the reader's table, and read from the Torah and the Prophets. God says to them . . . "Keep in mind not to hate, envy, quarrel with, or embarrass one another." (Midrash *Shir Hashirim Rabbah* 8)

Kingdom Present

MICHAEL S. KOGAN

I

"The children of Israel shall keep the Sabbath, observing the Sabbath throughout their generations as an everlasting covenant." (Exod. 31:16)

I will never forget a photograph I once saw at the Jewish Museum in New York. It was part of an exhibit on Lower East Side Jewish immigrant life. The photo had been much enlarged and took up most of a wall. In it could be seen the corner of a room in a slum dwelling, little more than a hovel really. In the foreground was a bearded Jew seated at a crude wooden table. The table was covered with a clean white cloth; on it was placed a braided challah. The man's face looked directly into the camera. It was etched with lines of toil and poverty and of bewilderment at the strange new world in which he seemed to be stranded. But on it too was written the assurance—the set jaw, the determined mouth—of a man who knew who he was. He sat erect; his eyes gleamed. After a moment so did mine. My tears were tears of sorrow for his poverty, for his loneliness in his wretched room, and for his apparent dislocation in a world incapable of knowing his heart.

But if my eyes gleamed with tears, they also shone with pride, with recognition, with shared identity. For if the world did not know this Jew's heart, I did. He was my brother, my twin, one with whom I shared a common origin and a common destiny. I doubt that I would have been so deeply moved had the picture not been of this man's humble, desperate, glorious observance of the Sabbath. There he sat, in the midst of poverty and degradation as the world defines such things. But he was a king, a Jew at his Sabbath table. And in this man, long dead, whose life was so distant and so different from my own, I found myself. It was the shared observance of the Sabbath that was the link—that has been the link from generation to generation, a common heritage of Jews at all times and in all places.

If God calls the Sabbath "a sign between me and the children of Israel forever," then to partake of it is to see oneself not only as an individual but as one of a people, an eternal people called at Sinai to witness to the Divine Presence in the human community. "All Israel is one fellowship," and on the Sabbath we feel that unity most deeply. Each Sabbath is a link in an endless chain binding us to all the generations which have gone before and will come after "for as long as the heavens remain over the earth." As in that haunting image in the photograph, Jews have kept the Sabbath through persecution and pogrom, exile and wandering. Often the Sabbath was their only home, their only refuge from the pain and cruelty of an alien environment. Today it can provide a connection for us to all of our struggling, suffering, vanished brothers and sisters. Through the Sabbath they are with us yet, bound by a shared consciousness and a shared observance.

On the Sabbath a Jew comes to know himself, not as twenty, or thirty, or sixty years old, but as four thousand years old, the bearer of an eternal witness of which the Sabbath is the sign. On the Sabbath we cease to be isolated and alienated egos and discover ourselves as part of the collective individual which is Israel, the people of God. We find that as Jews we have a place and a purpose in the world, a transcendent origin and destiny.

The Sabbath is the link with our future as well as our past. For if its observance provided a central focus for Jewish religious life in generations gone by, it can play the same role in years to come. Sabbath observance can offer us a weekly touchstone on which to ground our commitment to the Jewish future. For ultimately we are as much the link between past and future as is the Sabbath itself. The Sabbath is the sacred repository of Jewish memory. It is the renewed and renewing symbol of Jewish hope.

II

And He will turn the hearts of the parents to the children and the hearts of the children to the parents. (Mal. 4:6)

I have spoken of the Sabbath as uniting us with our people. But there is another unity which we seek and which the Sabbath can offer us as Jews in the modern world. Consider what shared family Sabbath observance can do to strengthen the ties between husbands and wives, parents and children. Contemporary existence is so varied and multifocused that it often results in the fragmentation of the family itself. Frequently parents and children no longer take meals together or spend time in each other's company. Dinners are rushed, inelegant affairs; entertainment is often sought alone, with each family member in a separate room watching his or her own television set.

But imagine another scene: the family is gathered around a carefully set dining table covered with a white cloth, the "good" china, and holiday foods. The Sabbath candles are blessed and lit. Parents bless their children and praise their spouse. God's gifts of bread and wine are acknowledged through the blessings. The family settles down to enjoy a leisurely festive meal, to share news of the past week, and to enjoy each other's company. If the implications of this Sabbath experience are taken seriously, family life cannot help but be enriched. The transcendent focus of the ceremonies call family members to see beyond petty disagreements and misunderstandings to appreciate what these loved ones really mean in their lives.

While the Sabbath is no cure-all for family ills, it can provide a glimpse of what family life can be at its best, as well as an opportunity to share a profound experience which binds all participants in a common framework of meaning.

Family synagogue attendance adds yet another dimension to Sabbath observance as an affirmation of familial identity within the larger family of Israel. These two senses of family can only reinforce and strengthen each other. The shared worship with its joyous song and solemn prayer can bring a family together as only the focus on a common, embracing reality can. The joy of being a Jewish family together in the midst of a warm and welcoming congregation must really be experienced to be fully appreciated.

Following services the focus of Sabbath observance returns to the home. Kiddush, luncheon, group singing of the Birkat Hamazon and Sabbath songs are followed by a relaxed afternoon where a walk or talk or nap may add to the sense of quiet well-being. No appointments loom; no duties distract. Our only thought is to rest and enjoy the peace and stillness of the day.

Sabbath afternoon is also the ideal time to deepen our knowledge of the spiritual and intellectual treasures of Jewish literature. Family study of the Torah or Midrash or reading aloud from a work of Jewish fiction, biography, or history can give added depth to the Sabbath experience. Specific practices will vary from home to home, but the Sabbath itself remains as a weekly oasis, a precious opportunity to renew and reaffirm the centrality of the family in Jewish life.

III

Those who celebrate the Sabbath rejoice in Your kingdom. (Sabbath Prayer Book)

The Sabbath can unite us with our people Israel through a shared weekly observance which has been a common focus of Jewish life in every age and in every corner of the world where Jews have lived. Sharing the warmth and fullness of the Sabbath—talking together, eating together, worshiping and studying together—can strengthen ties of intimacy between husband and wife, parents and children. It remains for us to discuss only the final and perhaps highest function of the Sabbath: that it provides a clearly defined, regularly recurring time devoted to strengthening the relationship between the Jewish people and God.

This crucial religious aspect of the Sabbath is not easily articulated since it deals with a reality beyond the descriptive power of human language. Ordinary words can only point to the divine dimension of experience but the attempt to express the inexpressible must be made if we are not to miss the essence of the Sabbath and of Judaism itself.

One way of approaching the great mystery of this relationship may be via Judaism's central conception of the Kingdom of God. This perennial Jewish idea has usually been expressed in terms of a final goal of human history, a future age of universal justice, human brotherhood, and profound and lasting inner and outer peace. In this ideal age to come, finite persons will at last come to see themselves as intimately related to the infinite, divine Life which is the source of all existence. But while it is the chief task of every Jew to labor diligently toward the up-building of God's Kingdom, the earthly realization of this lofty vision often seems very far away. Our century has seen so much of war and tyranny, of human suffering and inhuman cruelty, that it is sometimes very difficult to believe that progress is real or to keep one's spiritual eyes fixed upon the distant vision of the future Kingdom.

That is why we have the Sabbath. On this day we are given a foretaste of the Kingdom, an assurance of what life can be—will be—when God's purposes are at last realized in the midst of the human community. The Sabbath calls us not out of our world and into another but out of one dimension of this world into "another intensity" where human life may become humanized once again after a week of toil and distraction. The Sabbath holds up a mirror to each of us and reflects back the image of what we can be, freed of the claims of the workaday world to contemplate the spiritual potentiality of ourselves and our environment. As such the Sabbath is a present sign of God's future Kingdom.

The Sabbath is called "a remembrance of the work at the beginning." It is curious that this day when all work is forbidden should be seen as a remembrance of work. But the work referred to was God's work of creation and on the Sabbath we abstain from work precisely to acknowledge the Creator and to attune our finite lives to the infinite life of God. That divine life shines through and holds together all things. It is felt within us in the pulsation of the blood and the miraculous workings of our minds and bodies. It is sensed in the world around us, in the teeming life of the creation of which we are part.

The Sabbath calls us to see what we overlook in the preoccupation of the week's labors: that if a miracle is defined as any event with God as its source, then we live in the midst of miracles, immersed in a divinely grounded reality so all-embracing that we fail to recognize it. God's work of creation may have been "completed" on the seventh day, but that does not mean it was finished. The wholeness of the world was achieved by that first Sabbath, but the life of the creation pulses on to a rhythm which we hear most deeply when we pause on the Sabbath to listen. And when we do listen we come to know our own life as caught up in the universal life which surrounds us. Thus the Sabbath tells us that the Kingdom is not only the future potential of the world; it is what the world already is and what it, in a sense, becomes over and over again when human beings, the conscious element of creation, come to recognize it.

The Sabbath is also called "a remembrance of the going out from Egypt." As such it offers liberation from the tasks at which we toil all week long. We too need liberating as did our ancestors in Egypt. We are enslaved to the pharaohs of monetary success, social position, and career goals. When these things come to possess us, dominate our lives, and shape our consciousness, we recall the words of the psalmist, "Out of my distress I cried unto the Lord; He answered me by setting me free."

The Sabbath sets us free. What a relief to be able to lay down the pen, the briefcase, the tools of our various trades for twenty-four hours of peace, rest, and refreshment. By calling us away from our work, the Sabbath reminds us that "being" is both deeper and higher than "doing," that sometimes we have to stop doing what we do in order to start being who we are. To pause, to take stock of our lives, to contemplate the way we have come and the way we are going is not reserved for Yom Kippur alone; every Sabbath offers us an opportunity for self-assessment, a liberation from the structures that define us, so we may be free to define ourselves in the eternal light of the Infinite. On the Sabbath we are freed to stand before God and to "know before Whom we stand," from Whom we have come, to Whom we must give ultimate account of our lives.

This is the Kingdom of God available to the people of God each and every Sabbath, "Eternity's Day" in which we can see ourselves as integral elements of a divinely ordered creation, liberated to be God's own. This intimation of eternity does not illumine the Sabbath only, but all time. It enables us to look anew at the time-bound days of the week and see that time itself, properly understood, is made up of moments of eternity. This Sabbath insight can transform the experience of every day so that all time becomes, as it were, transparent, revealing the Eternal Reality beyond and within. Just as the Sabbath represents the full potential of every day, and the eternal the potential of time, so does the Kingdom of God reflect the potential of the kingdom of man.

In an age of materialism the Sabbath calls to us to sojourn in the Kingdom of the Eternal in the midst of time. In a world of isolation and alienation, it calls us to our true home among our people Israel. In a time too often characterized by narcissism and egoism, it calls us to renew the ties that bind us to parents, spouses, and children. In all these calls we hear the summons to self-transcendence, to move beyond what we merely are to what we *really* are, sons and daughters of a divine Father, members of an eternal fellowship, privileged, as were our forebears, to "observe the Sabbath day to keep it holy."

The Place of the Sabbath in Rabbinic Judaism

ROBERT GOLDENBERG

No understanding of Jewish religious life is complete unless it includes an account of the joy and peace of the seventh day. Jews over history have celebrated the Sabbath in quite varied ways, but this celebration in all its variety offers the key to the meaning of Jewish life. The Sabbath is the punctuation of Jewish existence, marking Jewish life off into intervals of seven days; it determines the rhythm of Jewish life more decisively than any of the annual festivals and more pervasively than any of the once-in-a-lifetime rites of passage by which the life span of a Jew can be divided. This paper cannot provide a thorough examination of all features of this great Jewish institution, but it will offer some insight into the role of the Sabbath in shaping Jewish life.

We begin with two stories, the first from the Bible and the second from the Babylonian Talmud. The biblical story, from the Book of Numbers, reads:

> The children of Israel were in the desert when they found a man gathering wood on the Sabbath day. Those who had found him gathering wood brought him up to Moses and Aaron and the whole congregation, and they put him under guard, for it had not been clearly stated what should be done to him. The Lord said to Moses, "The man must be put to death; let the entire congregation stone him outside the camp." The entire congregation took him outside the camp and stoned him, so he died, as the Lord had commanded Moses. (Num. 15:32–36)

The phrase [*mekoshesh etzim*] is unclear; modern translators give "gathering wood" or "gathering sticks." Whatever its precise nuance, however, the implications of this story for the present purpose are quite unambiguous. A man was found doing something on the Sabbath that was considered improper; on inquiry it was determined that his infraction had been a capital crime, so he was put to death. It seems that the people whose lives are reflected in this narrative took the Sabbath very seriously and that they understood the Sabbath to be a day on which certain activities were strictly forbidden.

The story from Numbers can now serve as background for a tale from the Babylonian Talmud tractate *Shabbat*:

> Caesar [i.e., the Roman emperor] said to R. Joshua b. Hananiah, "Why is this Sabbath food so fragrant?" He said, "We have a certain spice named Shabbat that we put into it and it renders the dish fragrant." He said, "Give us some of it." He said to him, "The spice is effective for anyone who keeps the Sabbath but will not work for anyone who does not keep the Sabbath." (*Shabbat* 119a)

This is a very different picture of what the Sabbath meant. Here the seventh day is a day of such pleasantness and joy that even the emperor of Rome envies the Jews for possessing such a treasure. It should be kept in mind that on the Sabbath observant Jews will not cook, that even keeping already cooked food hot on the Sabbath can be accomplished only under very restricted conditions. All cooked food eaten on the Sabbath is thus in some sense leftover food, and to say of such food that even Caesar wished he could have some is to make a remarkable claim. Whether any Roman would really have expressed such a wish is neither here nor there; the point of this story is that the Jews who told and retold it believed that he would have. They believed that the food prepared for their Sabbath table was by virtue of that very circumstance fit for a king.

The spice that so provokes the emperor's desire is itself called "Shabbat," that is, Sabbath. This little pun reflects the point just made that food prepared for the Sabbath—food containing Sabbath flavor, so to speak—is always very tasty, and it allows as well for another translation of the rabbi's final response. This translation ignores the point of the remark in context but greatly expands its general significance, for it can now be imagined that the rabbi's real point was this: Not only a certain spice but the Sabbath altogether only works for those who keep it; those who do not keep the Sabbath will never enjoy, will never even comprehend, its benefit. Understood in this way, the rabbi's quip reveals the heart of the

Jewish Sabbath, a secret place, so to speak, where strict regulation of behavior and the rigorous enforcement of taboo were combined with a kind
of serenity and gratification of body and spirit that would have been the
envy of the world if only the world had discovered it. The modern observer too will not understand the Sabbath at all until it has been seen as
the union of two themes: the Sabbath as a day of avoidance of labor and
the Sabbath as a day of heavenly rest.

The example of grim legalism was drawn from Scripture and the example of playful spirituality from the Talmud largely to poke fun at the usual
stereotypes associated with these two texts. In fact, although the Talmud
dates from a period when Jews no longer enjoyed the power to execute
Sabbath breakers, it is quite full of extremely complex rules and regulations. On the other hand, the very idea that the Sabbath should be made a
day of joy is derived from Scripture (see Isa. 58:13). The whole point is
that joy and abstention from labor together make the Sabbath what it is.
This is the point the Roman monarch had such trouble understanding.

Others throughout history have had similar difficulty. Nehemiah had
to station soldiers at the gates of Jerusalem to keep the people from widespread violation of the Sabbath (Neh. 13:15–22), whereas five hundred
years later the Christian apostle Paul, or someone writing in his name, apparently agreed with Nehemiah's contemporaries and condemned Sabbath observance as a kind of superstitious slavery (Rom. 14:5–6; Gal.
4:10; Col. 2:16). The rabbinic rules and traditions concerning the Sabbath
must be understood as attempting to achieve a state of joyful rest. It is
sometimes hard to understand them that way, but the challenge to the
modern inquirer who approaches these texts from outside their own cultural framework is to keep this reality in mind.

The biblical texts, while reminding their readers over and over again
that the Sabbath was very important, never say much at all about what it
was like. From the meager details Scripture supplies, one would never
have anticipated that the Mishnah and Talmud would devote two entire
tractates, one among the largest and one among the most complex, to detailed regulation of Sabbath rest.[1] Indeed, while the sages who compiled
the Mishnah probably did not mean for it to serve as a functioning code
of Jewish law, there is no denying that the Mishnah's treatment of the Sabbath consists largely of a very great accumulation of legal details. Where
Jeremiah was content to plead that his hearers (or readers) abstain from
carrying burdens on the Sabbath day (17:21–27), the Mishnah devotes
three chapters in tractate *Shabbat* to the task of defining how much of any

conceivable substance constitutes a burden in terms of this law. Whereas Exodus simply rules that every man must remain in his place on the Sabbath (16:29), tractate *Eruvin*, the other of the two Mishnaic Sabbath tractates, devotes several chapters to defining the limits of a person's "Sabbath resting place" and detailing procedures available to those who wish to expand those limits or shift that place from its natural location.

To be sure, the Mishnah does offer a generalized list of forbidden activities, which is the closest thing it has to a definition of forbidden labor. Even this list, however, appears to contain only random details; it is not even found where one would expect it, at the beginning of tractate *Shabbat*. The location of this list in the middle of things (7:2) seems only to compound the general confusion.

> The main categories of labor are forty less one: sowing, plowing, reaping, binding sheaves, threshing, winnowing, sorting,[2] grinding, sifting, kneading, baking; shearing wool, washing it, beating it, dyeing it, spinning, weaving, making two loops, weaving two threads, separating in order to sew two stitches; trapping a deer, slaughtering it, skinning it, salting it, curing its hide, scraping it, cutting it up; writing two letters, erasing in order to write two letters; building, tearing down, putting out a fire, kindling a fire, striking with a hammer, taking anything from one domain into another. These are the main categories of labor, forty less one.

At first glance, this seems to be a random assortment of activities, all of them no doubt forbidden on the Sabbath but otherwise connected by no common feature. The list is also noteworthy for its omissions, for there is no mention here of some of the activities that Jews avoided most carefully of all; there is no mention here of commercial activity, of buying or selling or lending or paying off debts, and there is no mention here of the avoidance of judicial proceedings on the Sabbath, even though Josephus repeatedly informs us that Jews cared so much about such avoidance that it had to be confirmed by numerous Roman authorities in the face of Greek harassment (see especially *Jewish Antiquities* 14.10; also 16.6). What then does this list really mean?

The Talmud itself assumes that the list details the activities that were needed to build the portable desert sanctuary that is described toward the end of the Book of Exodus. It bases this assumption on the fact that one of the Sabbath prohibitions in the Torah (Exod. 35:1–3) is inserted into the midst of the section describing the building of that sanctuary. This idea, however, is not convincing. The linkage is artificial; some of the inclusions and some of the omissions are surprising; and there is too much uncertainty in the Talmud itself about how the sanctuary was actually built, on the one hand, and what items this list should in fact contain, on the other.[3]

The nature of this list therefore cries out for further exploration. On more careful examination, it turns out to contain an early rabbinic enumeration of the fundamental activities of civilized life. The first portion of the sequence has to do with the preparation of food, using bread as the food par excellence. This part of the list starts with sowing, ends with baking, and identifies nine intermediate activities that are needed for the production of bread. The catalogue proceeds to the preparation of clothing, starting in the same way with the shearing of wool and ending with "tearing in order to sew two stitches." Food and clothing are followed by the preparation of parchment for writing (not meat, as might at first appear the case). The enumeration concludes with the preparation of shelter, a category that includes the use of fire and the division of the world into units of property. Food, clothing, writing, and shelter—these are the indispensable foundations of civilized life as the early rabbis understood them. These are also, it turns out, the materials that one must prepare before the Sabbath sets in, so that the sacred day itself can be devoted to the higher activities which these preparations make possible.

Food, clothing, and shelter are universal necessities of life, as every schoolchild learns, but this list is distinctive for the other category it includes, writing. The only writing the authors of this list could possibly have considered a necessity of life is the writing of the Torah. If the writing of the Torah must be done before the Sabbath, however, then the Sabbath must be a day for the study of the Torah thus prepared; the jumble of rabbinic law thus conceals a vision of the Sabbath that is not so distant from that of the first-century philosopher Philo:

> [Moses] forbade bodily labor on the Sabbath but permitted the nobler labors, those that concern the principles and teachings of virtue. . . . Moses does not allow any of those who use his sacred instruction to remain inactive at any time, but since we consist of body and soul he assigned to the body its proper tasks and to the soul what falls to it, so that each might be waiting to relieve the other. (*Special Laws* 2.61, 64)

To associate the Mishnah with Philo is not to suggest that all Jews in late antiquity devoted their Sabbath rest to arcane philosophical inquiry, nor should it be thought that the Mishnah itself is a philosophical treatise in disguise. This linkage does however reinforce the previous suggestion that the key to understanding the rabbinic Sabbath is to see how abstention from labor has somehow been connected with striving for a certain mental state or discipline. Another story from the Talmud carries this conception still further:

> A certain pious man once went into his vineyard on the Sabbath and saw there a break in its wall. He decided to repair it when the Sabbath was over, but afterward he said, "Since I decided on the Sabbath that I would repair it, I shall never do so at all." What did the Holy One, blessed be He, do for that man? He prepared a caper bush which grew into the opening, and the man supported himself off that bush for the rest of his life. (Jerusalem Talmud *Shabbat* 15:3, 15a–b)

It is clear that the "pious man" of whom this story is told never considered actually performing the indicated repair on the Sabbath; this is not a story designed to dissuade people from doing actual labor on the Sabbath. The question in the mind of the "pious man," and therefore the only question this story seeks to discuss, was whether even thinking about a forbidden activity is itself somehow blameworthy. The story thus suggests that actual Sabbath breaking was not a serious issue in the rabbinic narrators' community and instead reflects an effort to turn the Sabbath into an escape from everyday reality, into what A. J. Heschel in our own century termed a "palace in time."[4] This little tale seeks to convey the message that conscious refusal to pay attention to ordinary concerns on the Sabbath should not be confused with impractical neglect; on the contrary, those who act thus "impractically" on the Sabbath can expect a lavish and quite material reward from heaven."[5]

The rabbinic Sabbath was thus an attempt to blend elevated religious consciousness with the strict, detailed regulation of behavior. The rabbis' assumption was that each of these modes of self-discipline enhances the other, that the two together form the framework for a life of piety, even saintliness. The Pauline idea that detailed behavioral rules are somehow a block to true religious fulfillment ("the burden of the law") could not have differed more dramatically from this point of view.

The preceding general remarks provide a framework for the following comments about specific aspects of rabbinic Sabbath observance. This discussion will concentrate on certain customs and rituals that over the centuries have been preserved in many Jewish homes. This focus is designed to combat the natural tendency for Americans to think that it is in the nature of a holy day that people will celebrate it primarily in a house of public worship and that its most important features can be discovered by examining what the worshipers do once they are assembled. Furthermore, the rabbinic synagogue liturgy for the Sabbath is not in the end so very different from that for weekdays. There are some differences, to be sure: the prayers are recited a little more slowly and some are rather longer; in keeping with the studied "impracticality" of the Sabbath, the most materially petitionary sections of the liturgy are dropped; and, of course, the public reading of the Torah assumes a far greater role in the Sabbath morning service than it does on weekdays. However, the structure of the synagogue services for weekdays and for the Sabbath and many portions of the actual liturgical texts are very similar indeed.

On the other hand, the onset of the Sabbath dramatically changes the atmosphere in a traditional Jewish home. This has something to do with the need to carry out so much preparation in advance and the deep, quite sudden relaxation that follows when the preparations are done (it has already been mentioned, for example, that all food has to be cooked before the Sabbath has begun). It also reflects the fact that already in ancient times certain foods and certain activities had special meaning and special character on the Sabbath, so that Sabbath meals were different from others, Sabbath lighting different from weekday lighting, and so forth. Among mystics of later centuries even sexual intercourse on Sabbath nights acquired a special character, which received varied and quite graphic symbolic expression.[6]

No later than the first century, the physical materials of the customary Sabbath meal began to acquire some of the holiness of the day. The following enigmatic description by the first-century Roman satirist Persius offers an image of Jewish Sabbath observance that conveys contempt, dread, and fascination all at the same time:

> But when the day of Herod is come, and the lamps, put in greasy windows along with violets, emit their oily clouds of smoke; and when the tail of a tuna fish floats curled round in a red dish, and

the white jar is bulging with wine, you move your lips in silence and
turn pale at the circumcised Sabbath. (*Satires* 5.179–84)

Many of the aspects of Sabbath observance familiar from later times
through our own are already here, though quite strangely described: the
burning lights, the wine, the fish, the whispered prayers. With due al-
lowance for the hostility of the Roman writer and for his unfamiliarity
with the activities being described, it is not so hard to imagine that the
Roman Sabbath of which he writes was very like the Sabbath of the Mishnah, the Talmud, and the Middle Ages that followed them in turn.

In current practice, the Sabbath begins shortly before sunset with the
kindling of special Sabbath candles; this act is preceded by a benediction
that praises God as the one "who has sanctified us with Your commandments and instructed us to light the Sabbath lamp." The kindling of the
Sabbath lamps apparently began as a utilitarian act; the Torah as already
noted forbids the making of fire once the Sabbath has begun (Exod.
35:3).[7] Therefore, if people wanted light or heat on Sabbath nights, they
had to make sure a fire was burning before the sun went down and the
holy day began. By reciting a liturgical formula, however, this simple
practical act was turned into a ritual—in fact, one of the most emotionally
resonant in the entire tradition.[8]

At an earlier time, when gender roles in Jewish life were more sharply
distinguished, the Sabbath lights were usually kindled by the woman of
the house after the men had gone off to the synagogue for the evening
prayers; this assignment seems at least as old as the time of the Mishnah
(*Shabba*t 2:6; see also 2:7). Even now, in fact, and even in homes where no
one goes to the synagogue on Friday evening, it remains the case that this
particular ritual is considered the task or, as some prefer to say, the privilege of the mother of the home.[9]

The first Sabbath meal then begins when those who have gone to the
synagogue return home. This meal begins with a special recitation called
Kiddush that is pronounced over a cup of wine. The term *kiddush* means
"sanctification"; it is a slightly different form of the word used in Genesis
2:3 to describe the Creator's original sanctification of the seventh day.
Here, of course, the word denotes not a divine act transforming the day
but a human act acknowledging this divine transformation. The association of wine with this act of proclamation is a mystery; in fact, the ritual
drinking of wine in Jewish life is altogether a perplexing matter. It has no
roots in the Bible. The Bible knows that renouncing wine might be a sign

of special devotion to holiness. The Torah instructs that every sacrifice in the sanctuary be accompanied by a libation of wine onto the altar. Scripture is also aware that wine can make you feel good (an attractive but a dangerous feature at the same time), but nowhere in Scripture do people drink wine as a ritual act.[10] On the other hand, when one examines post-biblical Judaism, one discovers the drinking of wine everywhere: at weddings, at circumcisions, at the onset and the conclusion of every sacred day, in connection with the Grace after Meals at any especially solemn or formal occasion. Judging from the New Testament stories of the Last Supper, this use of wine was already taken for granted by the time of Jesus, and rabbinic materials confirm this impression for just a little later on. The passage from Persius, dating from about the same period, gives the same report for contemporary Rome. No one really knows how this happened. Erwin Goodenough thought that the custom must have been learned by ancient Jews from the pagan customs that surrounded them, and no more convincing proposal has come to this writer's attention.[11]

The Kiddush prayer, in the standard Ashkenazi version, begins with Genesis 2:1–3, a passage that describes the original institution of the Sabbath as the climax of creation. It then goes on:

> You are blessed, O Lord our God, King of the universe, who creates the fruit of the vine.
>
> You are blessed, O Lord our God, King of the universe, who has sanctified us by your commandments, taken delight in us, and in love and favor has allowed us to inherit the Sabbath as a remembrance of the deed of creation. For it is the first day of holy convocations, a reminder of the departure from Egypt. For you have chosen us and sanctified us from among all the nations, and have allowed us to inherit your holy Sabbath in love and in favor. You are blessed, O Lord, who sanctifies the Sabbath.

This brief prayer summarizes the importance of the Sabbath in later Jewish thought. The link with creation is here, along with the link to the Exodus and its reminder that a free people should stop every now and then for rest and spiritual refreshment. The importance of the Sabbath as a marker of Jewish identity is also acknowledged, though here it is theologized as a token of divine love, and not simply noted for its social or cultural significance.

The special Sabbath part of this text is preceded by a shorter blessing that refers only to the wine. According to rabbinic law, this blessing is to be recited whenever wine is drunk and is therefore not strictly a Sabbath prayer at all. The Mishnah reports that rabbinic authorities of the first century disagreed on whether the special Sabbath portion of the text should be recited first, since, after all, this part identifies the occasion for reciting the prayer altogether, or last, as the culmination of the whole (*Berakhot* 8:1; *Pesahim* 10:2).

In the course of time, this dispute expanded into one of the perennial themes of rabbinic discussion of the Sabbath: To what extent should the Sabbath be like all days only lovelier, and to what extent should it be made distinct, as different from other days as possible? It has been noted that certain portions of the synagogue service for the Sabbath are quite indistinguishable from their weekday counterparts, but others are entirely unique, especially the central portion of the Amidah prayer (in rabbinic parlance, "the" prayer par excellence) and the practice of reading through the entire Pentateuch over the course of the year. The same blend of similarity and difference that was noted in the Kiddush prayer at the beginning of the meal can be found at its end, in the Grace. With the exception of a single interpolated paragraph, this fairly lengthy prayer is virtually unchanged on the Sabbath, but in traditional homes it is then sung out loud, with leisurely tunes, rather than simply recited in an undertone, as would be the case during the week.[12]

This uncertainty over the uniqueness of the Sabbath is nicely captured in a story concerning two early masters:

> It was taught concerning Shammai the Elder that all his days he would eat in honor of the Sabbath. Having found a handsome animal he would say, "Let this be for the Sabbath." Having then found one more handsome, he would put aside the second [for the Sabbath] and eat the first [right away].
>
> Hillel the Elder had a different rule . . . as it is said, "Blessed be the Lord each day" (Ps. 68:20).
>
> The House of Shammai say, "From the first [day] of the week [direct your efforts] toward the Sabbath," but the House of Hillel say, "Blessed be the Lord each day." (Babylonian Talmud *Besah* 16a)

This looks like a story about trust in divine providence and seems related to remarks attributed to Jesus about not worrying about what one will eat tomorrow (Matt. 6:25–33; Luke 12:22–31), but this story has more to do with the question of the Sabbath. Shammai, along with the school bearing his name, is described as believing that the entire week exists for the sake of the Sabbath—one gets ready for the Sabbath; one makes sure one will be able to celebrate the Sabbath as one ought; and only after this is accomplished does one enjoy the rest of the week with any resources that are left. Shammai's Hillelite opponents will not allow one's relationship with the Creator to be focused so narrowly on just one day a week. The Sabbath has its own rules and its own special character, but these are embedded in a larger system that holds the Sabbath and the other days side by side.

In the home, the chief Sabbath ritual has always been the meal. Even the number of Sabbath meals marked off the day as special: in a culture where most people ate two meals a day, custom and eventually religious law required that on the Sabbath one eat three (Mishnah *Shabbat* 16:2; Babylonian Talmud *Shabbat* 118–19). These meals provided a fixed structure for the Sabbath, and synagogue services, like everything else, had to accommodate themselves to the schedule they created. As early as the time of Josephus it was considered a firm religious custom to begin one's midday meal on the Sabbath no later than noon (Josephus *Life* 54. 279). These meals had to be fancier and more leisurely than workday meals, and at least since the Middle Ages it has been the custom to prolong them by the singing of table songs devoted to various themes of the Sabbath celebration.[13]

The third of these meals, usually held just as the Sabbath is about to end, eventually developed a special character of its own. This, after all, was an emotionally difficult time; even the world seems mournful at the twilight hour when the so-called third meal takes place, and the Jew's brief escape from an often oppressive economic, social, and political reality was about to end. The holy day was about to give way once again to ordinary reality, but this unhappy consideration was offset by another. By tradition, the Messiah will not arrive on a Sabbath or a Sabbath eve (Babylonian Talmud *Eruvin* 43b); on those days, after all, the Jews will be too busy or too restricted to be able to receive him as he ought to be received. The end of the Sabbath, therefore, even though by itself it was a sad time, came to bring with it a kind of consolation: Now it was once again possible to hope that the Messiah might be on the way. Under the influence of kabbalistic messianism, the "third meal" came to be a time of serene, meditative song, a time for quiet communal waiting for redemption. The Havdalah (division) ceremony that formally ends the Sabbath came to be associated with the prophet Elijah, who since pre-Christian times has been considered the Messiah's herald. Perhaps in connection with these themes, we already find in the Talmud a prediction that the Messiah would in fact not arrive until all Israel had fully and properly observed two Sabbaths in a row (Babylonian Talmud *Shabbat* 118b). Perhaps as well this is why one early rabbi is reported to have said that observance of the Sabbath is like a foretaste of the pleasures of the world to come (Babylonian Talmud *Berakhot* 57b).

The biblical sources on which later conceptions of the Sabbath were built contributed two main ideas to those conceptions: on the one hand, the idea of life,[14] and, on the other, the idea that such restrictions ought to be joyous (see, e.g., Isa. 58:13). The various possible combinations of these two ideas, which could easily have been considered contradictory (and have been so considered from time to time), have formed the matrix of Jewish Sabbath observance throughout history. From the ancient world there are Sabbath laws found in the Book of Jubilees, the "Damascus Document" associated with the Dead Sea Scrolls,[15] and the two Mishnaic tractates *Shabbat* and *Eruvin* together with their talmudic elaborations. From the Middle Ages we have the enormous halakhic literature of the rabbinic tradition along with a parallel literature produced by the Karaites. Modern Jewish thought has given huge amounts of attention to the problem of maintaining this unstable combination under vastly altered circumstances.

It seems fair to say that the rabbinic tradition by and large gave more weight in this mixture to the element of joy and less to the element of restriction than did most of the other types of Jewish religion just listed. This is only a relative statement, to be sure, but still it is important to remember that, while other traditions demanded that people eat unheated food on the Sabbath in unlit rooms, the rabbinic tradition developed admittedly complex legal fictions that turned observance of the Sabbath into a much more comfortable, even enjoyable, experience. The complexity of these arrangements eventually came to be considered a fault, but to discuss that subject it is necessary to consider the question of Jewish Sabbath observance in the contemporary world.

Modern Jewish life has been characterized by a wholesale repudiation by many Jews of their previous loyalty to the religious law of the Torah. There are many reasons why this has taken place, and despite the apparently negative term, simple description is intended here, with no value judgment implied. Even as many Jews have rejected the authority of the religious law, however, they have remained eager to preserve some link to their ancestral culture. The Sabbath was an important part of that culture, and so the place of the Sabbath in Jewish life has somehow been preserved, even as Jewish life as a whole has undergone revolutionary change over the last two hundred years.

Examples of this phenomenon can be found everywhere. The State of Israel is dominated by a thoroughly secularized conception of Jewish life, yet on the seventh day of the week newspapers do not publish, mail goes undelivered, schools and offices stay closed, and buses in most places do not run. Here in America (and in Europe previously) the leaders of Reform Judaism got their followers to accept all sorts of radical changes in the prayer book, and they instituted alterations in synagogue ritual that made it almost unrecognizable to those familiar with more traditional services. They managed, nevertheless, to retain the allegiance of their laity. However, when the effort was made to shift the main service of the week (in most Reform temples the only service of the week) to Sunday morning, the effort failed: that somehow felt wrong. Today there are fewer than a dozen synagogues in all of North America where the Sunday service is the main religious event of the Jewish week.

Many important factors have contributed to this result. Economic pressure on Jewish wage earners to go to work on Saturday has been declining for decades, and American society has in general been moving toward the five-day work week. Therefore, the percentage of American Jews who would like to attend a synagogue but feel compelled to go to work on Saturday morning continues to decrease. Moreover, even Jews who must or choose to work on Saturday are usually free on Friday evening to attend services; fewer and fewer Jews work such long hours or come home so tired that they cannot get out of the house after dinner for a fairly brief visit to the synagogue. Cultural or economic need for a Sunday service, in other words, has virtually disappeared. By shifting the main service of the week from Saturday morning to Friday night, liberal movements in American Judaism have been able to achieve the same gains that the Sunday service aimed for, but without going the extra step that so many people found unacceptable. The Sabbath remains, as it has been, the central axis of Jewish religious life.

To be sure, the people who attend these Friday-evening services are by no means Sabbath observers in the traditional sense of the term. On Saturday afternoon these people go shopping or sailing or driving into the country, and even on Friday night many of them have their presynagogue dinner or postsynagogue dessert in a nearby restaurant. The point is simply that the shape of the Jewish week has been imprinted on their consciousness and will not go away.

That imprinting has become a little smudged, of course. Under the pressure of modern life the combination of joy through restriction that was for so long the distinctive feature of Jewish Sabbath observance has become harder to keep balanced than it used to be. Many Jews claim that the restrictions have grown to the point that they interfere with the joy. Some, though fewer, respond that joy without the restrictions is a false joy, a kind of forgery that entirely misses the true heavenly satisfaction that even the emperor of Rome knew enough to envy. This increasingly sharp dispute explains the battles in Israel over the question of movies on Friday night, along with all the similar issues receiving widespread if sometimes uncomprehending coverage in the American press.

Still, people throughout the Jewish world who feel no obligation to observe the old rules of Sabbath observance have nevertheless found ways to make that day the "Jewish" day of the week. Secularists and Yiddishists have opened schools that meet on Saturdays to transmit to the young their distinctive conceptions of Jewish life, and even synagogues run Saturday afternoon cultural programs for those who have no interest in attending the morning worship services. A new cultural institution, the *Oneg Shabbat*, has come into being, a gathering on Friday evening or Saturday afternoon where people come together primarily to enjoy relaxed fellowship and some sort of cultural enrichment. Modern Jewish life thus continues to confirm the observation of the great essayist Ahad Ha'am that the Sabbath has preserved the Jews over the centuries even more than the Jews have preserved the Sabbath.[16] For many Jews all over the world, the Sabbath remains the Jewish day of the week, the day for Jewish books, Jewish prayers, Jewish food, Jewish songs, Jewish peoplehood. As was the case many centuries ago, so it remains today: the regular celebration of the seventh day is one of the hallmarks of Jewish life. Through the lens of the Sabbath we can glimpse the Jewish vision of eternity.

Notes

1. This is why a famous passage in Mishnah *Hagigah* 1:8 describes the rules of Sabbath rest as "mountains hanging by a hair."

2. That is, grain from chaff.

3. See Yitzhak D. Gilat, "The Thirty-Nine Classes of Work Forbidden on the Sabbath," *Tarbiz* 29 (1960): 222–28 (Hebrew).

4. See A. J. Heschel, *The Sabbath: Its Meaning for Modern Man* (New York: Farrar, Straus and Giroux, 1951), 12–24.

5. For a modern treatment (chiefly for children) of this same theme, see S. Y. Agnon, "A Story about a Coin," in A. E. Millgram, *Sabbath: The Day of Delight* (Philadelphia: Jewish Publication Society of America, 1959), 128–30.

6. See the study by Elliot K. Ginsburg, *The Sabbath in the Classical Kabbalah* (Albany: State University of New York Press, 1989).

7. Recall as well the Mishnaic list of forbidden activities that was quoted previously.

8. See B. M. Levin, "On the History of the Sabbath Lamp," in *Essays and Studies in Memory of Linda R. Miller* (New York: Jewish Theological Seminary of America, 1938), Hebrew section, 55–68. According to Levin, the reasons for this transformation have to do with the great struggle between the rabbis of the early Middle Ages and their opponents, the Karaites, but the excerpt from Persius already quoted suggests that some sort of special Sabbath lamp was known long before the rise of Karaism.

9. This paper has not considered the question whether women and men have over the centuries experienced the Sabbath in a fundamentally different way. Although women throughout Jewish history have no doubt derived great enjoyment from Sabbath rest, it should be noted as well that in many cases the burden of cleaning and cooking has fallen largely onto their shoulders.

10. Renunciation as a mark of holiness (Num. 6:24); libation onto the altar (Num. 15:5, 7, 10); wine as source of joy (Judg. 9:13; Ps. 104:14; but see also Prov. 21:17, 32:4–5, and many other such warnings). "Nowhere in Scripture," needless to say, means nowhere in the Jewish Scriptures.

11. See Erwin Goodenough, *Jewish Symbols in the Greco-Roman Period* (New York: Pantheon, 1956), 6:219–20. This brief passage summarizes a discussion that has gone on for two hundred pages.

12. For sample liturgical texts, see Philip Birnbaum, *Daily Prayer Book* (New York: Hebrew Publishing Company, 1949), 71–97 (the core of the weekday morning service), 335–59 (Sabbath), 191–211 and 257–73 (evening services), and 760–69 (Grace after Meals).

13. For samples of these hymns, see Birnbaum, *Daily Prayer Book*, 291–97, 425–35.

14. Scripture calls these "labor," but until very recently no one thought that strenuous effort was really at the heart of the concept. In recent times, a powerful incentive to adopt this understanding has been the desire to justify setting the restrictions aside with the claim that everything nowadays is easier to do.

15. See the discussion by Lawrence Schiffman, *The Halakhah at Qumran* (Leiden: Brill, 1975), 77–133.

16. Ahad Ha'am, *Collected Works* (reprint, Tel Aviv: Dvir, 1965), 286 (Hebrew).

A Jewish Theology and Philosophy of the Sabbath

WALTER S. WURZBURGER

A n important caveat must be heeded in any discussion of the philosophy or theology of the Sabbath. Judaism constitutes a way of life
rather than the profession of a creed. Because it revolves around the observance of Halakah (religious law) rather than the affirmation of articles
of faith, precise dogmatic formulations are eschewed. No matter how far
theological beliefs may diverge from the mainstream of Jewish thought,
they qualify as perfectly legitimate expressions of Judaism, as long as they
are compatible with the acknowledgment of the binding authority of the
Halakah. As Abraham of Posquière put it in his strictures against Maimonides, one would not be excluded from the community of faith, even if
one would veer as far from the dominant theological view as to attribute
corporeal attributes to God.[1]

Since Judaism sanctions such enormous latitude in matters of belief, it
is impossible to develop a philosophy or theology of the Sabbath that can
lay claims to objective validity. All I hope to achieve in this paper is to
provide a conceptual framework for what the experience of the Sabbath
means to me and to show how the philosophy and theology I read into
the Sabbath contributes to the enhancement of my personal appreciation
and love of the Sabbath and enables me to treat Shabbat as the very focus
of my existence. My formulations are merely offered as possible interpretations of the postulates underlying the normative teachings of Judaism,
which are embodied in the Halakah.

In this connection it might be useful to refer to the *Pesiqta De'Rab Kahana*, which notes that the Sinaitic revelation addressed each individual in the voice appropriate for that person (12:25). Similarly, the Kabbalists point out that the divine revelation was heard by each individual in a different form. In keeping with this emphasis on the subjectivity that characterizes the realm of Aggadah as opposed to objectively binding halakic norms regulating conduct, my objective is a very limited one: I merely want to develop a philosophy or theology of the Sabbath, for which I make no claims except that it satisfies the needs of my personal existential situation.

To be sure, in striking contrast to the many areas of religious practice where classical biblical and rabbinic sources offer hardly any clue to their theological or philosophical meaning, we suffer from an embarrassment of riches in the attempt to explore the spiritual meaning of Sabbath observance. The numerous scriptural references to the Sabbath allude to a variety of themes, ranging from creation to the Exodus from Egypt, from constituting a day of rest for the individual to a summons to a "holy convocation." The Sabbath is portrayed also as a sign of the covenant between God and Israel that God created heaven and earth in six days (Exod. 31:17).

Especially revealing is the difference between the two versions of the Decalogue as presented in Exodus and in Deuteronomy. The former concerns itself exclusively with the creation theme and focuses on the theocentric aspects of the Sabbath, reminding humans that the world does not belong to them but to God. Refraining from work on the Sabbath primarily is interpreted as the acknowledgment of God as the Creator of the universe. A person's right to engage in creative activity is limited to what is explicitly sanctioned by God and contributes to the fulfillment of God's purposes. To be legitimate, human activity must conform to the pattern established by God, who stopped the process of creation on the Sabbath. In sharp contrast to this exclusive emphasis on the surrender to God, which seeks to guard humans against self-deification and the worship of their own powers, the version of the Decalogue in Deuteronomy includes, in addition to the creation theme, a reference to the Exodus from Egypt and dwells upon the benefits accruing to man and woman from the Sabbath as a day of liberation and rest. This humanistic motif is further elaborated in prophetic writings, which mandate that the Sabbath be proclaimed as a day of delight and be treated with the honor due to such a sacred and joyous event. The Tannaim developed these ideas by stressing that the Sabbath should not merely be treated as a commandment but be hailed as a special and unique gift that the Almighty had bestowed upon Israel (Babylonian Talmud *Shabbat* 10b).

Although with reference to the Sabbath, a relatively large number of themes is adumbrated in Scriptures and subsequently developed in rabbinic literature, it appears that, contrary to Hermann Cohen's opinion, acknowledgment of God as the Creator rather than the liberation of humanity constitutes the dominant motif of the Sabbath experience.[2] Notwithstanding the fact that the Torah enjoins the remembrance and the sanctification of the Sabbath as well as the cessation of whatever activity interferes with the observance of a day of rest, the drastic penalties that the biblical legal code provides for desecration of the Sabbath are reserved exclusively for violations of the prohibition against *melakhah* (work). Public desecration of the Sabbath through performance of *melakhah* is deemed the equivalent of the rejection of the entire Torah. According to talmudic law, any individual guilty of such conduct is deprived of many privileges associated with membership in the Jewish community and in some respects is treated as a non-Jew. Although according to many contemporary authorities the upheavals of the post-Emancipation era have for all practical purposes rendered this law inoperative, it is of the utmost importance to bear in mind that traditionally observance of the prohibitions against *melakhah* was a *conditio sine qua non* of membership in the Jewish community. Since the Sabbath functions as a sign between God and Israel that God is the Creator of heaven and earth, the desecration of the Sabbath amounts not merely to an act of disobedience but in effect to an outright denial of one of the most central tenets of Judaism—the affirmation of God as the Creator of the universe.

According to the rabbinic interpretation, no matter how strenuous an activity may be, it does not fall under the category of biblically prohibited work unless it constitutes *melekhet machshevet*, that is, an activity performed with design and purpose (Babylonian Talmud *Besah* 16a). To do so, it must not only resemble the thirty-nine types of work that according to Jewish tradition were necessary for the construction of the mobile sanctuary that was built in the desert; it must also follow the normal procedures and customary objectives associated with the activity in question. If an activity is carried out in an abnormal fashion (*kele'achar yad*), it is only rabbinically prohibited but does not constitute an infringement of the biblical prohibition against *melekhet machshevet*.

That designful activity rather than toil represents the defining characteristic of work sheds considerable light on the reason why the Sabbath plays such a pivotal role in the Jewish scale of values. It clearly indicates that such "social hygiene" functions as rest or relief from drudgery represent merely secondary considerations. Performing an activity in an awkward manner or without a purposeful, constructive intent would hardly affect the amount of effort expended. Were the suspension of toil and labor the primary goal of the Sabbath as a day of rest, the elements of purposeful activity could not be invoked as criteria determining whether or not a particular activity constitutes *melakhah*.[3]

The halakic definition of *melakhah* not as toil or labor but as purposeful work points to the specifically religious dimension of the Sabbath, which transcends considerations of social or psychological utility. If Isaiah (56:2,14) and Nehemiah (9:13) single out the Sabbath as the hallmark of faithfulness to the covenant, it was because they saw in the Sabbath the concretization of the most fundamental tenets regarding a person's relationship to God and to nature. Maimonides even declares that the original divine legislation issued at Marah provided only for the Sabbath and ethical laws; no other ritual laws were deemed necessary at that time (*Guide for the Perplexed* 3:32). Small wonder, then, that the Sabbath is regarded as the quintessence of Judaism. As Dayan I. Grunfeld phrased it so aptly, the "Sabbath epitomizes the whole of Judaism."[4] Viewed from this vantage point, the prohibition against *melakhah* emerges as a much-needed reminder to humans that for all their powers of creativity, they too are merely creatures of God.

To be sure, human creativity and dominion over nature represent perfectly legitimate activities. Judaism does not subscribe to the Promethean myth that condemns human creativity as an act of defiance of the heavenly powers.[5] There is really no basis for Erich Fromm's suggestion that the prohibition against work on the Sabbath aims at the reconciliation of humanity with nature and the restoration of the peace that has been disturbed as the result of human efforts to assert dominion over nature.[6] However appealing this explanation may be to an age that is becoming increasingly sensitivized to ecological issues, the Jewish religious tradition can hardly be invoked to justify such an antitechnological bias. According to an often-quoted midrashic statement, even under the idyllic conditions that prevailed in the Garden of Eden it was necessary for man to engage in work and to tend and guard the earth.[7] It is also highly significant that the act of circumcision, which according to numerous commentators symbolizes man's task to become a partner with God in helping perfect the world,[8] takes precedence over the prohibitions against work on the Sabbath. There is therefore scant plausibility to Fromm's suggestion that the Sabbath is intended as a protest against interference with nature. There is really nothing in the Jewish tradition to support the thesis that reconciliation with nature as evidenced by the cessation of human constructive activities constitutes an integral part of the messianic ideal of perfect *shalom*—the ultimate peace of which the Sabbath is the forerunner.

It therefore seems much more likely that the prohibitions against work on the Sabbath are grounded not in antitechnological attitudes but in the realization of the debilitating spiritual hazards posed by human creativity. It is one thing to endorse human creativity as the fulfillment of a God-given mandate to conquer the world and to harness the forces of nature for the satisfaction of human needs, and it is another to become oblivious to the enormous dangers to the image of God within humanity, which, as we have so painfully discovered in an age of secularization and desacralization, are likely to result from our technological triumphs. We are prone to become so intoxicated with our success in subduing nature that we may succumb to the danger of arrogant self-idolization and forget that the entire universe, including our own creative capacities, is not a self-contained cosmos but God's creation, which must recognize its dependence on him.

The regularity and order prevailing within the realm of nature tend to obscure the divine source of all existence. It is for this reason that it is precisely on the day when according to the biblical account the world began to function in accordance with the laws of nature that it is incumbent upon us to acknowledge God as the owner and master of the universe.

By abstaining on the Sabbath from productive activity in conscious imitation of the Creator, who "stopped" his work of creation on the Sabbath, we affirm that what appear to the secular mind as purely natural phenomena are in actuality manifestations of the divine. Thus the Sabbath reveals what nature conceals. It is interesting to recall in this context that, according to the *Zohar*, the letters of the term *E-lohim* suggest that this name of God reflects the quest for the ultimate meaning of reality, which can be apprehended only when we raise the question *Mi eleh* (Who are these?) (*Zohar* 1:1b). In a similar vein, Rabbi Shneur Zalman Mi'Liadi noted that the numerical equivalent of the term *teva* (nature) is *E-lohim*.[9] It is through the Sabbath experience that we are directed to penetrate beneath the surface to the core of reality and to become aware that the universe is not a self-sufficient cosmos but is created and sustained in its being by the divine Creator, the source of all reality.

Since the experience of the holiness of the Sabbath is the matrix of the formation of proper perspectives on the "secular" domain, it is readily understandable why the Jewish religious tradition looks upon the Sabbath as the very purpose of all of creation. Accordingly, the Sabbath was not primarily intended as a day of rest enabling a person to return refreshed to worldly tasks with renewed vigor and zest. Instead, the liturgy in the Friday-evening service extols the Sabbath as "the very goal of the making of the heaven and earth." Jewish life is supposed to be Sabbath-centered. The Jew does not rest on the Sabbath to prepare himself or herself for the tasks awaiting in the following week. Instead, the Jew literally lives for the Sabbath. He or she works six days in preparation for the goal of life—to enter the sacred precincts of the sanctuary in time that the Sabbath represents.

Nachmanides pointed out that the biblical commandment "Remember the Sabbath day to sanctify it" implies that the Sabbath is the only day of the week worthy of being designated by a name (*Commentary to Exodus* 20:8). The rest of the days are defined solely in terms of their relation to the Sabbath. In Hebrew there is no word for Sunday or Monday, etc.; they are simply the first or the second day of the week. It is noteworthy that the Midrash interprets the biblical phrase "God finished on the seventh day the work He had made" (Gen. 2:2) as implying not merely that the work was concluded on the seventh day but that the work became perfect only on the seventh day (*Genesis Rabbah* 10:10). As Rashi interpreted it, until the Sabbath was created, the world was without *menuchah* (tranquillity) (Rashi on Gen. 2:2).

Although the exclusively theocentric formulation of the fourth commandment in the Book of Exodus in describing the "Sabbath unto God" does not mention the social and psychological benefits accruing to one from its observance, the version of the Decalogue as presented in the Book of Deuteronomy adds the themes of liberation and rest to be enjoyed by all creatures. Both Hermann Cohen and Erich Fromm write from a basically humanistic perspective, which frowns on obedience to heteronomous norms as being devoid of all ethical worth.[10] They concentrate on what they regard as the ethical implications of the Sabbath as set forth in Deuteronomy, which are contrasted with what they describe as the mythological features contained in the creation story, which form the core of the fourth commandment in Exodus 19. It appears to me that this approach reflects a dogmatic insistence on forcing Judaism into a Procrustean bed of humanistic categories. The additional references in Deuteronomy to anthropocentric themes do not in any way detract from the theocentric aspects mandating total surrender to God as the Creator and master of the universe. Significantly, it is precisely in the version in which the humanistic benefits are introduced that the Torah stresses that the observance of the Sabbath is in conformity to a divine imperative ("as God has commanded thee").

This being the case, it would be far more appropriate to treat the anthropocentric and the theocentric dimensions of the Sabbath experience as reflections of the dialectical tension between these two components rather than as irreconcilable positions. Contrary to Feuerbach and Karl Marx, a person's unconditional submission to the Creator does not devalue human existence but adds an extra dimension of meaning and significance, which enables him or her to experience true dignity and freedom. The Sabbath experience makes us aware of the fact that our ontological status is based not on what we make but on what we are. As the bearer of the divine age, persons must not be "thingified" and reduced to self-alienated commodities or tools but must be accorded the dignity due to creatures endowed with infinite, intrinsic spiritual value. Through the observance and experience of the Sabbath, the Jew learns that in the divine economy, a person's worth does not depend upon social utility as an agent of production but derives from the intrinsic sanctity of the human personality.

At first blush it may strike us as strange that the observance of the Sabbath, which cuts a person down to size by mandating that his or her creative powers may be exercised only within the parameters approved by God, simultaneously elevates a person's dignity by providing us with a day of universal rest and liberation, which engenders the experience of *oneg Shabbat*—the enjoyment of delight, peace, and harmony. But it must be borne in mind that classical Jewish thought has always proceeded from the premise that it is only through submission to the authority of a transcendent God that humans achieve true dignity and inner freedom. In the often-cited formulation of the rabbinic sages, "one attains freedom only when one is engaged in Torah" (*Avot* 6:2).

The dialectical nature of the Sabbath experience is suggested also in a well-known midrash which states that "everything pertaining to the Sabbath is double . . . double Omer (of Mannah) . . . , double sacrifices . . . , double penalties . . . , double rewards . . . , double admonitions . . . and the Sabbath Psalm is double" (*Midrash Tehillim* on Ps. 92:1). The two loaves of bread that are *de rigueur* for Sabbath meals (Babylonian Talmud *Shabbat* 117b) reflect this emphasis on the duality characterizing the Sabbath observance. Significantly, the Talmud points out that the two versions of the fourth commandment were simultaneously commanded by God to Israel in one single pronouncement (Babylonian Talmud *Rosh Hashanah* 27a). The emphasis on the twofold nature of the Sabbath also comes to the fore in the rabbinic doctrine that with the arrival of the Sabbath the Jew is endowed with a *neshamah yeterah* (an additional soul), which departs at the end of Shabbat (Babylonian Talmud *Besah* 16a).

Since the Sabbath represents in a sense the bridge between the natural and the transcendent realms, the Talmud took it for granted that the Sinaitic revelation occurred on the Sabbath (*Shabbat* 86b). It seemed obvious to the rabbinic mind that the day which, according to the Bible, symbolized the incursion of the divine upon the world of nature, represented the ideal time for his revelation to Israel.

Another theme that is associated with the Sabbath is that of redemption. Although in the Torah the connection between the Sabbath and liberation is made only with reference to the Exodus from Egypt, rabbinic thought expands the concept by treating the Exodus as the prototype of the divine redemption—a process that will be completed only in the messianic redemption, when the kingdom of God will be acknowledged by all of humanity. The proper observance of the Sabbath, therefore, is regarded not merely as a reminder of the past liberation but also as a promise of the future realization of our eschatological hopes. It is for this reason that, in the opinion of the sages, the meticulous observance of the Sabbath on the part of the entire Jewish people would ensure the arrival of the Messiah (Babylonian Talmud *Shabbat* 118b). Because of the close association between the Sabbath and the redemption, the liturgy for welcoming the Sabbath includes a number of psalms that give vent to the feeling of exhilaration and jubilation that will be precipitated by the establishment of the kingdom of God.[11]

The Sabbath does not merely point to the redemption of the world from moral evil. Since the Sabbath atmosphere is supposed to make us oblivious to unfulfilled wants and unfinished tasks, it provides a foretaste of the world to come. This is why when the prayer of grace is recited after the Sabbath meal, the phrase "May the All-merciful One cause us to inherit the day which will be completely a Sabbath of rest and eternal life" is added to the weekday version.

It is interesting that the Talmud records two distinct modes of preparation that are appropriate for the proper encounter with the Sabbath. One Amora (talmudic sage) is reported to have urged his disciples to welcome the Sabbath as a queen, whereas another advocated that the Sabbath be greeted as a bride (Babylonian Talmud *Shabbat* 119a). In other words, one opinion emphasized the majesty, awe, and reverence with which Shabbat should be approached, whereas the other stressed the intimacy with the divine that should be engendered by the encounter with what the liturgy describes as "the most desirable of days." Since the two approaches need not contradict each other, they should be synthesized in the ideal Shabbat experience. Rabbinic authorities till this very day are divided over the question of whether there is a requirement to experience real *simchah* (joy) on the Sabbath or whether one is merely obligated to engage in activities that can be described as *oneg* (pleasant) but do not necessarily lead to the higher level of *simchah* which is mandated for holidays. Be that as it may, there is universal agreement that the Sabbath must be respected not only by refraining from work in the technical sense but by staying away from any activity that interferes with the atmosphere of holiness which ought to prevail on the Sabbath. The dignity of the Sabbath demands that one not only dress and eat differently from the rest of the week but that one's entire demeanor and conduct reflect the sanctity of the Sabbath. Subjects that disturb the spiritual atmosphere of the Sabbath are to be avoided in conversation (Babylonian Talmud *Shabbat* 69a).

For a proper appreciation of the sanctity of the Sabbath it should be borne in mind that the Sabbath, God's sanctuary in time, commands the kind of reverence that must be accorded to God's sanctuary in space. It is highly significant that the Torah juxtaposes the two types of sanctuary in the twice-repeated verse "Ye shall keep My Sabbaths and reverence My sanctuary" (Lev. 19:30 and 26:2). Moreover, the Torah harps repeatedly on the overriding importance of the observance of the Sabbath in connection with the demand to build a sanctuary for God. It is precisely this close linkage between the two types of sanctuaries that prompted the sages to define *melakhah* in terms of the categories of work that were needed for the construction of the sanctuary in the days of Moses.

Because the Sabbath is treated as a sanctuary of God, it is readily understandable that Jewish mystics employ spatial metaphors to describe the unique holiness that envelops the world with the arrival of the Sabbath. According to the *Zohar*, "On Friday evening a tabernacle of peace descends from heaven. . . . When Israel invites this tabernacle of peace to their homes as a holy guest, a divine sanctity comes down and spreads its wings over Israel like a mother encompassing her children" (*Zohar* Gen. 48a–b).

It must be realized, however, that the holiness of the Sabbath mandates not merely the cessation of certain types of "secular" activity but also the fulfillment of a number of specific positive obligations. Both the arrival and the departure of the Sabbath must be marked by special ceremonies (Kiddush and Havdalah). Moreover, according to Nachmanides' interpretation, the inclusion of the Sabbath among the days of "holy convocations" implies that Jews are not merely required to sanctify the Sabbath individually but are supposed to assemble for the purpose of divine worship and the reading of the Torah. In other words, the Sabbath experience is designed not only to impact upon the Jew individually but also to stimulate the formation of a unique sense of religious community. As a midrash puts it, Israel's loneliness can be overcome only by the realization that it is mated with the Sabbath—the symbol of its unique spiritual destiny (*Genesis Rabbah* 11:8).

It thus can be seen that, properly observed, the Sabbath is not just a day of rest and total inactivity. Notwithstanding the fact that already in the ancient world the Sabbath was maligned by anti-Semitic writers as evidence of the Jewish predilection to lassitude, which exacts a heavy price in terms of loss of productivity and usefulness, the Sabbath represents a day of spiritual creativity,[12] which, in the words of Ahad Ha'am, has made possible the very survival of the Jewish people. That the Sabbath is to be regarded as a day of positive achievement rather than of lack of activity can be seen from the fact that the Torah employs the term *la-asot* (to make) in conjunction with the admonition to keep the Sabbath (Exod. 31:16 and Deut. 5:14). As Rabbi Kook expressed it so aptly, the Sabbath figures not only as a day of rest but also as a day of holiness.[13] Abstention from activities aiming at the conquest of nature do not exhaust the meaning of the Sabbath. Physical rest must be utilized for all-out spiritual efforts to respond to the challenge posed by the dynamic ideal of holiness which constantly beckons us toward ever greater heights of religious and moral perfection in the never-ending quest of *imitatio Dei*. This is perhaps what was supposed to be conveyed by the daring kabbalistic doctrine that the Sabbath symbolizes the union between the male (active) and the female (passive) metaphysical principles, which, according to Jewish mysticism, provide the foundation of the universe.[14]

Notes

1. Abraham of Posquière, *Hasagot Hara'vad Lemishneh Torah ad Hilkhot Teshuvah* 3:7 (Jerusalem, 1984).

2. Hermann Cohen, *Religion der Vernunft* (trans. Ephraim Fischoff; Leipzig: G. Foch, 1919), 180–82.

3. See my article "Sabbath and Creation," in *Yavneh Shiron*, ed. Eugene Flink (New York: Yavneh Students Organization, 1968), 51–53.

4. D. I. Grunfeld, *The Sabbath: A Guide to Its Understanding and Observance* (London: Sabbath League of Great Britain, 1956), 11. Dayan Grunfeld has pioneered in popularizing the ideas of Samson R. Hirsch in the English-speaking world. Their influence can readily be perceived in my own treatment of the relationship between the Sabbath and the creation theme.

5. See my article "Orthodox Judaism and Human Purpose," in *Religion and Human Purpose*, ed. W. Horosz and T. Clements (Dordrecht: Nijhoff, 1986), 106–22.

6. Erich Fromm, *The Forgotten Language* (New York: Grove Press, 1985), 488–91.

7. *Avot De'Rabbi Natan* 11:1.

8. See *Sefer Hachinukh*, chap. 2.

9. R. Shneur Zalman Mi'Liadi, *Tanya, Sha'ar Hayichud Ve'ha'emunah* (Brooklyn: Kehot Publication Society, 1953), chap. 6.

10. Cohen, *Religion der Vernunft*, 180–82; Fromm, *Ye Shall Be as Gods* (New York: Holt, Rinehart & Winston, 1966), 193–99.

11. See Yechiel Michel Epstein, *Aruch Hashulchan, Orach Chayim* (New York: Halakhah Publishing, 1950), 277:2.

12. See Normann Lamm, "Ethics of Leisure" in *Faith and Doubt* (New York: Ktav, 1971), 197–98. I have also learned a great deal from Abraham J. Heschel, T*he Sabbath: Its Meaning for Modern Man* (New York: Farrar, Straus and Giroux, 1951), as well as from the profound insights of Yitzchak Hutner in his *Sefer Pachad Yitzchak* (Brooklyn: Gur Aryeh Institute, 1982).

13. Abraham Isaac Kook, *Olat Haraya* (Jerusalem: Mossad Harav Kook, 1949), 2:146.

14. See *Zohar* Exod. 135a–b; *Zohar* Gen. 48a–b; and Nachmanides, *Commentary to Exodus* 20:8.

Tradition and New Creation
in the Ritual of the Kabbalists

GERSHOM SCHOLEM

I t would be no exaggeration to call the Sabbath *the* day of the Kabbalah. On the Sabbath the light of the upper world bursts into the profane world in which man lives during the six days of the week. The light
of the Sabbath endures into the ensuing week, growing gradually dimmer,
to be relieved in the middle of the week by the rising light of the next Sabbath. It is the day on which a special pneuma, the "Sabbath soul," enters
into the believer, enabling him to participate in the right way in this day
which shares more than any other day in the secrets of the pneumatic
world. Consequently it was also regarded as a day specially consecrated to
the study of the Kabbalah.

The Kabbalists cited three separate passages in the Talmud, which
were brought together and presented in a new light by . . . [a] conception
of the Sabbath as a sacred marriage. The first tells us that on the eve of the
Sabbath certain rabbis used to wrap themselves in their cloaks and cry
out: Come, let us go to meet Queen Sabbath. Others cried: Come, O
Bride, come, O Bride. The second passage relates that on Friday evening
Simeon ben Yohai and his son saw an old man hurrying through the dusk
with bundles of myrtle. They asked him, What are you doing with those
bundles? He replied: I will honor the Sabbath with them.[1] The third passage tells us that Torah scholars used to perform marital intercourse precisely on Friday night.[2] These disparate reports are interpreted in the
kabbalistic books of ritual as indications that the Sabbath is indeed a marriage festival. The earthly union between man and woman, referred to in
the third passage, was taken as a symbolic reference to the heavenly mar-

riage.³ These themes were combined with the mystical symbolism identifying Bride, Sabbath, and *Shekhinah*. Still another mystical notion that played a part in the kabbalistic Sabbath ritual was the "field of holy apple trees,"⁴ as the *Shekhinah* is frequently called in the *Zohar*. In this metaphor the "field" is the feminine principle of the cosmos, while the apple trees define the *Shekhinah* as the expression of all the other *sefiroth*, or holy orchards, which flow into her and exert their influence through her. During the night before the Sabbath, the King is joined with the Sabbath–Bride; the holy field is fertilized, and from their sacred union the souls of the righteous are produced.

On the basis of these conceptions, which are set forth at length in the *Zohar*, the Safed Kabbalists, beginning in the middle of the sixteenth century, developed a solemn and highly impressive ritual which is not mentioned in earlier sources. Its dominant theme is the mystical marriage. A strange twilight atmosphere made possible an almost complete identification of the *Shekhinah*, not only with the Queen of the Sabbath, but also with every Jewish housewife who celebrates the Sabbath. This is what gave this ritual its enormous popularity. To this day the Sabbath ritual is pervaded by memories of the old kabbalistic rite, and certain of its features have been preserved intact.

I shall try to describe this ritual in its original and meaningful form.⁵ On Friday afternoon, sometime before the onset of the Sabbath, the Kabbalists of Safed and Jerusalem, usually clad in white—in any case neither in black nor red, which would have evoked the powers of stern judgment and limitation—went out of the city into an open field, which the advent of the *Shekhinah* transformed into the "holy apple orchard." They "went to meet the Bride." In the course of the procession the people sang special hymns to the Bride and psalms of joyful anticipation (such as Ps. 29 or Pss. 95–99). The most famous of these hymns was composed by Solomon Alkabez, a member of Moses Cordovero's group in Safed. It begins:

> *Go, my beloved, to meet the Bride,*
> *Let us receive the face of the Sabbath . . .*

In this hymn, which is still sung in the synagogue, mystical symbolism is explicitly combined with messianic hopes for the redemption of the *Shekhinah* from exile. When the actual procession into the fields was dropped, the congregation "met the Bride" in the court of the synagogue, and when this observance in turn fell into disuse, it became customary, as it is to this day, to turn westward at the last verse of the hymn and bow to the approaching Bride. It is recorded that Luria, standing on a hill near Safed, beheld in a vision the throngs of Sabbath-souls coming with the Sabbath–Bride. A number of our sources tell us that the Sabbath psalms were sung with closed eyes, for as the Kabbalists explained, the *Shekhinah* is designated in the *Zohar* as "the beautiful virgin who has no eyes," that is to say, who has lost her eyes from weeping in exile.[6] On Friday afternoon the Song of Songs, traditionally identified with the indissoluble bond between "the Holy One, blessed be He, and the Ecclesia of Israel," but here taken also as an epithalamion for the *Shekhinah*, was also intoned. Only after the meeting of the Bride were the traditional Sabbath prayers spoken.

After the prayer the mystical ritual was resumed at home. According to Isaac Luria, it was highly commendable and "rich in mystical significance" to kiss one's mother's hands on entering the house. Then the family marched solemnly around the table, from which they took in silence the two bundles of myrtle for the Bride and Bridegroom, and sang a greeting to the angels of the Sabbath, that is, the two angels who according to the Talmud[7] accompany each man to his home at the onset of the Sabbath. The four stanzas of the hymn to the angels, "Peace be with you, you angels of peace," are followed by recitation of the thirty-first chapter of Proverbs, which seems to sing the praises of the noble housewife and her activities, but which the Kabbalists interpreted line by line as a hymn to the *Shekhinah*. Strange to say, it was through the mystical reinterpretation of the Kabbalists that this praise of the Jewish housewife found its way into the Sabbath ritual. This "hymn to the matron" is to be sung in a melodious voice by the seated company. Then, before the meal, as the *Zohar* prescribes, the master of the house "explicitly utters the mystery of the meal," that is, he introduces the sacred action in words which describe its secret meaning and at the same time conjure the *Shekhinah* to partake of the meal with her Bridegroom ("Small-faced," or better "Impatient") and the "Holy Old One." This solemn Aramaic invocation runs:

> *Prepare the meal of perfect faith*
> *To rejoice the heart of the holy King,*
> *Prepare the meal of the King.*
> *This is the meal of the field of holy apples,*
> *And the Impatient and the Holy Old One—*
> *Behold, they come to partake of the meal with her.*

What happens in this sacred action is described in Isaac Luria's great hymn, one of the few authentic works that have come down to us from the hand of this greatest of the Safed Kabbalists. Luria wrote hymns of this kind for each of the Sabbath meals. In the solemn drapery of their Zoharic Aramaic, they suggest the grandiloquent gesture of a magician, conjuring up a marvelous pageant for all to see. They read like the hymns of a mystery religion. Here I should like to quote the hymn for the Friday-evening meal.

> *I sing in hymns*
> *to enter the gates,*
> *of the field of apples*
> *of holy ones.*
>
> *A new table*
> *we lay for her,*
> *a beautiful candelabrum*
> *sheds its light upon us.*
>
> *Between right and left*
> *the Bride approaches*
> *in holy jewels*
> *and festive garments.*
>
> *Her husband embraces her*
> *in her foundation,*[8]
> *gives her fulfillment,*
> *squeezes out his strength.*
>
> *Torment and cries*
> *are past.*
> *Now there are new faces*
> *and souls and spirits.*
>
> *He gives her joy*
> *in twofold measure.*
> *Lights shine*
> *and streams of blessing.*

Bridesmen, go forth,
and prepare the Bride,
victuals of many kinds
and all manner of fish.[9]

To beget souls
and new spirits
on the thirty-two paths
and three branches.[10]

She has seventy crowns
but above her the King,
that all may be crowned
in the Holy of Holies.

All worlds are formed
and sealed within her,
but all shine forth
from the "Old of Days."

To southward I set
the mystical candelabrum,
I make room in the north
for the table with the loaves.

With wine in beakers
and boughs of myrtle
to fortify the Betrothed,
for they are feeble.

We plait them wreaths
of precious words
for the coronation of the seventy
in fifty gates.

Let the Shekhinah *be surrounded*
by six Sabbath loaves
connected on every side
with the Heavenly Sanctuary.

Weakened and cast out
the impure powers,
the menacing demons
are now in fetters.

In the eyes of the Kabbalists, this hymn was in a class apart. Unlike other table songs for the eve of the Sabbath, which could be sung or not, as one pleased, it was an indispensable part of the ritual. In Luria's hymn new meaning was not injected into an old prayer by means of mystical exegesis or *kavvanah*; rather, an esoteric conception creates its own liturgical language and form. The culmination of the hymn, the chaining of the demons on the Sabbath, when they must flee "into the maw of the great abyss," recurs in Luria's hymns for the other two meals. The last song, sung at the dusk that ends the Sabbath day, strongly emphasizes this exorcism of the "insolent dogs," the powers of the other side—it is not a mere description of an exorcism, it is an exorcism:

The insolent dogs must remain outside and cannot come in,
I summon the "Old of Days" at evening until they are dispersed,
Until his will destroys the "shells."
He hurls them back into their abysses, they must hide deep in their
    caverns.
And all this now, in the evening, at the festival of *ze'ir anpin*.[11]

I shall not go into all the other Sabbath rites of the Kabbalists. But there is still one point I should like to bring up in this connection. Just as the "reception of the Bride" marks a beginning of the holy day even before the onset of the actual Sabbath, so some Kabbalists attached great importance to a fourth Sabbath meal (mentioned very briefly in the Talmud as the custom of a single individual) which takes place after the Havdalah, the prayer of division between Sabbath and weekday, and extends far into the night. This meal (at which among some of the Kabbalists nothing was eaten) escorts the Bride out of our domain, just as the ritual described above led her into it. Some Kabbalists attached the utmost importance to this mythical meal to "accompany the Queen." Whereas the three official Sabbath meals were associated with the patriarchs, Abraham, Isaac, and Jacob, this one was identified with David, the Lord's anointed, the Messiah. But according to the *Zohar*, these forefathers are the "feet of the divine throne," *or merkabah*. Small wonder that Nathan of

Gaza, the prophet and spokesman of the kabbalistic messiah Sabbatai Zevi, prolonged this fourth meal until midnight. "He used to say: This is the meal of the King Messiah, and made a great principle of it."[12]

NOTES

1. Cf. Moritz Zobel, *Der Sabbath* (Berlin, 1935), 59, 64.

2. *Kethuboth* 62b.

3. This symbolism contradicts the thought of Simeon ben Yohai in the early Midrash, who termed the Sabbath and the community of Israel bride and groom and interpreted the sanctification of the Sabbath in the Ten Commandments as a marriage concluded through the "hallowing" of the Bride–Sabbath. Cf. Zobel, *Der Sabbath*, 49.

4. On the strength of a talmudic phrase (*Ta'anith* 29a)—"like an apple orchard"— which in the Talmud however merely characterizes a particularly pleasant odor.

5. In the following I use chiefly the descriptions of the ritual given in the *Shulhan Arukh of Isaac Luria* and in *Hemdath Yamim*, vol. I. This is not the place for analyses of the development of the different parts of the ritual, such as are sadly lacking in the literature of Jewish studies.

6. In *Zohar* 2: 95a, this virgin is the Torah, and the literal meaning of the metaphor applied to a virgin "upon whom no eyes are directed" (whom no one sees).

7. *Shabbath* 119a.

8. The ninth *sefirah, yesod,* "the foundation," is correlated with the male and female sex organs.

9. The fish is a symbol of fertility. The widespread custom of eating fish on Friday is connected with the custom of consummating marriages on Friday night.

10. Souls issue from "Wisdom" by 32 paths. The two branches are grace, judgment, and appeasing love, the three "pillars" of the world of the *sefiroth,* from which come the souls. The seventy crowns of the Bride in the following line are mentioned in *Zohar* 2: 205a.

11. *Ze'ir anpin* means in the Zohar the "Impatient One" in contrast to the "Patient One" as an aspect of God. In Luria it is taken literally as "he with the little face." He is the Godhead in its endless development and growth, as Lord of the *Shekhinah.*

12. *'Inyane Shabbetai Zevi*, ed. A. Freimann (1913), 94. It is in this light that we must understand the prescriptions of the *Hemdath Yamim* and the significance of this meal in the hasidic movement.

Praising the Work of Valiant Women: A Feminist Endorsement of Eshet Hayil

AMY BARDACK

Give her credit for the products of her labor and let her works praise her in the gates. (Prov. 31:31)

F riday night, the candles have been lit, the table set, the meal cooked by the wife. The husband, having just returned from shul (synagogue), sits at the table. "Shalom Aleikhem" is sung, welcoming the Sabbath angels. The husband then sings to his wife Eshet Hayil (Valiant Woman, Prov. 31:10–31), a poem praising a wise, righteous woman for her accomplishments in business, education, and household management.

When I first encountered Eshet Hayil, I felt alienated by the overemphasized domesticity of its setting.[1] Sung at the Sabbath table, where the only visible signs of the woman's work are the products of housework, the message is clear: domestic chores are central to her worth. Eshet Hayil can thus be read as a gesture to the housewife, tacit recognition of the meal she has cooked and the house she has cleaned, in compensation for her exclusion from public worship. Unlike the dynamic protagonist of Eshet Hayil, her real-life referent is silent and passive, dependent entirely on her husband to praise her. Thus, the ritual seems to glorify the stereotypical Jewish wife and mother, catering selflessly to her family, denying herself—or being denied—opportunities for public and self-recognition.

But the contemporary ritual does not fully express the richness and complexity of the text. The Book of Proverbs, in which Eshet Hayil is found, is a compendium of teachings and aphorisms which give practical advice regarding ethics and day-to-day conduct. Removing Eshet Hayil from this context and restricting it to home and hearth has diluted the power of the poem. It deserves a second look, unfettered by its history of interpretation and ritualization.

The text praises the Valiant Woman for far more than "housework" in the modern sense. Although the Valiant Woman works from her home, she is by no means confined by its boundaries. She is in charge of a successful home-based economy—selling textile products of wool and flax (v.v. 24, 13), and using the income to buy a field where she plants a profitable vineyard (v. 16). That her work extends beyond the home is clear: "She is like a merchant fleet, bringing her food from afar" (v. 14).

In addition to her economic contributions, the Valiant Woman is responsible for management of a large household, which includes teaching morals and ethics (v.v. 26, 30). Her moral conscience is evident in acts of social justice (v. 20); she is generous with the needy rather than hoarding the profits of her labor. Her work is impressive enough to bring recognition at the city gate (v. 31), the locus of business and political activity from which most women were excluded.

Like the male heroes in Psalms, the Valiant Woman is known for her praiseworthy accomplishments, above beauty or pedigree. A comparison to male heroic warriors is further suggested by the pervasive military imagery in the text. For example, the word *hayil* denotes power and strength in a military sense. Numerous phrases with double meanings referring to war are complemented by several references to her physical strength.[2] The battle imagery signifies that her work is as vital to the survival of the community as that of a male heroic warrior.

This portrayal of a strong, active woman derives further significance from its location at the end of Proverbs. Such placement suggests that women's work is representative of the wise, righteous activities commended in the rest of the book. In her embodiment of practical knowledge, the Valiant Woman is not simply capable but pious as well. Proverbs makes clear that wisdom is at once mundane and holy since it is a quality bestowed upon us, and shared, by God. The Valiant Woman's tasks—which are manifestations of wisdom—take on some of the luster of God's own labor.

In the first nine chapters of the Book of Proverbs, wisdom is personified and deified as a woman. Numerous correlations between Wisdom, who opens the Book of Proverbs, and the Valiant Woman, who closes it, suggest that the authors and editors of Proverbs drew a deliberate analogy between the two figures.[3] We learn that the Valiant Woman's "mouth is full of wisdom" (v. 26) and that she is "a woman who fears God" (v. 30), a quality which the books of Proverbs and Psalms deem a prerequisite to wisdom.[4] Fear of God is also associated with the knowledge Wisdom bestows on her followers (1:29, 8:13). Both Wisdom and the Valiant Woman are deemed more valuable than rubies, and each recognizes her own worth.[5] Both figures seek and receive attention at the city gates (1:21, 8:3, 31:31). These parallels are buttressed by the passages' physical placement as brackets surrounding the Book of Proverbs: the book opens with Wisdom personified as female and closes with a woman who is wise.

The connection of the Valiant Woman with the figure of Wisdom signifies that women, through their daily activities, exhibit the shared human–divine characteristic of wisdom. The analogy with Wisdom places the public functions of the Valiant Woman on a par with her roles as wife and mother. Her worth is not dependent upon the praise of her family; rather, her works speak for themselves. The Valiant Woman is good to her husband and children, but it is by virtue of her activities—in business, teaching, household management, and charity to the poor—that she is wise. And her wisdom does not just earn her praise; it is, above all, a vehicle for holiness.

Despite these positive messages, some feminists see in the poem an endorsement of "superwoman," the unattainable, and therefore oppressive, ideal of a woman who can do everything well. Thus, Eshet Hayil is perceived as supporting the unreasonable expectations which society places upon women. Others think Eshet Hayil should be rejected outright insofar as it is a product of a patriarchal world view: that the Valiant Woman is a wife and mother implies a sanctioning of that lifestyle above others; that she is praised by her husband suggests that her worth is defined by him.

These criticisms are based, I believe, in a reading and experience of Eshet Hayil outside its biblical context. I choose not to abandon the ritual but to extend its application so that it can function as an appropriate tribute to contemporary women and do justice to the text. Eshet Hayil becomes more powerful when it is not sung exclusively by a husband to his wife.

In some communities, including some Orthodox circles, single, divorced, and widowed women recite Eshet Hayil and/or "receive" its recitation. Just as the Valiant Woman's works sing her praises, just as Wisdom promotes herself confidently, more women should feel free to sing it to themselves and to one another. As lesbian partners, unmarried hetero-

sexual couples, and single women adopt Eshet Hayil, it becomes a celebration of all women, not only wives.

I am not suggesting that we dispense entirely with the ritual of a husband singing to his wife. The meaning of Eshet Hayil need not necessarily
be distorted in a domestic setting. As women's productivity in private and
public arenas is acknowledged, the image of a wife in the home will conjure fewer associations with oppression and limited opportunity, and a
husband's singing Eshet Hayil to his wife at the table might resonate differently. Also, some women reciprocate their male partner's recitation of
Eshet Hayil with their own recitation of Psalm 112, which praises a God-
fearing man for many of the same qualities with which the Valiant Woman
is credited.

In keeping with Proverbs' conception of wisdom as encompassing all
facets of life, the setting of the ritual should be expanded beyond the Sabbath table to mark other occasions in which women excel with valor. It
could be sung in the synagogue, in honor of a woman's first time leading
services or reading Torah. It could be sung in celebration of a creative en-
deavor, job promotion, or graduation. Even our most secular pursuits are
appropriate to be sanctified in this manner. Eshet Hayil could be a vehicle
for rendering visible women's invisible passages.

In order to reinforce the holiness of the Valiant Woman's activities,
Eshet Hayil could be framed by Wisdom passages from Proverbs, such as
the following:

> Wisdom cries aloud in the street, raises her voice in the squares:
> "Receive my instruction rather than silver, knowledge rather than
> gold. Mine are counsel and resourcefulness; I am understanding;
> courage is mine. Whoever finds me finds life and receives favor
> from God."[6]

New tunes could be composed, incorporating Wisdom passages, and
Eshet Hayil could be complemented by verses which a woman, her family, or her friends choose or write.

Given difficulties with the poem and how it is used, some might opt to
start anew with an original text. There is, however, tremendous value in
reimaging, and thereby reappropriating, a traditional text. The words of
an ancient text carry with them the power of history and heritage. They
connect us to a past which, despite its devaluation of women in certain
areas, did nonetheless recognize and celebrate women's accomplish-

ments. By endorsing Eshet Hayil today, we rediscover and redeem that strain in Jewish tradition which praised women for their independent achievements and saw in women's work manifestations of Godlike wisdom. Taking our place among the generations of commentators who read Eshet Hayil in light of their own experience, we make our mark on tradition.

NOTES

1. Although the Sabbath dinner is the most prevalent setting of Eshet Hayil, the poem has undergone a variety of ritual adaptations at different times and in different communities, e.g., at funerals and weddings. See Yael Levin, "*Eshet Hayil*" (in Hebrew), *Beth Mikra* 31, no. 4 (1985/86): 339–47.

2. See verses 17 and 25 on her physical strength. The warlike connotations of phrases, coupled with the hymnlike structure of the poem, make Eshet Hayil akin both to poems in praise of valiant men and to hymns in praise of God. See Al Wolters, "Proverbs 31:10–31 as Heroic Hymn: A Form-Critical Analysis," *Vetus Testamentum* 38, no. 4 (October 1988): 446–57.

3. For further discussion, see Claudia V. Camp, *Wisdom and the Feminine in the Book of Proverbs* (Decatur, GA: Almono Press, 1985), 188–91.

4. Prov. 1:7, 2:2–5, 9:10, 15:33; Ps. 111:10.

5. Prov. 3:15, 8:11, 18; 31:10, 25.

6. Prov. 1:20, 8:10, 8:14, 8:35.

· II ·

SHABBAT
AS THE
ULTIMATE
MITZVAH

Law as Living Discipline: The Sabbath as Paradigm

NORMAN E. FRIMER

Man historically is not only a thinking and feeling being, but a "doing" being. His life is expressed in activity and relationship, in habit and structured productivity. When a thought or emotion moves him, he will not rest until he has converted it into objective form. Thus, man's life, like the product of genius, is one percent creativity and ninety-nine percent routine. Routine remains bearable only because of the nurture of creativity.

The same holds true for a community. In Milton Steinberg's words, "The ideas and ideals of a people may give it significance, but its group habits give it life." Whatever truths a group possesses must therefore be transmuted from abstractions and universals into group habits, the "stuff of life," which is particular and situational. Otherwise, they would remain lofty but ethereal, inspirational but nonoperative. Man can live neither by bread nor by principle alone.

Every social entity faces this problem. It was, however, central for the Jew. The presuppositions of his birth, existence, and destiny were unique and had to be uniquely embodied in the very bone and marrow of his daily activity. For this purpose, an all-embracing instrument was needed which could transform a slave rabble into a nation, inspire and direct the formation of a social order, withstand the shock of Israel's dispersion, and, by hurdling barriers of language and culture, serve as the great unifier of a people across time and space.

The force which undergirded the truths of Israel's life-view and translated them into daily routine—of home and marketplace, field and factory, school and sanctuary—was the dynamic folk conviction regarding Torah and mitzvot. Torah was the divine teaching and tradition out of which scholars and teachers in every generation were to forge whatever forms, practices, and institutions were needed for their own time. These were then to be built, as bricks and girders, into the very structure of life's demands and challenges and thereby be converted into repositories of Israel's heritage of truth. The mitzvah was to be the diurnal, but existentially crucial, act of life prescribed in the divine teaching by means of which the universal "ought" can be transformed for the individual, as member of the community, into a personal "I must," "I can," "I will." In a conjoined relationship, means and ends are fused into an indissoluble unity.

I

This process is illustrated, for example, by the way in which our forefathers sought to meet the challenge to fashion man's life in accordance with Judaism's faith-premise, viewing God as Creator and man as His creature.[1]

The stark fact is that for six-sevenths of every week man struggles to master his natural environment, to draw sustenance from its resources, and to bend it to his will for his enjoyment or advantage. This is good, for creative labor is good. It is a mitzvah commanded by God Himself.[2]

Yet several dangers lurk in the shadows of human productivity. First, man paradoxically tends to become dependent upon the very instruments he has fashioned to free and serve him. Gilbert Murray emphasizes this point in his analysis of *Five Stages of Greek Religion:* "On us the power of the material world has, through our very mastery of it, and the dependence which results from the mastery, both inwardly and outwardly increased its hold. *Capta ferit victorem cepit.* We have taken possession of it and now we cannot move without it."[3] Second, the danger is very real in modern industrial society that man, as worker, becomes depersonalized and functions merely as a human cog in a vast assembly line. Above all, however, there is the opposite danger—the danger that man, aware of his power and success in dominating nature, will begin to regard himself as the measure of what is right and the yardstick of the good. "Beware," warned Moses thirty centuries ago, ". . . lest when thou hast eaten and art satisfied, and hast built goodly houses [probably split-level ones], and dwelt therein and thy silver and thy gold is multiplied [when thine industrial plants and commercial enterprises have multiplied] . . . then thy heart be lifted up, and thou forget the Lord thy God . . . and thou say in thy heart: My power and the might of my hand hath gotten me this wealth."[4] Men are singularly susceptible to these spiritual foibles.

To balance this impulse, Judaism felt the need for a powerful reverse thrust. Only a counteracting spiritual force, operating radically and publicly in the social fabric of the community, might shake man out of his propensity for self-enslavement and self-deification. He must be compelled to stretch his spirit or shrink his ego so that he can begin to assume his authentic stature as man.

Consequently, Jewish law stepped in with boldness and an uncompromising demand. "Six days shalt thou labor, and do all thy work; but the seventh day is a Sabbath unto the Lord thy God, in it thou shalt not do any manner of work, thou nor thy son, nor thy daughter, nor thy manservant, nor thy maidservant, nor thy cattle, nor thy stranger that is within thy gates."[5] Make the whole machine-community come to a dead stop. Let inner man take over. Only the safety, security, and survival of an individual or the group can justify an exception.

Our oral tradition went beyond this generalization and spelled out the implications of labor in comprehensive detail.[6] Thirty-nine categories of productive and purposeful work were delineated and prohibited, each directed at breaking man's dependence or hold on nature and releasing his shackling grip on his fellow man. If you are a farmer, commands the Law, you must not plough, sow, reap, bind, thresh, winnow, grind, knead, or bake. Go and prepare your food in advance. If you are a shepherd or artisan, you must not shear, bleach, comb, dye, spin, weave, sew, tear. Prepare your clothing ahead of time. If you are a builder or craftsman, you must not construct or demolish, kindle fire or extinguish it, manufacture or ship your product. Close down the assembly line. This is Shabbat! Even if you represent management, you too must cease and desist. For on this day there are no employers and no employees. There are to be no exploiters and no exploited, no manipulators and no manipulated, no freemen and no slaves, no citizens and no strangers. On the Shabbat all are to stand equal in one human family before their one divine parent.

Yet even these specific details were considered inadequate. The sages of the Talmud developed additional categories enjoining any similar, related, or conducive task.[7] Moreover, Isaiah had long ago provided the rabbis with the scriptural grounds for outlawing any activity patently identified with the weekday world.[8] For him, even talking about commerce was desecration, let alone negotiating oral agreements and binding contracts.[9]

The extremes to which the rabbis went in building their halakhic "fences" and defenses reflect a twofold insight. One is their awareness of the gripping hold which work as job, career, or profession has on the life pattern of every human being. A job or profession is more than a means to one's material livelihood. In the moving words of the High Holy Day liturgy, *benafsho yavi lahmo*, man literally invests part of his very being in his task.[10] Craft and craftsman unite in a common partnership. In addition, however, the sages intuited the mortal struggle within every man between the twin forces of the creative and the acquisitive. God had intended man to use the acquisitive creatively; man persists in exploiting the creative acquisitively. Consequently, Jewish tradition pitted against this pair another set of twins, the affirming *zakhor* (remember) and restraining *shamor* (observe) of Sabbath power.[11] By arresting the acquisitive—through the negative *shamor*—Judaism aimed at releasing the creative, allowing it to come into its own. By encouraging the creative—through the positive *zakhor*—it redirected the flow toward the divine end for which it was originally intended.

Even a small measure of self-discipline and affirmative action can help man return to the deeper sources of his being—to his family, to his community, to himself, and to his God. For the problems of Western society are essentially no longer material. They are psychological and spiritual. As Lewis Mumford perceptively predicted in his *Condition of Man*, "At the very moment that mankind as a whole is clothed, fed, sheltered adequately, relieved from want and anxiety, there will arise new conditions calling equally for struggle, internal if not external conditions, derived precisely from the goods that have been achieved."[12] And it is regarding the alleviation of these crucial problems that Shabbat has much to say to contemporary man.

II

An entire community, however, in order to live by its faith and to retain the vitality of its seminal ideals, requires more than merely a formal knowledge of their origin and nature or a mechanical obedience to observances embodied in its tradition. A time may come when the hand of tradition begins to weigh too heavily upon us. If the past is to work dynamically through us, if its events and their derivative lessons are not to remain merely facts and statistics in the musty files of our intellectual archives, memory must become motive power, the experiential must become existential, "the past must become contemporary."

This is more than suggested by the biblical claim that the covenant with Israel at Sinai was not concluded with our ancestors alone. "Neither with you only do I make this *berit* and this oath, but with him that standeth here with us this day before the Lord our God, and also with him that is not here with us this day."[13] In some inexplicable way we, too, were involved.[14] For this *berit* to be alive and compelling, the voice of Sinai must also address us, this very day.[15] We must be with Abraham at Mount Moriah, with our Hebrew brethren in the lime pits of Egypt, by their side in their majestic procession of freedom toward Horeb, as well as with Elijah on Mount Carmel in his dramatic confrontation with the priests of Baal.

What was to be the power which would enable the Jew to acquire that sense of the eternal presentness of Sinai? According to an ancient tradition, revelation took place on the Sabbath Day.[16] Thus, when a Jew of piety and faith sits in the synagogue on Shabbat, wrapped in his prayer shawl, and listens to the voice of the reader reciting from the Torah, *Va-yomer Ha-Shem el Moshe,* "And the Lord spoke unto Moses, saying: 'Speak unto the children of Israel, and bid them,' "[17] he must somehow transcend time and space and be conscious that the biblical yesterday has become his today, and that Moses spoke not to his ancestors alone, but speaks to him. It is in this spirit that he is expected to listen to the reading of the Law and to proclaim aloud upon its termination: "This is the Torah which Moses placed before the children of Israel."[18]

This is no role-playing, no make-believe. It is a personal act of will, a personal leap of commitment, a personal identity of soul. The synagogue has been transmuted into an old–new Sinai, and Shabbat into a hallowed interlude in infinite experience. For the fraction of a second, there is no time–space dimension. There is only *am Yisrael hai,* the reality of a living Israel in a living relationship with its living God.

III

Unfortunately, this kind of ecstasy and union of souls is the gift of the rare man who stands at the peak of the mountain of the Lord. The rest of us stand only at its base or are, at most, on the ascent. Are we to be robbed of having any part in the experience of Shabbat? Was Judaism made only for the angelic, the saintly, the sage, and the mystic?

Eliezer Berkowitz, in his exposition of *God, Man and History*,[19] has underscored the fact that Judaism is more than just a "spiritual" or "intellectual" religion. It does not direct its call only to the soul or mind of man. For when man stands over against God in a one-to-one relationship (as all of us must ultimately do in our existential aloneness), the relationship is not partial, but total; not fragmentary, but full—involving the whole person. In this linkage the body, too, is partner with divinity. God created it. It is not profane unless man deliberately makes it so. Like the ark housing the Torah, the body enshrines the soul in an inextricable life-union. Neither can meet its maker without the other. The soul remains mute and helpless without the body; the body is cold and cloddish without the soul. As a divinely joined composite, however, they can aspire to fulfill the liturgical task enunciated in the Nishmat hymn of the Sabbath, "All my limbs do declare, O Lord, who is like unto Thee!"[20]

To implement this union, the Sabbath ordinances applied and explicated Isaiah's words, "Thou shalt proclaim the Sabbath joy."[21] How? By good food and good drink.[22] "And shalt honor it."[23] How? Through attractive clothing and decorous garments.[24] The whole personality of man stands before his King on the Sabbath Day. Clothed in the apparel of inner and outer dignity, every man, woman, and child may be received in audience before their God.

Can anything be too good in order to help celebrate this unique privilege? For God not only receives us but allows the *Shekhinah*, His Divine Presence, to come into our home as our special guest. For three full meals, gathered as a family in joyous repast, we are both His companions and His children. Consequently, the table must be bedecked with special linens. Flowers are to adorn the setting, wreathing the radiance and beauty that stream from the flickering Sabbath candles. The choicest wine is served, as are two loaves of white bread tastily baked. A leisurely meal of several courses is eaten, accompanied by joyous song. Moreover, on this day a Jew must not kindle any fire, especially not the fire of anger or personal controversy.

This Sabbath delight was never meant to be the monopoly of the affluent. Every Jew had the right and was to have the opportunity to share in its blessing. In order to celebrate the Sabbath, the Jew was required to give concrete evidence of a sensitivity and a responsiveness to the deprivation of others. He was admonished to contribute private *tzedakah* before kindling the Sabbath candles and to invite indigent or lonely guests for the Sabbath meal. In addition, Jewish law required every community to establish a welfare program for its needy citizens. No man must be reduced to the degradation of begging. Moreover, the allotment of food or funds adequate for an entire week was, by talmudic practice, to be distributed on Erev Shabbat. In this way, the poor family, too, would be able to honor and celebrate the hallowed day with joy, secure in the knowledge that the morrow was provided for as well. Otherwise, it would have been folly to chant on the Sabbath afternoon, "Let my soul leap up in blessing unto the Lord,"[25] having neglected the body which provides the springboard and the momentum for that winged leap. The popular mind might consider the stomach a good way to a man's heart. Jewish thought recommends it, along with learning and faith, as a conduit to the Jew's soul. Through this sacramental experience, he can literally "taste and see that the Lord is good."[26] In the concise words of Judah Ha-Levi, "The joyous observance of the Sabbath rites brings one closer to God than asceticism or monasticism."[27]

IV

Yet a complex problem remains. What can serve as a conveyor belt for such principles? Aristotle was more than theorizing when he insisted that "people do not become good by listening to lectures on moral philosophy." How then can ideals be transmitted from person to person and from one generation to the next?

"Ritual" has become a word of disdain for many young people, and "ceremonial" is often merely a synonym for distasteful pomp and circumstance. Yet, when used with integrity and earnestness, both are the indispensable tools of which every society must avail itself in order to hurdle the chasm of time. Existential appropriation is a gift for which few are ready, a capacity too private to make it socially operative. Yet ritual and ceremonial provide us with a nonverbal language whose idiomatic meaning can, by dint of repetition, become universally communicable and applicable to all ages. Jewish law has consequently availed itself of its usefulness and richly endowed the Sabbath with its eloquent beauty.

The Sabbath is basically a family celebration. Therefore, "he who is privileged to rejoice on the Sabbath, surrounded by sons and daughters, finds great favor in the eyes of the Almighty."[28] For, as the generations gather about the Sabbath table, they are not only bound by this expressive though silent symbolism one unto the other, but with all past generations of Israel.

In this setting, the flicker of the Sabbath candles, the words and chant of the Kiddush are the dramatic script and lighting effects for the depiction of the miracles of creation and Exodus. The two challot speak of God's providence and sustenance. The traditional washing of the hands links us with the High Priest in the ancient Temple, with the table as our altar and the food as the *mat'nat kehunah*, the portion of priestliness. Moreover, through the special medieval *zemirot* (Sabbath melodies), which even the smallest children may learn lispingly, tradition weaves its gossamer threads, which, with increasing strength, tie our children to the souls of such mystics as Rabbi Isaac Luria[29] and Rabbi Israel Al Najara.[30] Subtly and unknowingly, their hearts too may be filled with a heavenly yearning, which some day may spring forth as an unabashed love song unto God.

Similarly, the words of Torah—and no Shabbat table should be without them—form timeless linkages with patriarchs and prophets, sages and scholars, with the heroes and heralds who in every age pioneer and preserve our sacred way. More than that, Sabbath study is an *imitatio Dei*, an emulation of the ways of God who, after six days, rested only from His physical creation, but whose intellectual and spiritual essence remained undiminished. Therefore we are bidden, especially on this day, to immerse ourselves in the life-giving waters of Torah.[31]

V

Any treatment of Shabbat would, however, be incomplete if it limited itself to a description and interpretation of the parts alone. The parts are integrated into the wholeness of a living entity by that divine attribute which is the end purpose of its creation and the ultimate meaning of its observance—*kedushah*, freely translated as "holiness" or "sanctity." *Zachor et yom ha-Shabbat*, "Make the Sabbath a day of remembrance," commands Exodus; *lekadsho*, "to make it *kadosh*."[32] *Shamor et yom ha-Shabbat*, "Safeguard the Sabbath Day from all desecrations," enjoins Deuteronomy; again, *lekadsho*, "to make it *kadosh*."[33] *Kedushah* constitutes both a religious striving and a fulfillment.

It seems peculiar that the Jew is bidden to make the Sabbath *kadosh* when, according to the biblical record, the day already was *kedosh Ha-*

Shem, "the *kadosh* of God."[34] For when, at the very end of the beginning, the divine artisan had completed His physical task and found it to His satisfaction, He Himself bestowed upon the Sabbath His blessing, *vay'kadesh oto*, "and designated it *kadosh*."[35] Must man repeat this act?

It is Judaism's unique claim that everything in the course of history is shared by the effort of man. Man, for example, is God's partner—only a junior one, to be sure, but still a partner—in the completion of the work of creation.[36] Sinai, too, would not have seen the consummation of the covenant without Israel's assent[37] of *na'asseh v'nishma*.[38] The same, according to tradition, holds true for redemption. Unless the world is faced with utter annihilation necessitating an apocalyptic intervention, redemption, too, will be the accrued dividend of the divine–human investment.[39] Similarly, therefore, though God Himself designated the cosmic Sabbath of creation as *kadosh*, man, too, must carry his share of responsibility and make the human Sabbath of history worthy of being stamped with the seal of *kadosh*. This is why the Sabbath is proclaimed as an *ot*, "a binding sign" between God and Israel.[40] For just as God rested on the Sabbath *vayinafash*, "and ensouled the world," so must Israel, in celebrating its own Sabbath, never lose sight of its destiny and raison d'etre to "ensoul" all of history.

It is a high calling, and one for which there are few volunteers. Yet Jewish tradition insists that divinity has conspired to conscript us, and history has unerringly demonstrated time and again that there is no Tarshish to which a contemporary Jonah may escape. Ours, it seems, is not to reason why; ours is but to appropriate this sacred mission and to live in its fulfillment.

Nevertheless, it seems inevitable that even the best of us will grow weary in the fight against darkness and despair. Battle fatigue is the inevitable concomitant of long combat. Our exhaustion is not solely physical. It stems from a numbness of the soul, as we lose sight of our purpose. Our morale wanes quickly when the sources of our faith in our destiny begin to dry up. What healing and therapy can be provided for the fireless soul?

By its laws, Jewish tradition attempts to set up and place us in a temporary and temporal refuge to which the Jewish body and soul can move for haven and healing. It is not an escape from reality, for we act with full awareness of life about us. It is even less a flight from time, for we are to utilize it in full measure. Yet temporarily and spatially we are to live on a new level, in a new dimension. It is thus not withdrawal but an uplifting, a kind of second-story existence. We remain actively in history and time but try to reshape our entire social environment and refashion the stuff of its being into a new experience of living. For at least one complete day we strive to live according to an ideal vision of life as it can and ought to be, for both the individual and the community. It is the vision of a life in which man can have, not rest and peace *from*—which so often constitute our own Sabbath—but *for*, "the peace for self-perfection that Thou dost desire," "the rest for love and generosity," "the rest for peace and serenity, quietude and trust." No man can derive this quality of Shabbat from any other human being or from life without, "for from Thee alone cometh that brand of peace and rest."[41]

Thus, by making God sovereign over every segment of our life on Shabbat, we invest our individual lives with the *kadosh*. By joining together as a community and bearing witness to the glory of His mighty acts, we also renew our group vision of the messianic redemption and collectively move all of Israel (since we are one of its parts) one step closer to its destined task of becoming a *mamlekhet kohanim*, "a kingdom of priests" (or, in Nachmanides' translation, *meshortai*, "My servants"), *vegoy kadosh* (in parallel translation), a people of Him who alone merits the transcending designation of *kadosh, kadosh, kadosh*.[42]

Israel yearns to prolong this divine–human relationship beyond this single and singular day. It has always been man's yearning to extend ideal into real society. Yet man seems far from ready or willing to act out in reality what he is abundantly able to do in potentiality. Israel must, therefore, bide its time in patience and faith and prepare at the end of each Shabbat realistically but sadly for its return to the reality which is sundered and split. For in it there still is a separation of the sacred from the profane, of light from darkness, of Israel from the nations, of Sabbath from the workday week.

The Jew bids a plaintive farewell to this great day, but with zeal replenished and faith renewed. For his eyes are now lifted to a new Sabbath, a distant yet beckoning Sabbath, when life will be holy and one, humanity whole and one, and God's name perfect and one. He sees from afar the day of the *mizmor shir leyom ha-Shabbat, mizmor shir leatid lavo*, the day when the Sabbath will in and of itself be a psalm of song, a hymn to the future that can be. What kind of future? A *yom she'kuloh Shabbat umenuhah lehayei haolamim*, a "day which is totally Sabbath and tranquility unto all eternity."[43]

VI

This is the manner in which Jewish law performs its Sabbath tasks. It helps objectify the truths and principles of Judaism and wed them actively to the lived concrete. It holds captive the experiences of yesterday until man releases them into a situation of existential relationship that is contemporaneous and self-involving. The Sabbath laws join body and soul together, bind heart and spirit as one, so that in total union they encounter God in the wholeness of human personality. And, finally, the law marks out a chunk in life and hews out of its stuff an ideal living experience which is both memory and vision of man's potential and God's intention for personal and social achievement. By the strength of this renewed and renewing glimpse of the perfectible in expectation, Israel emerges from Shabbat refired and restored to stand as faithful and exemplary sentinels in vigil over those truths which alone can make Israel free and prove redemptive for all mankind.

This, of course, is Shabbat *in potentia*. As for the rest of the objective, we have not yet ceased to be the human partners of the divine, and thus continue to be charged with its actualization.

NOTES

1. Cf. Samuel Belkin, *In His Image* (New York, 1960), 20 ff.
2. M. M. Kasher, *Torah Shleymah*, 16:69, sec. 240. Cf. also note 240 and addendum, pp. 242 ff.
3. P. 114.
4. Deut. 8:11ff.
5. Exod. 20:9–10.
6. *Shabbat* 73a.
7. I. Grunfeld, *The Sabbath: A Guide to Its Understanding and Observance* (London, 1954), 33.
8. Isa. 58:13.
9. *Shabbat* 113a–b.
10. P. Birnbaum, *High Holyday Prayer Book*, 363.
11. Found in the two versions of the Ten Commandments (Exod. 20:8 and Deut. 5:12, respectively). According to tradition, they are an inseparable unit. See Rashi, *ad loc.*; also *Y. Nedarim*, chap. 3, sec. 2.
12. P. 337.

13. Deut. 29:13–14.

14 *Shabbat* 146a, *Shebuot* 39b.

15. Rashi (Rabbi Solomon ben Isaac, 1040–1105), commentary on Deut. 26:16 and 27:9.

16. *Shabbat* 86b.

17. Num. 15:37.

18. David de Sola Pool, *The Traditional Prayer Book*, 251.

19. Chap. 12, "The Holy Deed."

20. Pool, *The Traditional Prayer Book*, 175.

21. Isa. 58:13.

22. *Shabbat* 118b–119a.

23. Isa. 58:13.

24. *Shabbat* 113a.

25. Ps. 104:1.

26. Ps. 34:9.

27. *Kuzari*, pt. 2, chap. 50.

28. Pool, *The Traditional Prayer Book.*, 713.

29. Founder of Lurianic Kabalah (1534–72).

30. Prolific poet and liturgist (b. 1560).

31. *Y. Shabbat*, chap. 15, sec. 3. Cf. also Philo, *Moses* 2.3a.

32. Exod. 20:8.

33. Deut. 5:12.

34. Isa. 58:12.

35. Gen. 2:3.

36. Gen. 1:28, S. R. Hirsch, *Horeb* (ed. I. Grunfeld), 1: 62, sec. 139.

37. *Shabbat* 88a.

38. Exod. 24:7.

39. *San.* 88a.

40. Exod. 31:16.

41. Pool, *The Traditional Prayer Book*, 385.

42. Exod. 19:6. See commentary of Moses Nachmanides (1195–1270), ad loc.

43. Pool, *The Traditional Prayer Book*, 329; selection taken from the end of *Tamid* 37b.

Shabbat as a Reliving
of the Honeymoon

ALAN S. GREEN

As a man rejoices all the days of the wedding feast,
So does he rejoice on the Sabbath.
As the groom does no work on the day he is wed,
So he does none on Shabbat. (Al Nakawa)

B uoyant hearts within us sense the wonder of love as a gift of God.
Searching minds, reinforced by the teachings of sages, come ever
more to see it as an evidence of His nearness. *How then shall we find the
way* to pour out our thankfulness to Him, and to sustain forever these insights? The answer is: the Sabbath.

*For the Sabbath evening table is a dramatic celebration and exaltation of
human love.* This is a hidden truth, all too often unrecognized.

We are aware that the Sabbath encompasses many things, that it is the
sacred vessel that preserves the very essence of Jewish learning and longing. And many in our age are seeking to recapture the healing serenity
and spiritual reaffirmation of this special day.

We are acquainted with the moving explicit meanings of the ceremonies which usher it in within the sanctuary of our homes: The candle
flames are a sign of God's presence, of His guidance to light our path. The
wine stands for the delights of life, which He wants us to relish and to appreciate as evidence of His nearness and His care. The chant that goes
with it sings of God's special love and election of Israel. It recalls "the
work of creation," after which God "rested on the seventh day . . . and
hallowed it" (Gen. 2:2–3). It reminds us of the "deliverance from Egypt,"

where as slaves we learned firsthand the importance of providing a day of rest to all, including those who labor. It stresses that the Sabbath was the first, and remains primary, among all the holy days. Then the challah, or twisted loaf, bespeaks the gift of life itself and of the means to sustain it.

But now as a couple, our minds are opened to another dimension, deep within and not referred to by the words: When the wife sets the stage for the Sabbath to come in by blessing the candles, the world stops. The modest rays miraculously vanquish and blot out the harsh glare of tensions and pressures that may surround us. Business, carpools, disappointments, and debts are pushed aside. Fears slink off and disappear. And a husband, looking at his mate—exalted and beauteous in prayer, her eyes sparkling in the flame's reflections—will thank God for her: for her body and her soul, which are now all one to him as her true lover, and for the comfort and completion, the motivation and confidence which she has brought to him.

Then, as the husband raises the cup of wine and chants the Kiddush prayer with all the tenderness and melody of which he is capable (God grant him a sweet voice!), she looks upon him steadfastly and thanks the Creator for all the strength and sustenance, the promise of children, and the future which he has brought to her. The world which is always threatening to overwhelm and enslave us with its duties, demands, and deadliness—"getting and spending we lay waste our powers," wrote Wordsworth—has now been subdued. The subtler, more tender sentiments have their chance again and renew within us the intimations of happiness when first we met, the ecstacy of the reward when first we were wed, the purposiveness of all our being together. Shabbat is indeed the celebration of human love in the presence of God who made it His gift as part of His design.

The Sabbath is a reliving of the honeymoon. For what is a honeymoon but the declaration that the world and its pressures must give way to the two of us and our love! We proclaim that our occupations and varied pursuits—crucial, stature-nourishing, time-consuming as they are—must yet be kept in balance and made to enhance and nurture the ultimate satisfaction of our hearts: "Male and female He created them, and He blessed them, and called their name Adam."

The Hebrew idiom speaks not of honeymoon, but of *Shivat Y'me HaMishteh*, or Seven Days of the Wedding Feast—to which reference was made in the quotation which began this chapter. We could playfully coalesce the two languages and call it a honeyweek. Then we might say that

Shabbat enables us to recapture the wonder, vision, and avowals of the honeyweek weekly!

Around the Sabbath table we reaffirm that God has given us a sacred fire, that we are priest and priestess committed above all to tending it on our (His) altar, and that nothing must be allowed to dim or quench it. Shabbat, with its delicate sensibilities, its mood of peace and completion, its "foretaste of paradise," culminating in its marital intimacy as a special "mitzvah" (a good deed enjoined by God himself), is the honeymoon all over again. It is a day to be set apart, to renew and refresh the transcendence of our love. Once we awaken to this and cherish Shabbat accordingly, it can be an incalculable boon in keeping tenderness alive in the world which seems bent on stripping us of mystery and romance. Let it be so from the first Sabbath of our marriage, that its song and ceremony might capture and forever preserve the radiance and revelation of love's beginning.

Gates of Prayer, the New Union Prayer Book, declares, "Through the centuries, Israel has given itself to the Sabbath, seeing it as the climax of its life, even as it was the climax of creation." We must see it also as the climax of our love, even as it is of creation.

What a gift our forefathers have handed down to us! As children we could scarcely hope to understand all its roles. As adults we can scarcely afford not to.

Many a couple might have triumphed over the strains and differences inevitable in marriage and been spared much unhappiness or even separation had they observed the Sabbath each week, celebrating God and their love as their adventure supreme. The tension of concentrating on what I want might well have softened under the influence of what *my mate* wants, what *my marriage* wants, and what *God* wants and offers to me in His plan, during the quiet Sabbath atmosphere.

SEX—GOD—SABBATH: three concepts, yet see how they are intertwined! They are three aspects of a single reality: life coming into being, and then sustained, through love. Is there any reality closer to us than this? *Keep these joined in your thought and conduct: sex, God, and the Sabbath*, and you will be on your way to the bright purposiveness and to the security that you seek together.

There should be a place in every couple's schedule, sacred and welcomed, for each and all of these three. A time for sex when one is unhurried, unharried, and unexhausted. It is amazing that this drive, so insistent, can yet be neglected and shunted aside. The demands of careers and the ambitions of social status tend to monopolize our prime energies, allowing only scraps and leftovers for our life of love. Occasions, therefore, must be deliberately sought to cherish and renew the physical revelation of our bodies, when we are fresh and undistracted. Daytimes, if you choose, as well as night. Little honeymoons, away from home routines, and often closer to the woods and waves of God's creation.

A time for God, to search for Him, and to commune with Him in many ways. In the wordless intimations of nature. In the symbols and ceremonies of the sanctuary, eloquent with the memories of one's youth and the youth of one's people. In the evocative concepts of poets and singers. But time must be allotted, for the sense of God does not come instantaneously, as if by computer.

A time for Shabbat, whose very strength lies in the fact that it is fixed in time. You do not have to seek it out. It seeks you. There it is, every seventh day. And if you determine that you will greet it, and begin to observe its spoken and unspoken meanings, it will grow and so will its rewards.

The Sabbath provides a clear corrective to a problem which William Masters and Virginia Johnson cite in *The Pleasure Bond:*

> There is a danger of letting everyday chores and responsibilities come between you as husband and wife, so that you are always postponing the pleasure of having each other's company because there is work to be done.
>
> It would probably amaze you to know how many husbands and wives become sexually dysfunctional as a result of the so-called work ethic.

So let there be a Shabbat ethic!

Indeed, cherishing intimacy within the Sabbath setting is highly conducive to its success in many ways. Physically the couple is rested, having broken away from their outside labors and their household chores hopefully long before the Sabbath begins, and having refreshed themselves in preparation for the sacred day. The grace and manners about the Sabbath table prepare them with an added measure of tenderness toward each other. Spiritually they are exalted with the sense of the Presence felt so near their family. Little wonder that the "special mitzvah" of love's union on Shabbat became one of the most welcome and well observed of all the commandments.

One might speculate that the Marriage Encounter experience, which many are greeting with enthusiasm, is in a way a tribute and a parallel to this Sabbath of love, with its relaxed time for spirituality, affection, and communion on the upper reaches of man's capabilities!

As our falling in love may have opened our path to a sure sense of God, so the celebration of our love on Shabbat summons us now to the full and many-faceted splendor of this Seventh Day of Delight, in which our being, freed from material concerns and from the tyranny of success and failure, finds true rest and reward amid thoughts and values that are priceless and eternal.

Meditation and Sabbath

HARVEY COX

Even before I left Tibet-in-the-Rockies for Benares-on-the-Charles, I began to wrestle with what it means to be a Christian who practices a "Buddhist" form of meditation. For many people this would not pose any problems, because mixing assorted tidbits from different religious traditions comes easily to some. But it does not come easily to me. Others would simply sever previous affiliations, but I had not done that, either. I was not a convert and had no intention of becoming one. So the question remained: What role can meditation play in the life of a person who is neither a Buddhist nor a syncretist, but remains a Jew or a Christian?

For the past several years, Eastern meditation has been finding a larger and larger place in Christian practice. In monasteries from Maine to New Mexico, Roman Catholic contemplative orders have begun to integrate one or another form of sitting into their daily liturgical schedule. The Benedictine monks I visited in Vermont last winter began the day by "sitting" at 4:30 A.M., two hours before dawn, using cushions and postures similar to the ones I had encountered at Naropa. And in many churches, basic meditation techniques are taught to Christians, most of whom have no interest in becoming Hindus or Buddhists.

It should come as no surprise that certain Oriental spiritual disciplines are finding a resonance in the modern West. Christianity has its own contemplative tradition, much of which is highly reminiscent of such Oriental practices as sitting, breath concentration, and mantra chanting. According to the New Testament, Jesus himself, despite his turbulent life, often took out times to withdraw and be alone. The early desert fathers developed a wide range of contemplative techniques. In the Eastern Christian church, a practice known as "Hesychasm," the attempt to achieve "divine quietness"—for which the Greek word is *hesychia*—emerged. One of its early proponents, St. John Climacus, taught his followers to concentrate on each breath they took, using the name of Jesus as a kind of mantra to accompany this breathing. A later Hesychast, St. Nicephorus, instructed his disciples to attach a prayer to each breath and to focus their attention on the centers of their own bodies while meditating. Later Hesychasts believed that while in such a state of prayerful contemplation people could see the inner light of the Transfiguration. This will all sound familiar to any Westerner who has recently had instruction in a form of Oriental meditation in which breath concentration, chanting, or an inner light plays an important role.

Christian contemplative practices in the West developed in a somewhat more intellectual and moralistic direction. St. Ignatius Loyola, the founder of the Jesuit order, prescribed a rigorous form of spiritual discipline suitable for a soldier in Christ's army. Yet even the Ignatian *Spiritual Exercises* outline methods of introspection and patterned imagining which would seem familiar to practitioners of Oriental forms. Among Protestants, the practice of daily prayer and Bible reading was once held to be indispensable to Christian life. But the failure of most churches actually to teach people how to pray and the difficulties involved in learning the difference between reading, studying, and meditation on a text have produced a generation of Protestants who live with practically no spiritual discipline at all.

Still, despite similarities with Western practices, a vague uneasiness often bothers many Christians and Jews who meditate. Some feel uneasy because they seem to be filching someone else's spiritual inheritance. They suspect that to use the technique without the religious world view that comes with it is somehow dishonest, that it shows a disrespect for the whole philosophical structure within which meditational practices have come to the West. I respect the reservations these people have, and their reluctance. They are rightly suspicious of the groups that have cut meditation out of its metaphysical setting and reduced it to a mere psychological gimmick. They cannot accept the world view within which meditation has been integrated in Buddhism. Yet they have found that the practice of meditation undeniably resonates with something within them. What can they do?

I have come to believe that the answer to this question lies neither in swallowing the entire corpus of Buddhist philosophy nor in reducing meditation to a psychological self-help device. Rather, a third possibility presents itself. It consists in combining the serious practice of meditation with a patient rethinking of the biblical tradition and the history of Jewish and Christian spirituality—uncovering those points in our own spiritual tradition where the functional equivalents of meditation appear. I think there are many such points—that meditation need not be viewed as an exotic import but as something with roots in our own tradition.

I did not come to this conclusion easily, and as usual the basic insight—that Judeo-Christian spirituality has its own equivalent of the meditational practice—came to me first not from a book but through an experience that altered my way of thinking out the issue.

A few days before I was scheduled to leave Naropa, a rabbi who lives in a small town near Boulder invited me to join him and his tiny congregation in celebrating the weekly Sabbath—not just the religious service that took place in his backyard, but a genuine, old-fashioned Shabbat, a whole day of doing very little, enjoying the creation as it is, appreciating the world rather than fixing it up. I accepted the invitation and joined in the relaxed Sabbath, which lasted, as tradition dictates, from Friday sundown until sundown on Saturday. During those luminous hours, as we talked quietly, slept, ate, repeated the ancient Hebrew prayers, and savored just being rather than doing, it occurred to me that meditation is in essence a kind of miniature Sabbath. For twentieth-century Christians, and for many Jews as well, it provides a modern equivalent of what the observance of Sabbath once did but does no more.

The Jews did not invent the idea of Sabbath. Though its origins remain obscure, it undoubtedly had antecedents in the religious milieu of the ancient Near East. It is not impossible that the core insight from which Sabbath developed is identical with the one which, under different historical circumstances, eventually produced the practice of meditation. Both prescribe a regular time when human beings *do nothing*. This connection becomes even more evident when we realize that the word for Sabbath in Hebrew comes from a root meaning "to desist." Sabbath originally meant a time that was designated for ceasing all activity and simply acknowledging the goodness of creation. It was not, at first, a day for cultic acts or long worship services. It was a time set aside for affirming what is.

But meditation and Sabbath also differ, at least when we compare Sabbath with the theories of meditation as they are now frequently taught by neo-Oriental masters. Meditation, though it begins as something one does at a particular stated time, is also often interpreted as the key to a total way of life. Sabbath, on the other hand, is one day out of seven. It never becomes a complete way of life. It represents the Israelites' recognition that although human beings can catch a glimpse of the pure realm of unity and innocence, they also live in the fractured world of division, greed, and sorrow. Sabbath is Israel's ingenious attempt to live both in history and beyond it, both in time and eternity.

In the earliest recorded expression of the idea of Sabbath, in the Fourth Commandment of Moses, one day in every seven is set aside.

> Six days shalt thou labor and do all thy work; but the seventh is the Sabbath of Yahweh: in it thou shalt not do any work, thou nor thy son, nor thy daughter, thy manservant nor thy maidservant, nor thy cattle, nor thy stranger that is within thy gates; for in six days Yahweh made heaven and earth, the sea and all that in them is, and rested the seventh day; wherefore Yahweh blessed the Sabbath day and hallowed it.

At first reading, the suggestion that God "rested" after the toil of creation—the image is of a craftsman sitting down and wiping his brow—sounds quaintly anthropomorphic. The word "rest" literally means "to catch one's breath." God, like us, gets tired and has to restore himself. The passage may indeed depict a less exalted view of God than later emerges in Jewish faith. On further reflection, however, and with the anthropomorphic symbol somewhat decoded, a deeper truth appears and with it a possible link with the tradition of sitting meditation.

The first thing to notice about God's activity on the Sabbath is that it focuses on breathing. We all stop to draw breath after we have been exerting ourselves, and the passage may mean no more than this. But to depict God himself as one who ceases work and does nothing but breathe could suggest a deeper and older stratum of spiritual consciousness which lies behind the passage itself. Breath is a source of renewal, and God, like human beings, returns periodically to the source.

The second facet of this ancient passage is even more telling. Sabbath is the Jewish answer to the profound question all religions face about the relationship between doing and being, between what Indian mystics call *sat* (perfect being) and *prana* (spirit and energy). All religions must cope with the apparent contradiction between a vision of reality as ultimately changeless and one that contains contrast, opposition, and change. In the

Bible the key terms are not "being" and "energy" but "creation" and "rest." Viewed in this light, the idea of Sabbath is not naive or primitive at all. It is a highly sophisticated philosophical notion. It postulates an ultimate force in the universe which is not just passive and changeless but which acts and is acted upon. Yet it affirms what most religions also say about the ultimate: it is eternal and perfect. Sabbath links God and world and human beings in a dialectic of action and rest, of purposeful doing and "just sitting." The seventh day is holy to Yahweh, and one keeps it holy not by doing things for God or even for one's fellow human beings. One keeps it holy by doing nothing.

I think Hui-neng, the legendary sixth Zen patriarch, whose teaching constantly returned to learning how to do nothing, would understand Sabbath. I can almost see him, magically transported into a nineteenth-century hasidic shtetl or into an ancient Jewish village on the seventh day, smiling appreciatively: these barbarians certainly had an inkling of the truth one day of the week at least. But what would disturb Hui-neng is that after sundown on the Sabbath, the Jews do begin again to live as though work and effort and time are real, as though action does make a difference and salvation has not yet come in its fullness. Maybe Hui-neng would swat a few behinds with his fan, or pull a few beards. But his efforts would be useless, because his reality and the reality of Moses are not the same. The difference is that Hui-neng views the world either as total transience or total stillness, and for him there is no real difference between the two. The Hebrew vision sees both acting and being, doing and nondoing, as equally real and equally important. By observing the rhythmic return of Sabbath, human beings reflect the divine reality itself.

Pre-Israelite versions of Sabbath did not extend the provisions for rest to domestic animals, or to strangers and sojourners temporarily resident in someone's house. They probably did not apply to women either. The Hebrew Sabbath ordinance, on the other hand, is universal. Everyone, including animals, slaves, and guests, must stop work. There is no elitism. In the Orient, on the other hand, meditation is practiced mostly by a privileged, partially leisured class. The vast majority of Buddhists in the world do not meditate. They pray or chant on occasion. Meditation is left mostly to the monks. In fact, in most cultures, East and West, prayer and meditation are turned over to a special elite. But this approach presupposes a society where some people work while others meditate—not a very democratic form of spiritual discipline. Such elitism has also dogged the history of Western monasticism, which is Christianity's way of coping with the clash between the *via activa* and the *via contemplativa*. Some people worked while others prayed. For the Jews, however, there was no such spiritual elite. On the Sabbath everyone stopped and just sat.

Sabbath differs from meditation in another way. Not only is it universal, rather than elitist, it is also ethical. For Zen disciples, "just sitting" has no ethical significance whatever, at least not from a Western perspective in which distinguishing good, less good, and evil possibilities is important. In the Sabbath practice, on the other hand, the loftiest of all realities, God himself is linked to the human needs of the lowest bonded servant. The link is a rare Hebrew verb ("to rest") found only twice in the entire Bible. It means, as we have seen, "to draw one's breath." Both Yahweh and the exhausted slave need to stop and catch their breath, to look up from the task at hand. As the sovereign of the universe, Yahweh can presumably pause whenever he chooses. But the kitchen slave and the grape picker must be protected by divine law from the greed and insensitivity of the rich. The Sabbath discipline is not just an option. It is a legal mandate in order to insure the extension of its full benefits to the poor and the powerless. One ancient version of the Sabbath rule underlines its seriousness by imposing the death penalty on anyone who works or who *makes someone else work* on Sabbath.

Few Jewish practices are more misunderstood by Christians than the Sabbath. One reason for this misunderstanding is that several of the stories of Jesus in the Gospels depict him as deliberately breaking Sabbath rules, especially by healing people. Because of the way these stories are often interpreted in sermons and church-school lessons, many Christians grow up with an image of the Jewish Sabbath as an unsparingly legalistic straitjacket or an empty attempt to observe meaningless ritual rules. No doubt there were abuses of the spirit of the Sabbath in Jesus' time. But most Christian educational material fails utterly to point out why the Sabbath was instituted or to describe its ingenious blending of contemplative and ethical purposes. Its importance has been further obscured where Jews have changed it from an ethical-universal discipline into a badge of ethnic and religious identity, and where zealous Christian "sabbatarians" have tried to enforce blue laws against Sunday sports entertainment and closing hours, conveying the impression that a Sabbath (now a Sunday) is perversely designed to prevent anyone from enjoying anything.

The spirit of Sabbath is a biblical equivalent of meditation. It nurtures the same kind of awareness that meditation nurtures, for Sabbath is not just a day for doing nothing. It is a particular form of consciousness, a way of thinking and being that strongly resembles what the Buddhists call "mindfulness." In the hasidic tradition, where it reached its clearest expression, Sabbath not only excludes our ordinary forms of intervening and ordering, it also excludes manipulative ways of thinking about the world. Abraham Heschel repeats a story that exemplifies this point well. A certain rabbi, it seems, who was renowned for his wisdom and piety, and especially for his zeal in keeping Sabbath, once took a leisurely walk in his garden on the Sabbath day—an activity which even the severest interpreters allowed. Strolling in the shade of the branches, the rabbi noticed that one of the apple trees badly needed pruning. Recognizing, of course, that such a thing could not be done on the seventh day, the rabbi nonetheless made a mental note to himself that he would see to the pruning early the next week. The Sabbath passed. But when the rabbi went out to the tree a few days later with ladder and clippers, he found it shriveled and lifeless. God had destroyed the apple tree to teach the rabbi that even *thinking* about work on the Sabbath is a violation of the commandment and of the true spirit of the Holy Day.

It is a matter of consciousness. When we plan to prune a tree, we perceive it differently than we do when we are simply aware of it, allowing it—for the moment at least—simply to be as it is. The Buddhist scriptures make this same point in a distinction they frequently draw between two forms of consciousness, which are often confused with each other. The first they call *sati*, usually translated with the English word "mindfulness." This is the "bare awareness" which is strengthened by the practice of meditation. It is being aware, fully aware of the apple tree, but having no judgments, plans, or prospects for it. This *sati* is then often contrasted in the Buddhist texts with *sampajanna*, a form of consciousness which is sometimes translated as "clear comprehension." It refers to the attitude appropriate to doing something. *Sati* is receptive, open, passive. *Sampajanna* comes into play when action is required. According to the Buddhist notion, the two must be carefully distinguished and separately nourished before they can be correctly combined into what the texts call *satipatthana*, or "right mindfulness." Meditation is the cultivation of the first, receptive state of awareness, *sati*. Its purpose thus seems nearly identical with that of Sabbath.

Can we ever regain the glorious vision of Sabbath as a radiant queen, a jeweled sovereign who comes to visit bringing warmth and joy in her train? The poor and often inept hasidic Jews in the stories of Isaac Bashevis Singer may bicker and complain, and they surely suffer, but when the sun goes down and the lamps begin to flicker on Friday evening, a kind of magic touches their world. Special cakes have been baked, and now the sacred candles are lighted. Sabbath is eternity in time, as Abraham Heschel says; it is a cathedral made not with stones and glass but with hours and minutes. It is a sacred symbol that no one can tear down or destroy. It comes every week, inviting human beings not to strive and succeed, not even to pray very much, but to taste and know that God is good, that the earth and the flesh are there to be shared and enjoyed.

To rediscover in our time this underlying human meaning of the Sabbath should make Jewish young people think twice about whether they want to follow in the footsteps of "enlightened" parents who have shied away from Sabbath observance as an embarrassment. And it should cause Christians to wonder how some of the seventh-day spell, so spoiled by misguided Puritan opposition to enjoying its freedom, can be found again.

It is foolish, however, to imagine that a general observance of Sabbath can be reinstituted in our time. Bringing back an old-fashioned Sabbath would require either a religiously unified culture—which we obviously do not have—or a tight and self-conscious subculture, which Jews once had but do not have any longer. We already have empty time and major industries devoted to filling that time for us. Empty time is neither Sabbath nor meditation. What we need is a form of Sabbath observance which can function on an individual or a small group basis, but which restores the lost dialectic of action and repose, of intervention and letting be.

Meditation could become a modern equivalent of Sabbath. Sabbath is the key to a biblical understanding of meditation. True, meditation does not take the place of the gathered congregation, of celebrating and breaking bread. But it can restore the Sabbath insight that despite all the things that must be done in the world—to feed and liberate and heal—even God occasionally pauses to draw breath. Sabbath is a reminder that there will again be a time, as there once was a time, when toil and pain will cease, when play and song and just sitting will fill out the hours and days, when we will no longer require the rhythm of work and repose because there will be no real difference between them. Sabbath reminds us that that day will come, but it also reminds us that that day is not yet here. We need both reminders.

Our problem is that we need Sabbath but we live in a society whose pluralism militates against a particular day, shared by all, in which being replaces doing and affirming takes precedence over accumulating. It seems unlikely that a common Sabbath can be recovered. For the time being we will have to get along on a somewhat more personal version of the Sabbath. The person whose vision of the world is derived from biblical faith rather than from the wisdom of the Orient can incorporate meditation as a part of a daily dialectic of withdrawal and involvement, of clarification and action. For inevitably, on this earth and in our history, we cannot live in an eternal Sabbath. We always have to go back again to those other six days, days which, though suffused with the memory and anticipation of Sabbath, are still days when action makes a difference.

The greed of an acquisitive society, the pace of industrial production—signaled by lights that never go out and belts that move day and night, all week and all year—the historic Christian contempt for the Jewish religious vision, the compulsive rationalism of a truncated form of science, all these have conspired to create a mindset in the modern West for which the wisdom of the East, the inevitable shadow of self, is bound to hold an immense appeal. But the Eastern path, as its wisest interpreters know full well, will never accommodate more than a few converts. Its ultimate answer, or nonanswer, if it ever triumphed in the West, would do so at the cost of much that is valuable in the Western ethical and religious tradition. The wisest of the Zen masters will eventually inform us to look more closely at the land from which we have ridden off to seek enlightenment. If we do, we may discover that meditation can restore a lost treasure, the Fourth Commandment. It may be tarnished and twisted out of shape, but it still belongs to us; and as creatures who must live amid the contradictions and dislocations of history, the mini-Sabbath of meditation can be the gift of life itself.

I arrived back in Cambridge–Benares from the American Tibet not only having learned how to meditate but also with the beginnings of a way to integrate my meditational practice into my own religious tradition. This had come about because a wise rabbi had not abandoned God's gift of Sabbath. I had learned what it means to be a Christian who practices a "Buddhist" form of meditation—from the Jews.

The Meaning of the Sabbath

JEROME BRAUN

The Sabbath is one of those institutions that have been around so long most of us no longer remember their purpose. As with family or friendship, we are oblivious to their existence until we lose them. Then, for a moment, we realize what they're for. This illumination usually does not last long, and we continue on the way to forgetting entirely and so perhaps enter a new Dark Age of barbarism.

The secular world now is essentially pagan. People are trapped in various niches of society and live to fulfill the respective principles and perspectives governing these niches, which then dominate their lives. Money, power, politics, sensuality, competitiveness are just a few of them. As in the old days when the courtesan worshiped the Goddess of Love, the soldier the God of War, we too worship our obsessions. We do not rule our objects and our goals. They rule us.

Primitive society saw the entire world as being animate, and in their fear and anxiety sought the favor of these principles of nature. Now we see the entire world as mechanical, dead, inanimate. Emotionally, we might as well be living on the moon. The Sabbath is meant for this world too.

The secular world has ways of inviting rules to fill up the blank portions of our lives, but these rules have no moral meaning. For some it is the politeness of café society. For others it goes deeper. The conniving that lawyers often find a requirement in the practice of their profession, the development of social hierarchies that have little relation to moral character are examples of rules Jews have tried to eliminate. They do this by trying to preempt those spaces by better rules or, more likely, by setting boundaries that preserve freedom in these areas of our lives. The corollary to responsibility, which Judaism and life in general require, is that one does not demand rules where there are no rules, just individual freedom.

This is what the Sabbath does. By separating the sacred and profane, it preserves an area of freedom where human motives in all their purity can flow unhampered.

What is meant by the blurring of boundaries, mixing the sacred and profane, can best be illustrated by example. Nowadays the fact that people use sports as an outlet for all their tensions puts more pressure on sports than it can carry. Witness the decline of decorum and sportsmanship in professional sports as the audience goes crazy over games that serve as metaphors for their lives. Likewise, the game metaphor infiltrates all areas of life, as in competition at work, and puts more pressure on other institutions than they are meant to take. Giving one's all in a two-hour game is quite different from working hard sixty hours a week, all in the name of competitiveness. Thus by crossing boundaries meant to be kept separate, the distinction between game and real life begins to be lost, to the mutual disadvantage of both. A more serious lapse is blurring the distinction between friend and business partner, between spouse and casual sexual partner, between respecting others and exploiting them for one's own profit.

Ours is a secular world, and few places more so than America, which socializes people to compete from early childhood. Children are taught to be popular and successful, not to be themselves, but to learn to play guitar or to get on a team. Since to a large extent we have been led on, and the adult world offers a lot less opportunity for glory than we have been led to expect, we tend to relax by re-creating that world of childhood, striving to reduce our fears and to show we can deal with what we have learned to accept as the ultimate realities of life. This is not a world of spontaneity or of friendship but of social roles and only grudging social acceptance that has to be fought out and earned. Acceptance for playing a role is no substitute for the love of intimates, but how many people will ever know that? By endlessly striving for social prowess and status in our free time, we're still stuck in the world of work. We don't relax, we just purge our anxieties, never learning there is more to life than this anxious world of competition and work. We rarely overcome our childish fear of failure, and then we wonder why so many of us rarely enjoy what we do attain. What we have lost in the process of attaining is the ability to enjoy.

So how is the Sabbath different? The Sabbath provides an opportunity for the expression of the most important human feelings, for deep relationships with others, with God, and with ourselves, our own thoughts, our own feelings, our own aspirations. It is a meditative experience of a sort the Eastern religions place so much emphasis on but not a meditation of emptiness, of withdrawing from the world. It is a meditation on becoming *more* involved with the world, with others, with ourselves, and of course with God. What is cast out is the working week's obsessive drive to compete, to meet societal standards of honor and status; unfortunately, since there isn't time for everything, what is sacrificed in the process is the re-creation of deep relationships.

Perhaps the most important aspect of the Sabbath is that it is very much a human institution. We are so used in modern life to looking for a material input and a material output that we forget that it is the mental state of integrity, of self-respect, of psychological wholeness that is the output, not anything material.

Those who find the Sabbath meaningless have already forgotten what to look for or have never been told. When a tradition has broken down it is not easily repaired. Once, among Christians, Jews, Muslims, and others, the body was the home of the soul, either literally or metaphorically. Now the body is the soul, as if endless accumulations of possessions and pleasures to adorn and amuse the body can provide the happiness disordered social relationships and metaphysical relationships cannot.

Our recreation is thus an idealized version of work, having all the components of specialization and control that we take for granted in modern society. What is missing is achieving wholeness. Successful, obsessive, professional people only do more of the same on weekends. Those who consider themselves failures only seek to blot out reality in their free time. These extremes do not make for a balanced personality.

But a person who is accepted for being himself can never be a failure. And this is the ideal of the Sabbath.

The functions of the Sabbath can be conveyed only by those who have observed it. The Sabbath teaches man humility, that he is not master of the universe, and so defuses his obsessive drives for control and power.

Instead of providing opportunities for the exercise of power, it teaches self-control and modesty that reflect not a monkish asceticism but a realistic view of man's place in the universe. The Sabbath restores the ability to relate on the most human level.

No doubt there is a place for simple releasing of tension. For some this means drinking or getting high. For others it is watching football or collecting antiques. But isn't there also a possibility for spiritual renewal? That is the question the Sabbath answers.

Shabbat

BLU GREENBERG

The Seventh Day

Time. Jews have an amazing way with time. We create islands of time. Rope it off. Isolate it. Put it on another plane. In doing so, we create within that time a special aura around our everyday existence. Carving out special segments of holy time suits the human psyche perfectly, for ordinary human beings cannot live constantly at the peak of emotion. Thus, Shabbat,[1] holy time, gives us an opportunity to experience that emotional peak, to feel something extraordinary in an otherwise ordinary span of time.

You would not think of time as having texture, yet in a traditional Jewish household it becomes almost palpable. On Shabbat, I can almost feel the difference in the air I breathe, in the way the incandescent lamps give off light in my living room, in the way the children's skins glow, or the way the trees sway. Immediately after I light my candles, it is as if I flicked a switch that turned Shabbat on in the world, even though I know very well the world is not turned on to Shabbat. Remarkable as this experience is, even more remarkable is that it happens every seventh day of my life.

How does it happen? There will always be an element of mystery in transforming time from ordinary to extraordinary, but the human part of the process is not mysterious at all. It is not one great big leap or one awesome encounter with the Holy, but rather just so many small steps, like parts of a pattern pieced together.

Why do I or any other Orthodox Jew take these steps, week after week, month after month, year after year, with never a slipup? The first answer falls hard on untrained ears. I observe Shabbat the way I do because I am so commanded. Somewhere in that breathtaking desert, east of Egypt and south of Israel, Moses and the Jewish people received the Torah, including the commandment to observe Shabbat. Since I am a descendant of those people, my soul, too, was present at Sinai, encountered God, and accepted the commandments.

Now, I don't for a moment believe that God said at Sinai, "Do not carry money in your pockets on Shabbat," or, "Do not mow your front lawn," or even, "Go to synagogue to pray," but the cumulative experience of Revelation, plus the way that experience was defined and redefined in history for a hundred generations of my ancestors, carries great weight with me.

The biblical commandment to observe Shabbat has two reference points: God's creation of the world and the Exodus/freedom from slavery. True, these are events in history, yet, linked as they both are to Shabbat, they also suggest something else about the human condition: that there is a tension between the poles of one's life, mastery at the one end and enslavement at the other; mastery in drive, energy, creativity—and enslavement to the pressures and seduction of the hurly-burly world.

To some extent, Shabbat achieves what the song title suggests: "Stop the World, I Want to Get Off." Let me paraphrase the biblical injunction, as it speaks to me, a contemporary person:

> Six days shall you be a workaholic; on the seventh day, shall you join the serene company of human beings.
>
> Six days shall you take orders from your boss; on the seventh day, shall you be master/mistress of your own life.
>
> Six days shall you toil in the market; on the seventh day, shall you detach from money matters.
>
> Six days shall you create, drive, create, invent, push, drive; on the seventh day, shall you reflect.
>
> Six days shall you be the perfect success; on the seventh day, shall you remember that not everything is in your power.
>
> Six days shall you be a miserable failure; on the seventh day, shall you be on top of the world.
>
> Six days shall you enjoy the blessings of work; on the seventh day, shall you understand that being is as important as doing.

A friend has this bumper sticker affixed to the front of her refrigerator: HANG IN THERE, SHABBOS IS COMING. There definitely are weeks in my life when I feel that I will barely make it, but the prize of Shabbat carries me through.

It doesn't always work this way. There are times on Friday night that my best ideas come to me. I feel the urge to take pen in hand and write my magnum opus, but I am not allowed to write. There are those weeks when I am just not in the mood for a big Friday-night family dinner. There have been some Shabbat mornings when it might have been more fun on the tennis court than in shul, and there were some Saturday afternoons when I had to miss what I was sure was the world's best auction.

Happily, the negative moods are the exception and the positive ones the rule. (Were it otherwise, commanded or not, I might have walked away as most modern Jews have done—without, I am well aware, being struck down.) But more important is the fact that I never have to think about picking and choosing. I am committed to traditional Judaism. It has chosen me and I have chosen it back. And just as I am commanded to observe the laws on a Shabbat that rewards, pleases, heals, or nurtures me, so I am commanded on a Shabbat when it doesn't strike my fancy. So when that auction rolls around each year, I don't really suffer serious pangs of temptation. I go to shul, which might even happen to be tedious that particular Shabbat, but which offers me that which I could not buy for a bid of a hundred million dollars anywhere—community, family, faith, history, and a strong sense of myself.

There is something, too, about the power of habit and routine, regimentation and fixed parameters—stodgy old words—that I increasingly have come to appreciate. There are some things that spontaneity simply cannot offer—a steadiness and stability which, at its very least, has the emotional reward of familiarity and, at best, creates the possibility of investing time with special meaning, experience with special value, and life with a moment of transcendence.

And that goes for feelings, too. Those occasional Shabbat dinners when I am just not in the mood. When I don't feel like blessing anyone. Simply, I must be there. Involuntarily, almost against my will, a better mood overtakes me.

I find it fascinating that the Rabbis[2] of the Talmud speak of *kavannah* as the emotion that should accompany performance of ritual. *Kavannah* means intent, or directed purposefulness, rather than spirituality. Even in those more God-oriented times, the Rabbis knew you couldn't always drum up feeling. Try, they said, but it's all right, too, if it doesn't come. Often, meaning and feeling will come after the fact and not as a motivating force.

While it may sound sacrilegious, one can experience a beautiful Shabbat without thinking a great deal about God. Peak for a Jew does not always mean holy or having holy thoughts. Rather ordinary experiences often become sublime because of the special aura created by Shabbat.

On a recent Shabbat, in shul, my peak experience had nothing to do with prayers, God, Shabbat, or the Torah. As we all stood to sing a prayer toward the end of the service, my eye caught sight of Henri V. holding his two-year-old granddaughter Jordana in his arms. In that same line of vision, twenty rows ahead, I saw Lou B., whose wife was just recovering from surgery, holding his two-year-old grandson Jeremy in his arms. For a few seconds I felt a surge of spirit, a misting of the eyes, a moment of joy in the heart. For me that was Shabbat.

My peak experience the week before (and I don't have them every week) was even more "unholy." Three of our children had friends for Shabbat lunch. After *zemirot* and before the closing Grace, Moshe and two of his yeshiva high-school friends reviewed their terrible pranks of yesteryear. For an hour at the Shabbat table we all laughed over their antics. It wasn't very "*Shabbosdik*," but neither could it have happened at any other time—the warmth, the closeness, the leisure . . .

No system that engages a variety of human beings can be absolutely perfect. But, to the average Orthodox Jew, Shabbat comes very close to perfection. It is a day of release and of reenergizing; a day of family and of community; of spirit and of physical well-being. It is a day of prayer and of study; of synagogue and of home; a day of rest and of self-indulgence; of compassion and of self-esteem. It is ancient, yet contemporary; a day for all seasons. A gift and a responsibility. Without it I could not live.

Preparation

Islands of time do not appear on their own, nor merely as a result of imagination. There is a great deal of planning and preparation that goes into creating an island of time. For the well organized, this means starting on Wednesday; for most of us, it also includes a last-minute madness, the tension-producing countdown before candlelighting each week.

One should definitely not approach Shabbat the way I do, and each year I try to change my ways. But human nature being what it is, I suspect half the Orthodox Jews enter it leisurely and the other half pump adrenaline on Friday afternoons. The amazing thing is that when the moment of Shabbat descends upon us—as it inexorably does, for the sun will not stay another moment despite our pleas—an utter serenity falls over the frantic and the reposed alike. After I light my candles, always at the very last moment, I feel a sense of relaxation sweep through me, more total than I could ever dream of achieving in a yoga exercise class.

What must one do in advance to prepare for Shabbat? Everything!

On Shabbat itself, there is no cooking, no cleaning, no laundry, no shopping, no business, so literally everything needed for Saturday must be done before Friday-evening candlelighting. Some of these tasks can be done only at the last moment, although far fewer fall into this category than a brinkmanship mentality would allow. In fact, mental preparation for the coming Shabbat really begins early in the week. For example, if on Monday morning you are ordering something from a department store, unless it were essential, you would request not to have it delivered on Saturday. Receiving a chance delivery that doesn't involve an exchange of money is not forbidden; it's simply that the United Parcel Service man— his uniform, his truck, his department-store packages—intrudes the workaday world into a Sabbath household that has temporarily set that world aside.

The physical tasks fall into three broad categories: (1) getting the house in order, (2) preparing the meals, and (3) getting oneself ready. One would be hard put to call these tasks spiritual. (Who can find godliness in polishing a silver challah tray?) Yet, without this kind of preparation, one could not as easily be transported into holy time.

The House (Apartment)—Cleaning Up

The house should be cleaned or tidied well so that family, guests, the Sabbath angels, and the Sabbath Queen will notice the difference. No, Jews don't really believe in angels looking for dust on the coffee table. I speak here of the aura of Shabbat. If your house is spotless all the time, then bring in fresh flowers or something else to distinguish and honor the day.

You can't swab the kitchen floor or shovel the snow after dinner Friday night, or run the washing machine, or pick the tomatoes on Saturday morning, so plan ahead. Polish whatever silver you'll be using for Shabbat, such as wine cups, challah tray and knife, candlesticks, wine bottle, cake knife, and serving pieces; silver polishing is prohibited on Shabbat and cannot be done after sunset. Many families try to change their bed linens on Friday in honor of Shabbat, although it gets a little tough to do everything on those short winter Fridays.

Reflections

I must admit to a bit of ambivalence about the electric-light situation. While I wouldn't want the law reinterpreted—as Conservative and Reform Judaism have done—I do feel conscious of the problems of energy waste under a system that doesn't permit the flexibility of flicking a switch. For example, we don't use the upstairs hall lights or bathroom lights except for occasional moments throughout the Shabbat, yet you can't program when someone is going to walk through the hall or use the toilet, so the light must burn continuously.

We have done two things. One is to cut down. Unless it's an emergency, or a special situation, such as the need to do a lot of quiet reading, we don't leave on the lights in the bedrooms. In our hallway, we turn on a wall lamp that uses half of what the regular ceiling fixtures use. In our bathrooms, we unscrew all but one bulb of the three-to four-bulb fixtures. Unspiritual as it is, that, too—going into a dimly lit bathroom—is part of the ambiance. If we've invited guests who are not Sabbath observant and who would automatically turn off the bathroom lights, we tape the switch in its on position before Shabbat begins.

The second thing I do is rationalize. I say to myself that, by and large, our family, as a unit, doesn't use any more light than we would on an ordinary weekday if everyone went up to his/her own bedroom after dinner and switched on the lights.

Whatever the arrangement, at times it can be rather inconvenient, such as when you want to read in bed in the middle of the night and forgot to set up your bed lamp on a Shabbos clock, or worse, when someone thoughtlessly leaves the light on in the bedroom and you have to sleep with a pair of bleepers over your eyes all night. (One thing we've learned: never put a white, cotton bedspread over a lamp to block out the light. Fall into a deep sleep and the whole place will go up in smoke.)

Moreover, of all the restrictions of Shabbat that are linked to the biblical categories of labor, creativeness, and the kindling of fire, this one seems most remote of all.

Nevertheless! Electric lights are part of the total package, one piece of the whole gift of Shabbat. It is a commitment of our own choosing, one that we have lovingly made; it is the manner in which we identify ourselves. Having done so, then if our lights should happen to be on or off inappropriately, we simply take that in our stride.

On the positive side, inconvenience or not, somehow walking into a room and not being able to flick a light switch does contribute to the total mood and feeling of the day. And in a covert sort of way, it serves another function: It generates a sense of family time that goes beyond special mealtimes. There is something nice about family and associated friends gathering in the living spaces of the house instead of each going his or her own way. Sometimes two or three of us sit in the living room on Friday night after dinner, reading or talking quietly, while we hear the sounds of laughter from the breakfast room where some of the children sit and snack with their friends, or two or three of them lie sprawled out on the carpet under the lamp in the hallway, playing a board game.

And finally, lest you think Orthodox Jews can't find a way in every instance to observe the law in comfort, some enterprising souls have invented a Shabbos lamp (as opposed to a Shabbos clock), a fluorescent lamp with a shade that slides over it to block out the light. Some say this is a legal fiction which circumvents the law. I prefer to see it as a technique by which one finds oneself relatively undiscomfited yet reminded that the day and all of its human actions are special.

To one who is completely unfamiliar with the law, it seems almost petty and silly to go to such lengths over such a little thing as throwing a light switch. But this is one of the many basic steps in creating that special aura of Shabbat.

The Telephone

People will generally know not to call an Orthodox Jew's home on Shabbat. Our phone rings every ten minutes on a normal evening, but rarely ever does it ring on Shabbat. However, even an occasional jangling can interrupt the mood. Rather than take it off the hook altogether, before Shabbat we put the ringer on low and stick the phone into a drawer so it is barely audible.

Some people think the lack of use of the phone is constricting and inconvenient. It surely sometimes is, as when you're expecting company and you don't know whether or not they'll come in this driving rain, or how your mother is fighting the flu bug that attacked her yesterday.

But as one who does a lot of business—social, managerial, and professional—on the telephone, to be released from it on Shabbat is worth the entire effort. On Shabbat, I am freed from the ringing of the telephone. I am simply not available to whoever might want the immediate access a telephone brings. I have the freedom to savor the peace and privacy of my family and my home.

Emergencies notwithstanding, my mother doesn't expect or want me or anyone else to call her on this day; and our friends will know that we will wait half an hour for them and then conclude that they've decided not to weather the storm.

However, in case of medical emergency, the Sabbath not only may be violated, it must be violated. Lifesaving comes above everything else, and there's a good deal of leeway in interpreting what lifesaving means. Once, when J.J. was fifteen, he began fighting with his sister over who would cut the cake. He grabbed the knife and sliced a deep cut through his finger. It bled heavily for about twenty minutes. We called the doctor (a friend who is Orthodox); he came immediately and said the finger must be stitched. We asked if it could wait five hours until Shabbat was over. "No," was the answer, there was a measure of risk. He called the surgeon, who said come right over. J.J. and his father walked; if it hadn't been close by, J.J. would have taken a cab. Despite what the New Testament says about Jewish legalism, this is just how our ancestors, the Pharisees, would have done it.

Having said all that, modern Jews have gone a step further. The same ingenious scientists and scholars who invented the Shabbos lamp have invented a Shabbos telephone. These are members of the Institute for Science and Halacha in Jerusalem, whose basic principle is that there is nothing that needs to be done that cannot be done according to Halacha. Inventing something called a "grama switch," they are able to activate electricity in a manner that is consonant with Halacha. The grama switch turns on an electrical device without violating the Sabbath. How? It works like this: An electric capacitor stores voltage from a constant power source. From somewhere nearby, an electric eye beams light rays at the capacitor, dissipating the voltage. To activate the switch, a Sabbath observer slides a piece of plastic between the two devices, blocking the light rays from reaching the capacitor. The voltage then builds up unhindered until it reaches the necessary level to start whatever is hooked up to it.

What makes this a Shabbos telephone? It does not directly generate electricity; instead, it acts by preventing it—the pieces of plastic inhibit rather than activate. This, the modern rabbis have determined, is permissible. They base their contemporary interpretation on a talmudic precedent: one may close a window on the Sabbath in order to stop a breeze that might blow out a candle, even though closing the window makes the candle burn more brightly.

However, even a Shabbos telephone must conform to another principle of Jewish law—the spirit of Shabbat. So while it may be used for medical and other urgencies, its use is checked in order to preserve the sanctity of the holy day.

Some of what we have learned from Shabbat carries over to the weekday, and the telephone is a good example. Why not preserve an island of family time each day? we asked ourselves. With five teenagers the phones are always ringing. First we told our children to ask their friends not to call at dinnertime, and then we lower the ringer and just ignore the thing until we're all through with our meal. Four of them accept it nicely. The fifth gives us a song and dance every night about the possible emergencies we are missing by not answering—but I've noticed his litany is becoming less dramatic.

Spiritual Preparation

Some Jewish men, Chasidim in particular, go to the *mikvah* (ritual bath) on Friday afternoon. It is a lovely custom, for *mikvah* not only symbolizes a spiritual cleansing, it also offers a few moments of private time to reflect, to relax, to disengage from the past week, to think about the coming experience of Shabbat. However, if their wives are home frenziedly preparing for Shabbat, caring for eight kids, it's not altogether fair, nor is it in the spirit of the day. Similarly, in those families where a woman has the leisure to sit in a beauty parlor for three hours on a Friday afternoon while her husband is frantically winding up a hard week, there might be a better distribution of responsibility so that a man will have the time to come a bit more restfully into Shabbat.

Before Shabbat begins, it is a custom to put some money into a *pushke*, a charity box. Nowadays, *tzedakah* (charity) being a bigger business, what with appeals, dinners, guests of honor, checks, and IRS deductions, this custom of slipping a few coins into a slotted tin box is of less impact. Yet, it is a sweet thing for children to observe, to do, and to learn from. And it's one more act associated with the special preparations for Shabbat.

Some people also are able to set aside time to meditate or study quietly before Shabbat. These are wonderful ways to prepare spiritually for the day. My husband often studies his daily quota of Talmud right before Shabbat. Somehow, I never have the time or discipline to distance myself this way until the very last minute. Perhaps this is my conditioning as a woman who, like most women, has been largely responsible for the physical preparations in the home and who gleans the sense of sacredness and holiness from those endeavors; but for those who can get themselves spiritually as well as physically ready, there is a different foretaste altogether of Shabbat.

Inasmuch as one should review the biblical portion of the week at least once before it is read in shul on Shabbat morning, this is an excellent subject for quiet study on a Friday afternoon.

Hachnasat Orchim—*Hospitality*

Although tradition requires that Jews fulfill the mitzvah of *hachnasat orchim* whenever the opportunity or need presents itself, for most of us modern urbanites Shabbat and holidays seem to be the preferred times for inviting guests. There is more time to spend leisurely with old friends, and more time to get to know acquaintances better. In addition, Shabbat and holidays are experiences of sacred time and of family tone. Those are added gifts to share with people who are lonely or unconnected to family and/or tradition.

And finally, *hachnasat orchim* is a wonderful mitzvah for children: (a) it is a concrete model from which to learn the art of sharing; (b) children have an opportunity to become acquainted with all different kinds of people, including non-Jews; (c) it reminds them, periodically, that they are not the center of the universe. . . .

Like all good things, we must learn to balance openness and sharing with our own needs for privacy and rest. Like all good things, we must plan ahead to fulfill this mitzvah. Erev Shabbat is too late to invite guests for that evening, but it is a good time to think ahead and act. It is easy to invite people we like; but, occasionally, we have to extend ourselves and invite those who otherwise might not have, yet would greatly appreciate, the experience of a family Shabbat. Most often, they, too, become our friends. In other words, Shabbat is a great occasion for enlarging one's circle of friends.

Shabbat

On Thursday and Friday I called the butcher, the baker, the fish store, and the vegetable man and gave them my orders, most of which were delivered. I made up a menu and talked it over with my housekeeper. When I returned home on Friday afternoon, everything had been done, except for the following: setting the lights and the Shabbos clock, picking up the bakery order, fish order, and some last-minute supermarket items, checking the [pre-torn] tissues and towels in the bathroom, baking a home-made cake, chilling the wine, putting up the kettle of water, burning in the candles' bottoms, prodding the kids, getting the *blech* [a burner cover] set up, and everyone showering, polishing shoes, and dressing. All of these tasks were divided, and the last-minute tensions were kept to a bare minimum. (Without a little hysteria, it just wouldn't be a real Erev Shabbat.)

I can't say that I missed the cooking, cleaning, and setting up, no matter how much it heightened the difference between week work and Shabbat. If someone else fills my house with Shabbat cooking odors and spanking cleanliness, that's just fine. Several years ago, I was assigned to supervise a lab that officially closed at 4:00 P.M. on Fridays. I ordered most of my food ready-made and would stay as late as possible toward closing time. This meant that on certain Fridays of the year I didn't get home until twenty minutes before Shabbat. I remember once coming home to find my candles lit for me. It was a half-hour before Shabbat, and I couldn't figure out who had done it. Yitz had picked me up at school, so I knew it wasn't he. The children were all under seven, so it couldn't have been any of them. It turned out that the housekeeper, who had been with me only three weeks and had seen me light candles during the previous weeks, wanted everything to be just perfect for Shabbat when I arrived home.

I recall my father was very unhappy about my Friday-afternoon routine that entire year, with so little preparation on my part. He felt that it just wasn't the same and that I wasn't creating for the children the proper memories and associations and smells of Friday in a traditional Jewish home, memories my mother certainly gave me. I wasn't quite liberated at that time, and it would never have occurred to me to say, even respectfully, to my father, "If you think it's so wonderful, how come men don't take over the preparations for Shabbat?" All I could tell him was that my appreciation of Shabbat after a hard day at work was as great as it was staying home all day and preparing. I still feel that way, even though I know that our children don't get the same flavor of the day unless all of us are involved.

I treasure my moment of candlelighting. When we speak today of men and women sharing rituals that have been traditionally male, such as Kiddush and *aliyot* (calling men up for the Torah blessings in the synagogue), a little fear creeps up inside of me. I don't want Shabbat candles to be taken from me. . . . If I were starting out now, I might do it a bit differently. I would expect all the family to be in attendance as I light, much as they are for Kiddush and Havdalah. But having done it this way for so many years, my pleasure comes from the private rather than the public experience, enhanced if some of the family are there at the moment, but not diminished if I light alone.

For many years my husband would stand by while I lit, but that ended when he became a pulpit rabbi and had to leave early for shul. When the children all were younger, I used to let each of them light a candle or ignite the match (which, to a five-year-old, is an even bigger prize). Now that they are grown, and I have less control over their time, their presence at candlelighting is a sometime thing. A friend, a young widow with three teen daughters, sets up a pair of candlesticks for each to light, and they all do it together every Friday night. It's a lovely sight to behold.

Some Jews, particularly the Lubavitch Chasidim, have embarked on a campaign to have all young Jewish girls light one Shabbat candle. Though Jewish law does not explicitly require it, many consider it important for educational training purposes. This practice is still not universally observed. In most Orthodox homes, the mother will light for the entire household. However, when an unmarried woman sets up her own household, she is responsible for Shabbat candles. So is a man, when there is no woman in the household. There are many Jewish college students living in dormitories who light Shabbat candles every week. A pair of candlesticks makes a fine gift for a student, male or female, going away to college.

If one has women guests, at least two candles should be prepared for each of them. If there are young girls present, it is thoughtful to inquire whether they, too, wish to light their own candles. One doesn't need a whole lot of extra candlesticks. Almost anything flat and lined with aluminum foil will do. Shabbat candles are short and stubby, and if the bottoms are burned in, they will stand safely on just about anything. But do not use thin glass or porcelain as a base. When the candles burn down, their heat will shatter that beautiful Limoges bonbon tray. . . .

I've added another brief ritual to my candlelighting, a very private one. Several years ago I was chatting one evening in Jerusalem with a middle-aged couple who had settled in Israel four years earlier. They had come without their three children and had left America as their youngest daughter was entering Barnard College. Planning ahead for the day when our children go their own ways, I asked Mrs. F., "Do you miss them? Do you think about them a lot? Do you imagine what they are doing at any given moment?" "No," she said, "I love seeing them" (usually twice a year, as things worked out), "receiving their letters, and writing to them, but I don't miss them. . . . In fact, I began to realize that if I didn't remind myself of them, a week or two could go by without my thinking about them at all. So I decided that at candlelighting each Friday night, I would let my thoughts dwell for a moment on each child, picture their faces, and think about their lives. I once mentioned it to them, and now they all light candles on Friday night and think for a few moments about us."

So as I light my candles each week, I reflect for a few seconds about my husband and about each child, and then I remove my hands from my eyes and say, "Good Shabbos," and kiss whoever happens to be standing by.

After candlelighting, the men go off to shul for Minchah, Kabbalat Shabbat, and Maariv prayers. Minchah, the afternoon prayer, really belongs to the weekday, but it is scheduled back to back with the evening prayer for convenience. Minchah is recited at the last possible moment of the afternoon, and Maariv, the evening prayer, at earliest evening, with the Kabbalat Shabbat service (welcoming the Sabbath) as the highlight wedged between the two. In an urbanized society, it is difficult to run back and forth to shul three times a day, especially on a short Friday, and the Rabbis took these practical problems into consideration as they formulated ritual.

Some women go to shul for Friday-evening services, but far fewer than go on a Shabbat morning. Most of the Friday-night women's crowd consists of little girls, teenagers, and older women. At times our daughters go, but often they stay home, and the three of us pray together. We should go more often because the Friday-night shul davening (prayer) is the most beautiful of all, with more communal singing than at any other time. But on Friday night I like to luxuriate in the sudden peacefulness of the house between candlelighting and dinner and in the prayer with my daughters, parts of which we sing together.

One of the special prayers of Kabbalat Shabbat is the Lecha Dodi, welcoming the beloved Sabbath. There are several beautiful melodies for these words. On Friday nights, as I sing the Lecha Dodi, an image of the sixteenth-century mystics of Safed springs into my mind.[3] I picture them as lean men, dressed in white caftans, their fine faces tanned from sun and wind, and glowing from their ritual immersion. I see them standing atop the mountain crest, facing toward Jerusalem and the setting sun, and singing Lecha Dodi. Could they ever have imagined that four hundred years later a New York Jew, in a modern house, would be singing "their" song? I wonder if the Beatles will have such longevity.

Even better than shul is my mother-in-law's Friday-night davening. Occasionally, she spends a Shabbat with us. As I lurk around a corner, and listen intently, I feel as if I am privy to a private audience with God. She finishes up the regular Friday-night prayers, and then, in a barely audible whisper, and looking into her Siddur all the while, she proceeds to carry on a one-way conversation with Him.

With eighty-five years behind her, my mother-in-law brings God up to date on the whereabouts and doings of each child, grandchild, and great-grandchild, occasionally summing up past favors and events of yesteryear. Once, more than fifteen years after I had been married, she reminded God that her son had married a nice *yiddishe maidele* (Jewish girl). After describing what each of us was doing, she turned His attention to the grandchildren—which school each attended, who was graduating, who was in a cast with a torn cartilage, and who was going to camp for a month. Rarely does she make an outright plea, but once she mentioned in passing that my brother-in-law's blood pressure was too high. Yet another time, she informed her beloved God that her grandson, then twenty-eight, chief resident at Peter Bent Brigham Hospital in Boston, was working very hard and had no time yet to look for a wife (hint, hint). Systematically, every Friday night she parades the entire family before God. Without ever using those words, it is a prayer of thanksgiving. May I be forgiven for eavesdropping, hers are truly among the most moving prayers I have ever heard.

NOTES

1. In writing of the Sabbath, I have used interchangeably its two Hebrew pronunciations: Shabbat or Shabbos. I chose one or the other depending on what I believe to be its most common pronunciation in that particular context.

2. At times the word *rabbi* is spelled with a capital R. This signifies a special group of rabbis, those of the talmudic period whose decisions have served as the basis for rabbinic activity throughout history, including modern times.

3. In the sixteenth century, Jewish mystics, known as the Kabbalists, went up to settle in the Holy Land in the city of Safed. It was they who created the Kabbalat Shabbat service, including in it the Lecha Dodi prayer which was written by one of their own.

Serenity Lost—and Found

HAROLD M. SCHULWEIS

In my youth the Sabbath was a wet blanket, a puritanical litany of prohibited joys, a series of proscriptions and negations that inhibited productivity, creativity, and fun. The Sabbath was the day of "no"—no, you cannot play ball, listen to the radio, ride your bike. "You shall not do any manner of work." Why, I wondered, is the Torah so insistent about forbidding labor? I could understand prohibitions against immoral behavior, but who needs a law against working?

Endless work is a curse. After Adam transgressed, God punished him. "In toil shalt thou eat of it all the days of your life. In the sweat of thy brow, in the seat of thy face shalt thou eat bread till you return to the ground."

Why, then, are so many of us willingly embracing the curse of all-consuming work? Why do we want to toil not six days but all seven? Because we are afraid not to work.

We fear the Sabbath as slaves fear freedom. If I have free time, with what shall I fill it? With whom shall I spend it? How can I live without schedule, without deadlines, without orders? We complain, of course, of insufficient time for family and friends, but left with twenty-four hours of unstructured time, we become ill at ease. We are frightened of boredom, which the philosopher Soren Kierkegaard called "the root of all evil." We know how children go crazy when they are bored; it goes double for adults.

Therapists are familiar with this odd phobia: the fear of vacations, of relaxation, of retirement, of leisure. Even the terms themselves are filled with negation. The root of vacation is "vacate," to cause to be empty or unoccupied. Relaxation is defined as "an absence or reduction of muscle retention." Retirement comes from the French *retirer*, which means "to withdraw." The dread of having a single day away from the office produces in many people what psychologists Ferenzi and Karl Abraham call "Sunday neurosis." Some of us grow depressed and even ill when the stock market prices stop marching across the screen.

The seduction of work has drained us of our poetry, romance, and intimacy. And, if one follows the psychological literature, it has brought tens of thousands of people to a state of anhedonia, an inability to achieve joy in intimacy.

Sigmund Freud called work and love "the parents of human civilization." But at the dawn of the twenty-first century, work—not love—is our chief joy. In *The Overworked American*, economist Judith Schor informs us that, in the last two decades, the average worker has added on an extra 164 hours—an entire month—to the work year! Vacations have shortened by fourteen percent, and in white households parental time available to children has fallen ten hours per week. In his bestseller, *The Time Bind*, Arlie Russell Hochschild contends there is a profound reversal in our social psyche: both men and women favor the workplace over home.

Why? Because the workplace is more interesting and more fun than the home. The office is an escape from unwashed dishes, unresolved quarrels, testy tots, and unresponsive mates. Women report that the rewards of caring and feeding the family cannot compare to the satisfaction, recognition, and respect they receive at the office. The historian Kay Hamod writes, "I love scholarly work because you force a manuscript into shape. It's not like sitting alone for nine months waiting for something to happen to you."

An important revolutionary reversal is taking place in our culture. Yesterday we spoofed the office, the factory, speed, scheduling. Charlie Chaplin's *Modern Times* offered a satiric, sharp insight into the technological, industrial world of the late 1930s. Workers no longer had to stop for lunch; they were fed by a revolving plate with an automatic food pusher, and an automatic soup plate arrived with a compressed air blower so the workers didn't even have to blow on the soup.

A different scenario suggests itself for our modern times. If Chaplin's feeding machine hurried the worker, the modern parent hurries the child. The culture of the workplace has taken over that of the home. In a recent advertisement for a popular oatmeal, a working mother feeds her tot in just under ninety seconds. "Sherri Greenberg" holds four-and-a-half-year-old Nicky in her arms and declares: "Nicky is a very picky eater. With Instant Quaker Oatmeal, I can give him a terrific hot breakfast in just ninety seconds, and I don't have to spend any time coaxing him to eat it." The ad concludes, "Instant Quaker Oatmeal for moms who have a lot of love but not a lot of time." Some technological advances take a bit longer: "two-minute rice," "five-minute chicken casserole," and "seven-minute Chinese feasts."

Hallmark has just the card for busy parents. One is to be placed on the child's bed: "Sorry I can't be there to tuck you in." Another is to be put on the breakfast table: "Sorry I can't say good morning."

Surely, work is not the culprit. Judaism does not oppose work. The six days do not stand in opposition to the seventh day. It is all within the same commandment: "Six days you shall labor and do all your work, but the seventh day is a Sabbath unto the Lord" (Exod. 20:9–10). Judaism pleads that we attain some degree of independence from the store, from the factory, from the office, from the culture of commerce, from the adulation of commodities.

The Sabbath challenges us to break our addiction to work. Shabbat is a cry for sanity, for freedom from the omnivorous monster that eats at our soul and robs us of our family, our friends, and the gentleness in us.

On Yom Kippur the Haftarah from the prophet Isaiah 58 concludes: "If you refrain from trampling the Sabbath, from pursuing your business on My holy day, if you call the Sabbath a delight and call the holy day honorable, if you honor it and go not to your own ways nor look to your own affairs nor pursue your business nor speak thereof, then shalt thou delight yourself in the Lord and I will feed you with the heritage of Jacob." For the Sabbath to be a delight, it must go beyond lighting candles, reciting Kiddush, and blessing the challah. If the table talk is filled with the making of "deals" or of a "killing" in the market, the challah turns hard and dry. If the table talk is acerbic, sarcastic, and full of gossip, or speaks to the children only of their progress in school and not of their hopes and dreams, the Kiddush wine turns sour. If there is shouting at the Sabbath table, the candles are extinguished.

Judaism asks for equilibrium. The Sabbath is a declaration of a truce, an armistice for the sake of our liberation.

We are lopsided, out of kilter. We need one day out of seven to restore our sanity.

One day out of seven let us erect a barrier to keep out the culture of business, its toughness, its hardness, its obsessiveness, its competition.

One day out of seven let us close our pocketbooks.

One day out of seven let us liberate "In God we trust" from the dollar bill and put it into our lives.

One day in seven let us halt the motor.

One day in seven let us not purchase what we covet.

One day out of seven let us disconnect the TV, fax, and computer; instead, let us take our time, talking and listening to those whom we love.

One day out of seven let us create the balance indispensable for our sanity, our health, and the solidity of our family lives.

On Shabbat we can begin to take back control of our lives. The Sabbath is our time; the home is our place.

· III ·

JEWS CELEBRATE SHABBAT

Sabbath Eve

MARK ZBOROWSKI

AND ELIZABETH HERZOG

It is told that God said to Israel, "If you accept my Torah and observe my Laws, I will give you for all eternity the most precious thing that I have in my possession."

"And what," asked Israel, "is that precious thing Thou wilt give us if we obey Thy Torah?"

God: "The future world."

Israel: "But even in this world should we have a foretaste of that other?"

God: "The Sabbath will give you this foretaste."

Sabbath brings the joy of the future life into the shtetl. This is the climax of the week, "a different world, no worry, no work." One lives from Sabbath to Sabbath, working all week to earn for it. The days of the week fall into place around the Sabbath. Wednesday, Thursday, and Friday are "before Sabbath," and they draw holiness from the Sabbath that is coming. Sunday, Monday, and Tuesday are "after Sabbath," and they draw holiness from the Sabbath that is past. Any delicacy that one finds during the week should be bought and kept, if possible, "for Sabbath."

The Sabbath is a day of rest, joy, and devotion to God. None must work, none must mourn, none must worry, none must hunger on that day. Any Jew who lacks a Sabbath meal should be helped by those who have more than he. But of course one hopes not to need help, for no matter how poor a man may be he counts on the Lord to provide for the Sabbath meal. Some stroke of luck, some sudden opportunity to earn the price of a fish and a fowl will surely turn up at the last moment—if only one goes after it hard enough. Many stories and legends describe miracles by which God at the last moment provided Sabbath fare for a devout Jew who lacked means to "make Sabbath."

Sabbath is a Queen and a Bride; and on the Sabbath, "every Jew is a king."

Perhaps not every Sabbath in every shtetl was alike for all the Jews of Eastern Europe. Perhaps everyone did not always enjoy a happy Sabbath. Yet the memories that live through the years have a glowing uniformity. On no point is there more unanimity than on the significance and the feeling of Sabbath in the shtetl. It is remembered as a time of ecstasy—father in a silken caftan and velvet skullcap, mother in black silk and pearls; the glow of candles, the waves of peace and joy, the glad sense that it is good to be a Jew, the distant pity for those who have been denied this foretaste of heaven.

Friday is the day of the eve of Sabbath, Erev Shabbes. It is set apart from other days because, although it is not a holiday, it is the day on which one makes ready to greet the Sabbath. The shtetl housewife wakes up earlier than usual with the thought, "Today is Erev Shabbes—I must hurry!" Even if she usually works at the shop or market, on this day she will try to stay home to prepare for the reception of the Queen Sabbath. First of all she pours over her hands the "fingernail water"—the water that stood by her bed overnight in a glass or a cup to be at hand for the ritual ablution that must start each day and says the short morning prayer with which each day must begin. Then she puts on her oldest dress, her work apron, ties a kerchief over her head, and rolls up her sleeves.

Before the others are awake she "fires the oven" with logs so that it will be ready for use. She feeds the family as they appear, as quickly as possible, and bundles the boys off to school. Meanwhile she inspects the dough that she set to rise last night for the Sabbath loaf, the challah. She begins to clean the chicken that she bought yesterday, watching anxiously—"it shouldn't happen!"—for any forbidden flecks of blood, blister on the gizzard, or other calamity that would raise doubts whether her chicken was kosher—ritually fit to eat.

If it did happen, someone would have to hurry to the rabbi asking breathlessly, "Is it kosher?" and waiting in painful suspense until the rabbi, after studying the chicken and the relevant laws, declared, "Kosher!"

The fish, also purchased on Thursday, must be cleaned, chopped, seasoned, prepared for cooking. "Without fish," the saying goes, "there is no Sabbath." All the rest of the Sabbath food must be prepared as well, for after sundown no fire may be lit, no work may be done. There will be noodles, which the housewife kneads and flattens out, rolling the thin sheet into a long floury coil, slicing it and spreading the fine slivers to dry on a clean cloth.

Next she braids the dough into "twists" ready for baking. Before the loaves are placed on the hot bricks, she throws a bit of dough into the fire, saying, "Blessed be Thou, O Lord our God, King of the Universe, who hast hallowed us by His commandments and commanded to take of the challah."

This is one of the three rituals known as the "womanly" duties. Without this offering, challah would not be fit for its part in the Sabbath feast. If by mischance she forgets it, however, she can "take challah" when she removes the loaves from the oven.

From sunrise to sunset the day is a race with time. The whole house must be cleaned, the floors swept and sanded, the woodwork washed, the kitchen tables and benches scrubbed, the towels changed. The housewife darts from broom to oven and back again, peering, stirring, prodding, dusting, giving commands to her daughters, and ordering all males to keep from underfoot.

The day whirls on: the challah has been lifted out with a long-handled shovel and glazed with white of egg. The loaves are high and light—God has answered the prayer whispered while she was kneading the dough, and she will not be ashamed before her husband, her family, and the neighbors.

To fit each task in with all the others requires a high order of domestic engineering, especially since the boys come home from school at noon on Friday and must be disposed of with a snack—perhaps with a smack. Of a woman who has trouble coping with the domestic routine and runs a confused house, it is said scornfully, "For her every day is Erev Shabbes."

Meanwhile the beggars make the rounds of houses and stores, for in most places Friday is the beggars' day. Each beggar has his regular beat and each household has its pile of coins ready, probably presided over by one of the children. Each beggar is known, and in turn knows the amount he may expect from each household. If he is given two kopeks where three are the rule, there will be no end to his rage and complaints. Sometimes food will be given instead of money, and a privileged beggar may be given both.

Each Friday the same duties are done in the same order and each Friday brings the same anxiety that Sabbath may arrive before all is ready. A woman knows the tasks and their order from long experience, reaching back to childhood in her mother's house; and from her mother's house she also knows the Friday fear that the sun may set too soon. The fear is sharpest when the whole routine must be fitted into the "short Friday" of midwinter.

After the house is cleaned, she turns to the children, who must be washed from the tops of their crowns to the tips of their toes and dressed in clean clothes from inside out. Their heads must be doused, soaped, and finally rinsed with kerosene, and the odor of their cleanliness is an aura about them. After they are dressed, they are stiff with the command to keep their clothes clean for the Sabbath.

A pile of clean clothes must be prepared for each of the men and older boys. Carefully folded on top of the bundle is the *talis koton* that they must always wear, and wear in such a way that it is visible. It is a large square of white wool with black stripes along two edges and with a hole in the middle so that it can be slipped over the head. At each corner are knotted fringes, and the knots must be the correct kind and number. It is also called "four corners," *arba kanfos.*

A male Jew wears it from the time he begins to walk and is forbidden to move about without the *talis koton.* A child cannot wear it before he is trained to be "clean," however, for there would be danger that it might be defiled. Some men wear it even in bed. A blessing must always be said when it is put on, and although almost no women wear it, the regulations stipulate that a woman who does so must say the blessing.

When the men return from their shops and market stalls, or from their journeying, the bundles will be ready for them. Wherever one is, he will try to reach home in time to greet the Sabbath with his own family. The peddler traveling from village to village, the itinerant tailor, shoemaker, cobbler, the merchant off on a trip, all will plan, push, hurry, trying to reach home before sunset on Friday evening.

As they press homeward the *shammes* calls through the streets of the shtetl, "Jews to the bathhouse!" A functionary of the synagogue, the *shammes* is a combination of sexton and beadle. He speaks with an authority more than his own, for when he calls, "Jews to the bathhouse," he is summoning them to a commandment.

All who can respond. The women are usually so caught in the tangle of their preparations that they must perform their ablutions at home. But the men and boys seize their clean clothing and from all the streets they bear down on the bathhouse, their bundles under their arms. There they will be cleansed in the bath and purified by three ceremonial immersions in the pool of "living water" known as the *mikva*. Meanwhile, they will be entertained by the conversation of their peers. The bath is like a turkish bath and those who are prosperous enough to stop work early can plan to linger, chatting in the steam, slapping themselves with "brooms" made of supple twigs, and basking. For the others the ceremony must be brisk, since Sabbath is almost here.

Coming home from the bathhouse, dressed in their clean clothes, they put away the soiled garments and cover themselves with the carefully cherished Sabbath caftan, tying in its fullness with a silken girdle. The Sabbath caftan is usually of "silk." It may be sateen if the man is very poor, and the black fabric, whatever it is, may be green with age, frayed and mended. But the Sabbath caftan is made of "silk" and is a very special garment, stored away during the week with the rest of the Sabbath and holiday clothes. There is a Sabbath cap too, also of a precious fabric—satin or velvet perhaps for the opulent. The coat pockets must be emptied of all money, since none may be touched or carried on the Sabbath. If by any chance the coat is put on after sundown, children will happily perform the duty of emptying Father's pockets, rewarded by the privilege of keeping for themselves any stray coins they may find.

The boys, down to the very smallest, are dressed like their fathers in long black caftan and black cap or hat. The very little ones may have short trousers underneath, and childish socks peeking out from under the hem of the dignified coat.

At last the housewife, with house and family furbished for the taste of heaven on earth, turns to preparing herself. By the time she is ready, the men have returned from the bathhouse, still racing against time—for they must be at the synagogue by sundown. They depart quickly while she puts the last touches on her own costume. The kerchief is replaced by the wig, or *sheytl*, that covers her cropped hair, and her splashed and rumpled cotton dress is replaced by the Sabbath dress of black silk, enriched with whatever jewelry she has to mark her dignity as a wife and mother.

For many women a Sabbath without jewelry would be almost like a Sabbath without chicken or fish. The ideal Sabbath jewel is a necklace of pearls. It is said that even if hard times forced one to pawn her pearls, she might hope to have them back for the Sabbath. "On Monday morning,

Mother returned her pearls (to the pawnbroker) and then on Friday night he would bring them to her again."

As the sun sets, Queen Sabbath enters the shtetl, to be greeted by the men and boys at the synagogue, by the women and girls at home. The precise moment when each Sabbath begins is noted on the official calendar and is announced by the *shammes*. Then the mother in her *sheytl*, her Sabbath dress and pearls, performs the ritual of lighting the candles. No household will have less than two, and those that can afford it will have one for each living member of the home family, in a five-or seven-branch candlestick of silver or brass—with additional holders if they are needed. Probably the candlestick is a family heirloom handed down from mother to daughter through the generations. There are few heirlooms in the shtetl, but most households have their treasured Sabbath candlesticks. If a family should have to leave—"God forbid"—whatever else may be abandoned, the candlestick will be kept.

The woman of the house lights the candles, praying as she does so, "Blessed art Thou, O Lord our God, King of the Universe, who hast hallowed us by His commandments and commanded us to kindle the Sabbath light!" She says the prayer in Hebrew, which she may or may not understand, for Hebrew is the language of religion. Her prayer is almost inaudible to earthly ears. Men say some prayers aloud, but a woman usually moves her lips and barely murmurs the words. Having lighted the candles, she moves her arms over them in a gesture of embrace, drawing to her the holiness that rises from their flames. She draws the holiness to herself, but not for herself only, for she represents her household.

In the glow of the flames and of their sanctity she covers her eyes with her hands, and now she says her own prayer, dictated by her heart. This prayer is not in the language of ritual but in Yiddish, her own vernacular. She is free to pray as she will, but she will probably repeat one of the familiar forms that have been used through the years, begging for the welfare of each member of her household, adding only the few special phrases and pleas that mark the prayer as her own.

Often she weeps as she prays and it would be hard to say to what extent the tears themselves are part of the ritual. For so many generations women have wept as they prayed over the Sabbath candles, tears of grief or of gratitude, of hope or of fear, tears for themselves, for their families, for their people. Through the years little girls have seen their mothers standing rapt and the tears between their fingers shining in the candlelight, seeming to be part of the prayer.

Lighting the candles is another of the three commandments special to women. The third is the ritual purification at the *mikva* after menstruation. If a woman performs her three commandments without fail, she may feel secure about her future life.

Once the candles have been lighted, Sabbath is within the home. All is ready. The race is won, anxiety vanishes, the breathless rush of the day changes to slow serenity which will continue until the new week begins. The table is prepared, with its white cloth, two Sabbath loaves set out on it and covered with a napkin—if possible, an embroidered one. The housewife herself is dressed and ready; no work need be done nor is any permitted. Therefore on Friday evening, in the first peace of Sabbath, she may sit at ease with no sense of guilt for idleness, and open her book. This is the special prayer book for women, containing the prayers women need to know, with Yiddish translations of the ones that are in Hebrew. In the book also are legends, sermons, and homilies to help her fulfill her duties as a Jewish wife and mother. So she may sit quietly reading—if she knows how to read—until the men return from the synagogue.

She will not have long to wait, for the Friday evening service at the synagogue is short. Its main feature is the welcoming by the Chosen People of the Sabbath, their Bride. "Come, O Cherished One, and meet the Bride! Let us welcome the face of Sabbath! . . ."

There is little time for musing and reading before the men return, the head of the household and his sons, and perhaps the *oyrekh*, the guest for the Sabbath meal. If the household can afford it, there will surely be an *oyrekh*, for without a guest no Sabbath is truly complete. He may be a stranger from some other community who was unable to get home for the Sabbath. He may be a delegate, traveling to collect funds for some educational institution. He may be, poor fellow, a Jewish conscript posted in town. Or he may be a rabbinical student studying day and night and fed by different households in turn so that in a sense his board constitutes a community fellowship.

Whoever he is, any stranger in need will come to the synagogue on Friday evening and at the end of the service he will expect to be invited to some home. First rights of hospitality usually go to the more prosperous. The *shammes* may bustle up to a rich man and tell him, "I have a guest." Or the rich man may ask the *shammes*, "Anyone for the Sabbath?"

There is a legend that every Sabbath God sends the prophet Elijah, dressed as a needy stranger, to visit the Jews and observe the way they are fulfilling His commandments. Accordingly, the stranger one brings home may be the prophet. No legend is required, however, to stimulate Sabbath hospitality. Prophet or beggar, to feed the hungry is a "good deed," especially if the stranger is a Jew who can eat only kosher food. Therefore it is a privilege to share the Sabbath feast, even if by ill luck it is a meager one.

The first words as the men and boys enter are "*Gut Shabbes*," the weekly greeting exchanged with all the holiday zest of an annual Happy New Year. The man of the house recites his greeting to the Sabbath angels. "Peace be unto you, ye ministering angels, messengers of the Most High . . ." He does not murmur as did his wife but speaks audibly, slowly pacing the room as he prays, with his head bent slightly and his hands behind his back. Little boys imitate their father's words, his posture, his gait, and the *oyrekh* joins them. When the small boy becomes a father and his little sister a housewife, the words of the prayers, the gestures, the intonations will already have become part of them.

The father says a second prayer, the chapter "in praise of the virtuous wife" from the Proverbs of Solomon. "A woman of worth—who can find her? For her price is far above rubies. The heart of her husband trusteth in her . . ."

Now the head of the family fills the ceremonial goblet with wine, takes it into his hands, and chants the Kiddush—the prayer consecrating the Sabbath—and the blessing over wine. He fills the cup to the brim, symbolizing abundance, and all stand while he "makes Kiddush."

When the father finishes, he takes a sip from the goblet and hands it to his wife. The wife, daughters, and younger children say the blessing over wine, but not the Kiddush, and each takes a sip. The older boys and the *oyrekh* say Kiddush after the father, also over a full cup of wine. If a very honored guest is present—a grandfather or a learned man—he is given the privilege of saying Kiddush first. The word *kiddush* means consecration. The ritual establishes the presence of the Queen Sabbath in the family and the participation of all its members in the Sabbath holiness.

The Sabbath meal, like every meal, is preceded by the ceremonial washing of the hands, pouring water over them three times as the blessing is said. Before sitting down, the father removes the hat in which he returned from the synagogue and almost with the same gesture substitutes a skullcap from his pocket, since it is commanded that his head be covered at all times. Then at last the family gather around the table set with the best linen and the best dishes. During the week, meals may be hurried and irregular, eaten in snatches and in solitude, whenever one has time or feels hungry. During the week, the mother may never find time to sit at the table. But on Sabbath all sit down together, men and boys on one side, women and girls on the other. The father sits at the head, the mother at his right. The festive table is set in the best room—if they have one—which during the week is little used except as a retreat in which the father can study.

The lengthy meal begins with the blessing of the challah. The father silently and deliberately removes the napkin, lifts the two loaves, holding them together, then sets them down again. He passes the knife over one of them, then cuts the other in half and gives each person a slice. Each one breaks a bit from his slice, dips it in salt, and "makes the blessing" for bread. All blessings are in Hebrew and while they are being pronounced no word of a profane language must be spoken. Therefore during the ritual prologue of the meal the only words uttered are in Hebrew and—except for the Kiddush—are murmured rather than spoken aloud.

The rule against breaking into the sacred language with the vernacular may lead to embarrassment. If the father suddenly finds there is no towel to wipe his hands after the handwashing, or no knife for the blessing of the challah, or no salt for it, he cannot ask in Yiddish for the missing article, and even if he knows the word in Hebrew, his wife may not. Therefore he must resort to dumb show, gesticulation, and inarticulate grunts to announce the emergency.

When the ritual prologue is finished, the mother brings in the fish, spiced and perhaps sweetened, and gives each one a piece. The father receives the head in deference to his family status, and he may then present it to his wife in token of her excellence and his esteem. The fish is followed by chicken broth—"clear like amber"—with the finely cut noodles, after which comes boiled beef or chicken, or both.

The delicacies of Sabbath are enjoyed slowly, with time to appreciate each mouthful, and with pauses between each course. The mother's hard work is rewarded by admiring comments about her skill—the flavor of the fish gravy, the golden color of the fat on the soup, the tenderness of the fowl—"it falls apart in your mouth." This is the time when she receives her weekly recompense of praise.

The waits between courses give time for learned conversation between father and sons, for comments on community affairs, or for plying the *oyrekh* with questions about his own shtetl, and about what he has seen and heard on his travels. As the men converse, the girls and women listen eagerly, their eyes active and their tongues still.

At the end of the meal all pour a few drops of water on their hands.

Knives, symbolic of bloody weapons, are covered or taken away and *zmiros* are sung—a series of songs praising God and celebrating good cheer. The placid *zmiros* melodies, associated with the happy, peaceful afterglow of the Sabbath meal, are among the favorite Jewish tunes and the ones most apt to be hummed during hours of work or meditation.

The Sabbath candles burn lower as the meal comes to an end. No member of the family may blow them out or move the candle holders because on the Sabbath a Jew must avoid all contact with fire or with anything related to it. Therefore at bedtime all lights will be extinguished and all fires taken care of by someone who is not subject to the severe Sabbath regulations. Often some non-Jew, a *shabbes goy*, is paid by the community for this service. As he goes from house to house, he may also be rewarded by the individual families with a piece of challah, different in appearance and taste from the dark bread of his everyday menu.

As the family go to bed, they know that every other Jewish household in the shtetl has enjoyed the prescribed observances in the same way. They know too that all are enjoying release from care. Not only weekday acts but even weekday thoughts are forbidden on the Sabbath. One must put aside all concern about business, money, family problems, and think only of God and His Law; for Sabbath is a foretaste of the future life in which there will be no worry, but only happiness and the pleasure of studying the Holy Words.

Even the soul is different, for on Sabbath an additional soul, *nshomeh yeseyreh*, is joined to it. All week this soul is with God, but on the Sabbath *nshomeh yeseyreh* is added to each man, woman, and child; and while it is present no cares or worries can spoil the joy that is a foretaste of the future.

Not only does each Jew know that all those in the shtetl are sharing his Sabbath experience. He feels, beyond that, a community with Jews who are celebrating the Sabbath all over the world. This is a major strand in the Sabbath feeling—a sense of proud and joyous identification with the tradition, the past, the ancestors, with all the Jewish world living or gone. On the Sabbath the shtetl feels most strongly and most gladly that "it is good to be a Jew."

A Niggun for Shabbat

ELIE WIESEL

For *shalosh seudot* [the third meal] in Wizsnitz or in Sighet we sat at the Wizsnitzer rebbe's table. It was dark. The beautiful part of *shalosh seudot* was the darkness, when you saw only shadows, shadows that suddenly began to sing.

I remember the song we used to sing. It was on Shabbat, of course, the most sacred day of the week; and the most sacred hour of Shabbat was *shalosh seudot*. All the books I could write and all the words I could use are nothing but pale reflections, if not pale substitutes, for those songs that I shall never forget and that somehow still vibrate in me.

During *shalosh seudot* we used to sit in the darkness—in the semidarkness—and of course we could not distinguish one from the other, poor from rich, the erudite from the *am ha'aretzim*. There were no *am ha'aretzim* among the Hasidim—only the Misnagdim would say that. At one point the rebbe would begin singing in Yiddish: "*Ven ich volt gehaht kaeakh, volt ich in di gahssen gelohfn, un ich volt geshrien haeakh, 'Shabbes, haeliker Shabbes'*"— "If I had the strength, I would run in the streets shouting and screaming with all my might, 'Shabbes, holy shabbes.'" Legend had it that, as long as the rebbe would sing, Shabbat would stay. I adored that song. I used to sing it not only on Shabbat. When I sang it, I made my own Shabbat.

If I miss something today, it is not so much Yom Kippur or even the holidays in Sighet; it is Shabbes. There was something special about it, something that can never be experienced again because the world of Sighet is gone, because Shabbat is no longer the same. Not even in Israel do I feel the same Shabbat, not even in Jerusalem. Why? Because Shabbat meant Jerusalem to us. On Shabbat in Sighet or in Lodz or in any other place in Eastern Europe, we were all in Jerusalem. But even if you are in Jerusalem, it is still not the same. Someone once asked me where I feel at home. And I said, "I feel most at home in Jerusalem—when I am not in Jerusalem."

There is a saying that if the Jews were to observe Shabbat twice in a row, the *Geulah* [redemption] would come immediately. If we could observe Shabbat as it should be, the *Geulah* would come because there would be no need for *Geulah*. That would *be Geulah*. That would be redemption. That would be the messianic time.

So I miss my Shabbat. And if I write about Shabbat, it is because I try to re-create it. And if I sing Shabbat, it is because I try to recapture those melodies that I heard and that are somehow still within me.

Sabbath Candles

ARI L. GOLDMAN

When an old woman who had served in her youth in the household of Rabbi Elimelech was importuned for stories about the master and his ways, she said: "Nought has remained with me in my remembrance, save only this. During the week, there were often quarrels in the kitchen, and upbraidings between the maidenfolk, as in other households. But in this we differed from others: on the eve of each Sabbath, we fell around each other's neck, and we begged forgiveness for any harsh words spoken during the week."

For me, Sabbath candles still held their magic. There was a perfect moment of silence when Shira would light them in our apartment in Somerville as the sun went down Friday evenings. She would wave her hands three times over the blue-and-white flames, cover her eyes, and recite her private prayers. "What do you say?" I would ask when she had finished, knowing that, for her, the formulaic blessing ("Blessed art Thou . . . who sanctified us with the commandment of lighting Sabbath candles") would not suffice. Shira would always answer my inquiry with a smile, which was all I really wanted anyway.

With the arrival of Shabbat, as we called it, our house would be transformed. The TV, the radio, the record player, the food processor, and the word processor were shut off. Cooking and cleaning ceased. Exams and term papers were behind me. Deadlines and interviews were behind Shira. There were only the three of us.

Adam, just a few months past his first birthday, was at a most delicious state—half boy, half baby. He would toddle, cuddle, giggle, and tumble, never letting go of the bottle in his mouth. He was trying out his first words, one of which was "light," which took on new meaning for him when he pointed to the candles ablaze over the white Shabbat tablecloth.

At times we would open up our little circle and invite a few guests for the Friday-night dinner. When we lived in Manhattan, these were usually Jews who, if not observant, were at least familiar with our Sabbath songs and the blessings we made over the wine and challah. In Somerville, we decided to open things up even more. After all, at the Div School [Harvard Divinity School], I was interested not only in learning but in sharing.

The cross-cultural possibilities were exciting. One Friday night we had over Jan, a Roman Catholic student who lived in Poland and was given a special visa to study religion at Harvard; Fran, a graduate student in the Div School who worked part-time for her church, the First Church of Christ, Scientist; and Anna, a bright undergraduate religion major who was Jewish and in my world religions class. On another occasion, two other classmates—Gary, my gay friend from California, and Edward, who was straight and from England—joined us. My dream was to get my two favorite teachers there on one night, but it couldn't be arranged. Instead, Rabbi Louis Jacobs came with his wife, Shula, one night and Professor Eck came another.

The discussions at our Sabbath table ranged widely and deeply, going well beyond the formality of a classroom or the niceties of a dinner party. Shira and I found that the sharing of our Sabbath rituals broke down barriers rather than created them. As we made the blessing over the wine, ritually poured water from a cup on our hands, and cut the challah, our guests questioned and compared and shared their own religious experiences. They talked about their lives, their families, their religious awakenings and disappointments and the meaning they derived from them.

On one Friday night, Lisa, a classmate who once managed a health-food restaurant, joined us with her live-in boyfriend, Jim, a graphic artist who had trained at the School of Visual Arts in Manhattan. Lisa and I talked about the courses we were taking and general Div School gossip that nobody but a student there could care about, like whether the seminar on the morality of nuclear war should be open to undergraduates. Shira and Jim were talking about the virtues of living in Boston versus New York. Jim didn't show any interest in things religious until we gathered around the Sabbath table and I recited the Hebrew prayer over the wine. "What does that mean?" Jim asked.

"It's from Genesis," I told him, offering a rough translation, "And God finished creating the heavens and the earth and rested on the seventh day."

"Chapter two, verse one," Jim said, with a nod of his head. "Thus the heavens and the earth were finished, and all the host of them." He went on like this, quoting the King James Bible in perfect preaching cadence. He saw he had a surprised and appreciative audience, so he continued with such fervor that I was afraid he would wake Adam. "And the name of the third river is Hiddekel: that is it which goeth toward the east of Assyria. And the fourth river is Euphrates." He didn't stop until he had finished the chapter. "And they were both naked, the man and his wife, and were not ashamed."

"I am the son of a Southern Baptist preacher from Louisiana," Jim told us over dinner. "It was a bit like growing up as a monk, except that you still had to live with your family. Grace before eating. Study the Bible, the unerring word of God. And beware of Catholics. And girls? Oh, there were girls, but don't get caught with one. Remember, social dancing is the work of the Devil!" We laughed and talked about growing up until the differences between a Southern Baptist from Louisiana and an Orthodox Jew from New York seemed minuscule.

As they were ready to leave, Lisa and Jim asked us the question we got most often about our Sabbath ritual: "You do this every Friday night?" We had to answer in truth that we did. There was no party, no show, no dance, no assignment, no opening that could stop us. "Why?" No, it was not the biblical mandate to observe the Sabbath or its rabbinic interpretation, although these figured into our observance. Our greatest motivation was also the most inexplicable: it was the magic that happened when Shira lit the candles.

Sleeping through Sunrise

ILANA NAVA KURSHAN

My computer screen stares back at me from across my desk. Stacks of papers spill into my lap. My various textbooks are stashed randomly on the bookshelf to my right. A trail of cornflakes and overdue library books snakes behind the bookshelf to the table and fridge next to the door. From my desk I can just reach my bed, a dangerous temptation when I'm writing a paper late at night. Out of the corner of my eye I see our TV, where my roommate and I watch the eleven o'clock news each evening to break from our studies. At my desk in the dorm, I see my whole life laid out before me, with no walls separating where I work from where I relax and where I eat from where I sleep.

I am not used to containing my whole life in one room. Back home, the computer screen glows in my father's study downstairs and the refrigerator hums in the kitchen. When I want to relax, I do not substitute Colleen McCullough for Harold Bloom; I concede to my younger brother's plea to play basketball with him on the driveway. When I am hungry, I don't pull a granola bar out of my bottom desk drawer; I head down to the kitchen and fix myself a tuna sandwich to eat at the table. And when I need to talk to someone, I don't switch from WordPerfect to Eudora; I climb onto the foot of my parents' warm, cozy bed and find a spot between the lumps of their feet to discuss what is troubling me.

Here in my dorm room, I can reach everything I need from my desk. I had assumed that college would be such a broadening experience, but instead, my whole world is contracted into the 12 x 25 feet of my dorm room. Since coming to college, all the boundaries between places and moments have dissolved. I can no longer locate distinct points on the coordinate axes of space and time; these axes seem to collapse into themselves, becoming a vortex of ambiguity and confusion.

E-mail, the way in which everyone on campus receives information from friends, clubs, and teaching fellows, has also challenged my notions of space and time. Messages no longer travel; they are sent and they arrive at the same instant, so that movement through space does not correspond to any movement through time. While it is convenient to know that my message shows up on someone else's screen the moment it leaves mine, it is also disconcerting. "Technical civilization is man's conquest of space," writes twentieth-century theologian Abraham Joshua Heschel.[1] This is true of cars and televisions and radios, but E-mail is the conquest of time as well. With E-mail, I can reach people and be contacted by them at any hour of the day. E-mail has dissolved boundaries of time, just as sharing a room has dissolved boundaries of space.

I have often wondered whether I could solve one of my problems of space by removing my bed. I spend so little time in it that it hardly merits the room it occupies. But when I don't get sleep, the distinction between one day and the next begins to blur, leaving me confused and disoriented. I go to sleep not to wake up well rested, but simply so that I can wake up. I must sleep, even if for only an hour, to create a boundary between night and day. Otherwise, my life will dissolve into ambiguity, like the black image fading into white in M. C. Escher's "Day and Night" lithograph.

Some nights I get little more than an hour of sleep. I stay up until five o'clock writing a paper and then meet Caroline in the bathroom. Caroline is the cyclist who lives down the hall. She wakes up every morning at five o'clock to pull black spandex over her legs and bury her long red hair in a helmet before biking ten miles along the Charles River. When we finish brushing our teeth together, I wish her good morning and she wishes me good night. Then I rush back to my room, clamber up to the top bunk, and collapse into bed. I want to be asleep before the boundary between night and day begins to dissolve. I need to sleep through sunrise. I would like to forget that there is that moment of both lightness and darkness that isn't day and isn't night, that moment of dawn indistinguishable from dusk.

Without boundaries, places and moments overlap and lose their meaning. I have begun to see time as Escher depicts space. In his lithograph "Mosaic II," Escher divides his canvas into the positive foreground of dark snails and elephants, and the negative background of white animals filling in the space between the dark ones. Both foreground and background bear clearly defined images. My initial response to the absence of designated space and time in my life is to fill my schedule with activities and structure every moment of the day. In my life, positive time is structured, devoted to either classes or activities. Negative time used to be my free time. But, like Escher's background, I divide up all my negative time to write articles or attend play rehearsals. There are no moments when I do not hope to accomplish or achieve. Instead of creating boundaries between the hours of my day, I spend all my time at work. I write my papers with an eye to deadlines and length requirements, stifling the love of learning that once illuminated my words and set my ideas aflame. In regimenting my schedule militaristically, I try to control time; to my consternation, I find that time controls me.

I often find myself defining time in economic terms: time is a resource that is managed, spent, and wasted. But I'm beginning to realize that there is another way of perceiving time, a way that restores the boundaries between places and moments, a way that adds meaning instead of detracting from it. This is the Jewish view of time. For Jews, time is meant not to be consumed but consecrated. We don't simply structure our time; we sanctify it. We distinguish between minutes and hours not to regiment them but to set aside moments of holiness.

Each week, we set aside Shabbat, the Sabbath, to stop working and to reflect upon the world. We remember that God created the world for six days, but on the seventh day He rested. Just as God blessed Shabbat and made it holy, creating a definite distinction between this day and the other six days of the week, we set Shabbat apart through the rituals we perform and the customs we observe. Observant Jews refrain from using electronic devices and from writing or working; as Heschel writes, we turn "from the world of creation to the creation of the world."[2] We contemplate instead of creating; Shabbat is a time for prayer and reflection.

In college, I anticipate Shabbat all week. Each night, I peer over the Escher drawings that decorate the walls of my dorm to read the poster that hangs above the door: "Hang in there, baby, Shabbat is coming." I look forward to Friday afternoons because I can take off the heavy bookbag which has weighed down my shoulders all week. In its place, as is customary on Shabbat, I carry a *neshamah yetairah*, an extra soul. After my last class on Friday, I come back to the room, shower, and slip my loose white dress over my head, so that the hemline dances along my ankles. As I walk over to Hillel, the wind blows through my hair, carrying away all the burdens of the week. The sun sets behind me and the leaves crunch beneath my feet, and I realize that the most beautiful moments of the day are moments of transition, moments when the sun sets and leaves change color, marking boundaries between the days and seasons. In the Friday-evening service, the prayers we recite welcome the Sabbath queen whose spirit descends upon us. We are surrounded by the peacefulness of spiritual life instead of the frenzy of daily life. Heschel notes this distinction: "It is one thing to race or be driven by the vicissitudes that menace life, and another thing to stand still and to embrace the presence of an eternal moment."[3]

Jewish practice is steeped in other demarcations that sanctify our lives. *Kashrut*, the dietary laws, requires that we separate milk from meat and distinguish between permitted and proscribed foods. Although no one knows exactly why the Torah requires that we observe these particular dietary restrictions, many theologians believe that it is not the rules themselves that are important, but rather the fact that they create boundaries. Since we cannot eat meat and milk simultaneously, we check that we have not eaten meat in the last three hours before sitting down to a dairy meal. By stopping to think before we eat, we are distinguishing ourselves from animals: for us, even the satisfaction of the basic need for sustenance has a spiritual dimension. Thus, the distinction between kosher and *treif* (nonkosher) is in service of the much more elevated distinction between humans and animals. Unlike all other creatures, we have a spark of the divine within us, so we can infuse even the natural, instinctive act of eating with spiritual meaning.

Though all the boundaries in my life at college seem to be dissolving, by living as an observant Jew I ensure that there are some boundaries that will always remain intact. Judaism forces us to note the passing of time because we mark time with prayer, setting aside a few moments each day for reflection. Heschel speaks of the importance of consecrating these moments: "Judaism teaches us to be attached to holiness in time. . . . It is, for example, the evening, morning, or afternoon that brings with it the call to prayer."[4] I worry that two hours of sleep will feel like no sleep at all, but because of the prayers I recite when I go to sleep and when I awaken, I set aside night as a distinct entity from day. As I fall into bed each evening, I recite Kriat Shma Al Hamita, a prayer in which we entrust our spirits to God while we sleep. Then, when my alarm goes off in the morning, instead of groaning that I just fell asleep, I thank God for returning my soul when I pray Modeh Ani. Night is distinctly defined from day, not as time that is not day, not as the absence of light, but as something inherently positive, as sacred time in which our souls are in God's care.

Judaism, I now realize, provides me with some of the boundaries and distinctions that are vital if my life is to have any meaning. Although I cannot look to Judaism to find a way of knowing when I am at school and when I am at home or to regain a sense of privacy and personal space, I can nevertheless look to Jewish practice for a model of how to restore these boundaries in my daily life as a college student. Heschel writes, "When a day like Wednesday arrives, the hours are blank, and unless we lend significance to them, they remain without character."[5] I must make the conscious decision to infuse my life with purpose. Just as God set aside the seventh day for rest, I must set aside moments each day for relaxation and reflection.

One of the Hebrew names for God is *Makom*, place; indeed, we can feel God's presence not just by consecrating time but by setting aside places as well. I have found a home for myself in the stacks of Widener Library, where the ceilings are low and the aisles dark. I climb up to the sixth floor, where the Judaica volumes cause the shelves to sag slightly, as if unable to bear the weight of history. Hebrew words are exchanged between rabbis with white beards and dark suits, and carrels are overflowing with leatherbound volumes of Talmud and Midrash. I sit in a stall in the back corner of the library. It belongs to a professor who never studies here, so I run my fingers along his bookshelf and brush the dust off the tomes. I lean back in the stiff wooden chair to write or to think, surrounded by thousands of years of Jewish history and rabbinic lore. This is the space I have made my own here at Harvard.

In setting aside places and moments, I am distinguishing them from the other buildings on campus and the other hours in the day. When I decide where and when I will work and where and when I will have fun, I create my own boundaries that restore the sense of meaning in my life. Heschel beautifully articulates our responsibility as God's partners in creation: "Creation, we are taught, is not an act that happened once upon a time, once and for ever. The act of bringing the world into existence is a continuous process."[6] Every instant and every moment can be set aside and sanctified; college is not the dissolution of boundaries, but the opportunity to create my own.

I create a boundary every Saturday evening when I perform the service to end Shabbat. I join with a group of friends on the patio in front of our dorm. As soon as there are three stars in the sky, we light the long braided candle and hold it high as the wax drips down on our fingers, each drop a lingering memory of Shabbat. We pass around a container of ground cinnamon from the dining hall which serves as the besamim, the spices we traditionally smell so that the sweetness of Shabbat will remain with us throughout the week. But the rest of the week will not be as sweet because it is distinct; it is separated by this service, Havdalah, the Hebrew word for separation. Before we blow out the candle, we recite one final prayer: "Blessed are You, O Lord our God, who distinguishes between the sacred and the secular." Blessed is God who distinguishes between moments and places. Blessed is God whose presence sanctifies space and time set aside, and the boundaries I create to consecrate my life.

NOTES

1. Abraham Joshua Heschel, *The Sabbath,* from *The Earth Is the Lord's and The Sabbath* (New York: Harper & Row, 1966), 3.
  2. Ibid., 10.
  3. Ibid., 29.
  4. Ibid., 8.
  5. Ibid., 20.
  6. Ibid., 100.

Erev Shabbas

DANNY SIEGEL

I t's so stupid,
Wednesday afternoon,
soaked in the idiotica of errands
and all those "things to do"
that steal a man's minutes, his years—
I forgot the Queen.
Her Majesty was due at four-eighteen
on Friday, not a minute later,
and I was wasting hands, words, steps,
racing to a rushing finish-line
of roaring insignificance
I just as well could fill
with preparations for the royal entourage:
cleaning and cleansing each act's doing,
each word's saying,
in anticipation of the Great Event of Shabbas.

Who am I that she should wish
to spend the day with me?
I dry out my strengths, cook, move dust,
casually insensitive to all the songs
reminding me that she, the Queen,
in diamond-ruby-emerald-glow tiara,
would come to grace my table.

She comes,
no matter how the week was spent,
in joy or in silliness,
yet she comes.
And I am her host,
laying a linen flower tablecloth
that is white,
that is all the colors of the rainbow.

This is the Jews' sense of royalty:
she never does not spend one day a week
with me, and every Jew,
in the open air of freedom,
or lightening the misery of prisoners
in stinking Russian prisons
or the ghettoes of Damascus.

Come, my Shabbas Queen,
embodiment of Worlds-to-Be:
Your gracious kindness is our breath of life,
and though we once, twice, all-too-often
fail to say, "How beautiful your cape!
How lovely your hair, your *Shechina*-eyes!"
we will not always be so lax,
apathetic to your grace, your presence.
Touch us again this week
with your most unique love's tenderness,
and we shall sing to you our songs,
dance our dances in your honor,
and sigh for you our sighs
of longing, peace, and hope.

First a Spark

SANDY EISENBERG SASSO

First a spark
    then candle glow.

I watched you at sunset time
    eyes sparkling in Shabbat light.

Circling above the flames,
    my hands pulled
    the warmth of Shabbat peace inside.

Praying for a good week and for blessing.

Take time—the lights beckon
    for dreams and wonder,
    for the candles grow smaller,
    the children taller,
    even as we pray.

Hold this sunset moment and let it go
    into morning light.

Another generation's candlesticks
    receive the next generation's lights.

And somewhere in the middle
    we stand, holding hands
    with yesterday and tomorrow,
    linking echoes of ancient melodies
    with the breath of our children.

Finding God and hope in their embrace,
    renewing days of creation.

In ordinary time—remember—
First a spark
    and then candle glow.

A Letter to Our Niece
and Nephew

ALBERT AND JEANNETTE KALL

D ear Children,

"Remember the Sabbath day, to keep it holy!" These are God's words, expressed to the Jewish people, urging us to work six days but to keep the seventh day hallowed as a day of rest. One of the ways we manifest this is in the lighting of the Sabbath candles.

As your marriage goes on and you are blessed with children, religion will play an increasingly important part in your family's existence and growth, and in the fulfillment of your roles on this earth. It is not too much to say that this candle holder, which we are giving you as an engagement present from us and which was patterned closely after the one that your late Grandmom Bessie used for all the years that her children can remember, will form a central core of spiritual feeling and goodness that can come from no other source.

Mackie and Steve—we don't want to try to impose anything on you that you may not at first be able to follow in the face of all the pressures of the early years of your marriage. In our own case, we did not have a regular religious Sabbath night until a few years after we were married. But now we are happy that we started to keep Friday night as a special night at home and that our children were born and raised in that atmosphere and have become closely attached to it. Our children realize that Friday-night dinner—with the blessing over the challah and wine and the brightly lit candles, with Mother's prayer over them and a silently mumbled blessing for all of us, our family, for Israel, and our entire people—is indeed something special, and we have every reason to want to continue it.

Our religion is sorely in need of whatever help it can get, to sustain and nurture it in the face of its detractors and those who would forsake it. By lighting the Sabbath candles you will be keeping a covenant with God and carrying on a tradition that has survived for over three housand years and constituted one of the powerful forces that have kept our religion alive in a hostile world. This simple act is one of the vital links that bind our people together and which we pass on from one generation to the other.

The glow of the candles radiates a warmth and a spirit that cannot be compared with any other light. The significance of the burning candles adds meaning to the household and the Friday-night dinner. The very act represents the fulfillment of a God-given commandment, or mitzvah, which is little enough to pay for the privilege of being a Jew and the very miracle of being alive.

We can only say, in conclusion, that *"benching licht"* on Friday night is one of the most beautiful and moving experiences in our own lives, and we hope it will be in yours. May God bless you both with a long and happy married life together.

With love, from your Aunt Jeannette and Uncle Albert

To Kindle the Sabbath Lights

NAHUM M. WALDMAN

A single ritual does not make a Sabbath. This holy day is a sanctification of time, which embraces the Jew from candlelighting to Havdalah. In the view of the poet-philosopher Judah Halevi, it is an acknowledgment of God's omnipotence and an affirmation of creation. It is also the "fruit" of the week, establishing man's connection with the divine power so that he may serve God with joy. Sabbath, by its very nature, cannot be abbreviated or condensed.

One observance, however, is charged with extra religious and sentimental power. *Hadlakat ha-nerot*—the kindling of the Sabbath lights—draws upon the full range of the Sabbath's richness, concentrating it into one point. The practical benefit of light is elevated into an encounter with holiness.

When did this rite begin? Our Rabbis never questioned its binding quality or antiquity. Our matriarch Sarah, they believed, lit the Sabbath lamps. The holiness which dwelt in her household was symbolized by the cloud, representing the Divine Presence, which hovered over the door of her tent. All the doors were open to wayfarers. When she died, candlelighting ceased, the doors were shut, and the Divine Presence vanished, to return when Isaac took Rebecca as his wife.

Our Rabbis devoted much discussion and commentary to the subject of the Sabbath lights, although they were concerned not with the root of the commandment but with its branches: what oils and wicks are permitted? Yet, when we reach the end of the technical discussion, a warm, human note crosses the pages and years. We hear the father's voice checking with the family at twilight to see that all the Sabbath preparations have been made. When he is satisfied that they have been, he gently urges them, "Kindle the Sabbath lights." Let us note that father, mother, and the members of the family are all involved in the preparation for the Sabbath. This is an important point.

Light is not only useful and practical; it has many meanings. "Light is Torah," says the Talmud. The presence of God may be expressed by light, as it was when Moses saw the burning bush. The soul of man is compared to a lamp (Prov. 20:27). Light symbolizes wisdom. We pray, "Illumine our eyes through Thy Torah." The light of God's countenance, in the priestly benediction, connotes His favor.

A house which is lit up on the Sabbath is one in which peace and harmony are likely to dwell. A familiar legend tells of two angels, one good and one bad, who accompany a man home from the synagogue. When they enter a house where the lamp is lit, the table set, and the bed prepared, the good angel happily says, "May it be thus the following Sabbath." The bad angel, even though reluctantly, must answer, "Amen."

This legend has suggested various thoughts to commentators. One is that the kindled lamp is a symbol of the proper fulfillment of all the commandments of the Sabbath. The good angel is man's good inclination (*yetzer ha-tov*) which controls his base impulses, represented by the bad angel (*yetzer ha-ra*), the evil inclination.

Another commentator relates the legend to a statement in the *Zohar*, the great document of medieval mystical teaching, to the effect that, when the table is set, the lamp lit, and a man's wife happy, the *Shekhinah*, the Divine Presence, dwells in that home and takes delight in Israel.

The related themes of light and peace are forcibly brought out by Moses Maimonides in his discussion of Hanukkah. If a man is so poor that he cannot afford both wine for Kiddush and Hanukkah lights (on Shabbat Hanukkah), he must buy Hanukkah lights. It is important to recall and celebrate the miracle. However, if he must choose between Hanukkah and Sabbath lamps, the Sabbath lights are more important. The reason is "peace in the household." Then the great legislator becomes lyrical and concludes, "Great is peace, for the entire Torah was given in order to create peace in the world, as it is written [Prov. 3:17], 'Its ways are ways of pleasantness and all its paths are peace.' "

We may consult the talmudic commentators for some very practical views of the relationship between light and peace. Sitting in the dark occasions gloom, and stumbling in a dark room engenders the very opposite of a peaceful mood. The Sabbath meal must be eaten in a brightly lit place, because thus we fulfill the commandment of *oneg*, pleasure on the Sabbath.

One legal note is that all the rooms that are used should be illuminated. The Karaites, who rejected Rabbinic Judaism, interpreted the biblical prohibition of kindling fire on the Sabbath so literally that they sat in dark, cold rooms. Rabbinic Judaism, on the other hand, realizing that light leads to Sabbath joy, ordained that fire and lamps be kindled in advance and enjoyed during the Sabbath.

The concepts of peace and harmony are connected with the Sabbath in still another way. A man, states the Torah, must provide his wife with food, clothing, and marital relations (Exod. 21:11). The Talmud elaborates upon this, setting up definite times and limits, depending on the husband's work and the amount of time he is at home or away from it.

Scholars of Torah were generally away all week at their studies, and on Friday evening they attended to conjugal relations. Rabbi David Feldman's outstanding work, *Birth Control in Jewish Law*, points out that the association of conjugal relations and Friday evening appears in the Talmud, in the mystical *Zohar*, and in the moralistic literature. It is carried to its highest level in the Siddur of Rabbi Jacob Emden (1679–1776). There the laws of marital relations are uniquely arranged so that they appear with the Friday-evening prayers. We witness a triumph of life-affirmation when we read his description of the ideal sexual relationship between husband and wife as embodying love, modesty, holiness, and benefit to body and mind (Feldman, *Birth Control*, 100–103).

Family harmony, expressed through the Sabbath lamps and the beautiful intimacy of husband and wife, are associated together on the Sabbath. They are two aspects of *shalom*, "peace." The Talmud offers a number of interpretations of the verse "My soul is bereft of peace. I have forgotten what happiness is" (Lam. 3:17). Rabbi Abbahu relates "peace" to the Sabbath lamps, while Rabbi Abba sees "happiness" in connection with the scholar whose bed is prepared and whose wife is adorned on Friday evening.

Both men and women have the obligation of kindling the Sabbath lights. A man who is unmarried or whose wife is unable to perform this duty must himself light the candles and recite the blessing. The primary responsibility rests upon the woman, because she is generally at home and concerned with the affairs of the household. The legal authorities Moses Maimonides and Joseph Caro exclude the further reason that is given in the Midrash, that the woman must kindle the Sabbath lights because woman—Eve—extinguished the soul of Adam, that is, brought about mortality by giving him to eat of the forbidden fruit. (This seems to overlook the fact that Adam could and should have said no. Does this shifting of responsibility represent a midrashic male chauvinism?)

In reality, the role of the woman was elevated to prime importance through the influence of the Kabbalists on the Sabbath ritual. Gershom Scholem, one of the outstanding contemporary authorities on Jewish mysticism, informs us that the mystics interpreted the Sabbath as a sacred marriage festival. The union of earthly husband and wife was seen to be symbolic of the union of God and the Divine Presence, the *Shekhinah*. The human union was an act that would initiate the heavenly event. "Bride" and *Shekhinah* were identified.

It was highly commendable and rich in mystical significance, taught Isaac Luria, the renowned medieval mystic, to kiss the hands of one's mother upon entering the house on Sabbath eve. Following the singing of "Shalom Alaykhem," greeting the visiting angels, the family would sing Ayshet Ha'yil, "A Woman of Valor" (Prov. 31), praising the Jewish housewife and the Divine Presence she represents. In this context, too, we must interpret the great value placed upon marital relations on Sabbath (G. Scholem, *On the Kabbalah and Its Symbolism,* 139–45).

Preparing for the Sabbath involved the entire family. The great Rabbis of the Talmud performed menial tasks in order to share in this preparation. Rav Pappa would twist the wicks, and Rab Hunah would light them in preparation for their later kindling.

Our sources have many views on how many lights should be lit and what these represent. While the Talmud speaks only of *ner*, "lamp," at least two lights are required by law, one for *shamor*, "observe," and the other for *zakhor*, "remember" (the Sabbath day, to keep it holy). These occur in the two versions of the Ten Commandments (Exod. 20; Deut. 5), one stressing practical observance and the other the mental attitude of inner peace. Both the inner and the outer aspects of Sabbath rest must be realized.

Another authority cites the custom of lighting three or four lamps, while yet another recommends seven lights, symbolizing the days of the week. The custom of lighting a candle for each member of the family is well known, and there is even recorded the exceptional lighting of thirty-six lamps. This symbolizes the original light of the beginning of creation, which was hidden after thirty-six hours. It is also recorded that brides lit candles on a weekday, the day of their wedding. This, it is explained, was to teach them their responsibilities as Jewish women.

Candlelighting time is an occasion for personal prayer and meditation on the part of the woman. The Talmud states, "Whoever is faithful about kindling Sabbath lights will have sons who are scholars of Torah." Thus women would pray at candlelighting for sons "whose eyes shine with the light of Torah." Here, of course, a wonderful opportunity for unprescribed, heartfelt personal prayer is afforded.

One example is found in the *Tekhina*, the Yiddish prayer book used by our mothers and grandmothers in Eastern Europe. It reads, in part, "'Your word is a light to my feet' (Ps. 119:105). May my children walk in God's way. May my performance of the commandment of candlelighting be accepted so that my children's eyes will shine with our beloved holy Torah. I beseech You, dear, blessed God, that my lighting of the candles be accepted like the lamp which burned eternally in the menorah in our holy Temple. . . . May the constellations of my children shine brightly in heaven so that they can support their wives and children in a generous manner."

The woman covers her face when she recites the benediction: *Barukh Atah Adonai, Elohaynu Melekh ha-olam, asher kideshanu bemitzvotav, ve-tzivanu lehadlik ner shel Shabbat,* "Blessed art Thou, O Lord our God, who has sanctified us by Thy commandments and has commanded us to kindle the Sabbath lamp." This is a beautiful moment of meditation, peace, and spiritual elevation for the woman and her family. Poets and storytellers have described the impact of this moment upon them. Bella Chagall, the first wife of the artist Marc Chagall, has left us an imaginative and touching description. In her reminiscences, *Burning Lights,* she writes:

> With a match in her hands she lights one candle after another. All the seven candles begin to quiver. The flames blaze into Mother's face. As though an enchantment were falling upon her, she lowers her eyes. Slowly, three times in succession, she encircles the candles with both her arms: she seems to be taking them into her heart. And with the candles her weekday worries melt away.
>
> She blesses the candles. She whispers quiet benedictions through her fingers and they add heat to the flames. Mother's hands over the candles shine like the tablets of the Decalogue over the holy ark. . . .

I hear Mother in her benediction mention now one name, now another. She names Father, the children, her own father and mother. Now my name has fallen into the flame of the candles. My throat becomes hot.

"May the Highest One give them His blessings," concludes Mother, dropping her hands at last.

"Amen," I say in a choking voice, behind my fingers.

"Good shabbes," Mother calls out loudly. Her face, all opened, looks purified. I think it has absorbed the illumination of the Sabbath candles (*Burning Lights*, 48–49).

The covering of the face, which has such emotional associations, seems to have originated in a technical legal dispute. The question was, When, exactly, did the Sabbath begin? Originally, it was not thought to begin with candlelighting. In ancient times a *shofar* was sounded to announce its coming. At the third *shofar* blast, the lamps were lit. A certain amount of time was allowed for small preparations, and the Sabbath began with another blast of *tekiah, teruah*, and *tekiah*. Later scholars maintained that Sabbath began when Ma'ariv, the evening prayer, was recited.

There was another view, however, which claimed that the Sabbath began when the blessing over the candles was recited. But here came a problem. A blessing had to come before the act. If the woman first recited the blessing, it would be Sabbath, and she would not be allowed to kindle the lights. A compromise was reached. She would light the candles and cover her face, as if she did not see them. She would recite the blessing and then uncover her face. This legal fiction insured that the blessing would come before the seeing of the lights.

There were other solutions, and serious objections by scholars who held to the first view, that the blessing does *not* mark the beginning of the Sabbath. Yet the second view prevailed and became the basis of current practice. Sabbath begins with candlelighting for the woman only. For the rest of the family, it begins with Ma'ariv. The outcome of this technical dispute has been to give added significance to candlelighting. For the woman, at least, it marks the boundary between the profane and the holy. The holy day does not merely come in upon her, but she actively brings it. Her act defines the sphere of holiness and makes possible for her a deeply religious experience.

Jewish artists and craftsmen have attempted to live up to the injunction of Jewish law that we must have "a beautiful lamp." There are seven-pointed star-shaped lamps, filled with oil and hung from chains in the ceiling, which were common in German Jewish homes. There are various types of candle holders created in days past, and now in the modern idiom. The real beauty of the rite, however, is drawn from the spirit of Sabbath peace and family harmony in which it is performed.

For some, candlelighting inaugurates a full day of Sabbath observance. For others, it is a fragment of holiness, the remnant, after secularism has all but destroyed the Sabbath. For yet others, candlelighting may be the mitzvah of inauguration not only of the Sabbath but of a personal pattern of Jewish living. A hasidic group is currently conducting a campaign urging men to put on *tefillin*, phylacteries, in the hope that this mitzvah will lead to a life of mitzvot. Perhaps candlelighting can serve the same function for Jewish women.

Young girls should be encouraged to emulate their mothers. Just as Jewish law requires men away from home, studying at school, to light Sabbath candles, so should Jewish college girls do the same. There is no justification for the "when-the-children-are-old-enough-for-Jewish-education" syndrome. Religion is a personal commitment, not a "put on" for our children. Indeed, who perceives pretense better than children?

We cannot present Judaism as a series of rituals unconnected to each other or unrelated to a religious commitment and a human-oriented value system. *Hadlakat ha-nerot*, candlelighting, offers an opportunity for rich and meaningful fulfillment, leading, for those who take it, to the rewarding temple of Jewish thought, feelings, and action.

Candlelighting Prayers
for Erev Shabbat

Before reciting the blessing on lighting the Shabbat candles, women often make personal prayers to God. These prayers, or supplications, are called *tehinot (tkhines* in Yiddish). Throughout the Middle Ages, *tehinot*, prayers for women, were collected and circulated.

The following selection of *tehinot* appeared in a manual on Jewish practices for married women, a book privately commissioned by an Italian gentleman, Giuseppi Coen, as a gift for his wife, Yehudit Kutscher Coen, in 1786. The excerpts below are from Nina Beth Cardin's translation of this book, *Out of the Depths I Call to You: A Book of Prayers for the Married Jewish Woman*, interspersed with her own modern commentary.

Tehinot

NINA BETH CARDIN

Master of the Universe, even from Your exalted throne You can see that I attend to the task of lighting the candles of the holy Shabbat in order to fulfill and preserve the commandments of my Creator, in love and gladness of heart just as You have commanded me.

Commentary: God does not want dutiful but vacuous, precise but cold, performance of rituals. Warmth and love, joy and gladness are as essential to the proper performance of the ritual as is calculated attendance to the detail.

Abiding by God's commandments, by definition, appears to be an act of obedience and not an act of volition. Yet in the twentieth century, to be willing to accept upon ourselves the mitzvot as binding commandments of God is to submit ourselves voluntarily to the commanding nature of God's law. Such is the paradox of faith entwined with modernity, freedom, and divine law.

The [above] prayer in the original offers, parenthetically, all the permutations for how it should be said, depending upon whether the day is Shabbat, a holiday, or both.

Therefore, Almighty, God of Israel, may it be Your desire to radiate light, joy, happiness, honor, goodness, mercy, prosperity, blessing, and peace upon those in the heavens and those here below; and bathe us, our souls, and our spirit in the light of Your luminous countenance. "For the radiance of a king's face grants life" (Prov. 16:15). "For in You is the source of all life; by Your light do we see light" (Ps. 36:10). "Light is sown for the righteous" (Ps. 97:11). "The Lord is my light and my help" (Ps. 27:1). "The Lord is God, who sheds light upon us" (Ps. 118:27). "May the Lord be gracious to us and bless us. May He shine His countenance upon us. Selah" (Ps. 67:2). "May He shine His countenance upon us and be gracious to us" (adapted from Num. 6:25), extending graciousness through the concealed light, the light of all life, about which it is written, "And the Lord said, 'Let there be light. And there was light' " (Gen. 1:3). Amen, Selah.

As she lights the candles for Shabbat or the holidays, she says:
Blessed are You, Lord our God, King of the Universe, who sanctified us through His commandments and commanded us to kindle the light of [on Shabbat] the holy Sabbath; [on a holiday] this holiday, a day of sacred assembly; [when Shabbat and a holiday coincide] the holy Sabbath and this holiday, a day of sacred assembly.

Disparate images of light tumble forward in a heap of verses reminding the petitioner of all the good we see in light. Light is blessing and guidance, security and life. Reference to the concealed light recalls the popular rabbinic explanation of the enigma of the creation of light: if the sun and the moon and the stars were created on the fourth day (Gen. 1:14–19), how could light be created on the first day (Gen. 1:3–5)? The primordial light, not bound by an orb, lit up the entire universe and enabled vision beyond the now-natural limits of sight. However, anticipating humanity's factious and arrogant behavior, God withdrew the fullness of the light, and hence the full power of sight, and created the limiting orbs in the sky. But the primordial light was not destroyed. It is being stored in God's special place of treasures, waiting for the end of time when it will once again illumine the world for the righteous (Hagigah 12a).

And then she says:
God of Israel, may it be Your will to be gracious to me and to my husband [and if she has children, add: and to my children] and to all my family and the people of Israel. Grant us long life and full health, security from all evil, prosperity in all good. Think well of us; bless us. Be mindful of our needs for care and mercy. Bless us with many blessings. Fill our household with everything that is good. Let Your holy presence dwell among us. May there not be counted among us a childless man or a barren woman, a widow or widower. May our children not die in our lifetime. May we be spared all suffering. Grant that I be worthy of giving life to knowing, wise, and distinguished children and grandchildren who love the Lord and who are God-fearing and God-struck. May they light up the world through their learning and kindness, doing the work of their Creator. Please, now hear my plea; for the sake of Sarah, Rebecca, Rachel, and Leah, our mothers. Let our candle shine forth. May it neither flicker nor ever be extinguished. Shine Your face upon us, so we will be saved, we and all Israel, speedily and in our day. Amen. Selah.

The prayers in the traditional Siddur are mostly communal. The prayers in this Siddur are mostly personal. The woman here petitions on her own behalf, and on behalf of her loved ones. But, since no Jew approaches God alone, the woman's personal prayer quickly enlarges to encompass requests for the well-being of all Israel. Personal good is embedded in the communal good. And the apparent humility of the petitioner (apparent because any noncommanded approach to God assumes a dash of bravado) is bolstered by the righteous worthiness of the matriarchs.

The theme of conceiving and bearing children, only touched upon here, is paramount throughout the rest of this Siddur.

Contemporary Prayers

WOMAN'S INSTITUTE FOR
CONTINUING JEWISH EDUCATION

The following collection of contemporary prayers for candlelighting is
part of a creative Shabbat service written in 1984.

I

God, You are within my candle
You are the flame
That draws us together.
At first, unignited, silent, waiting. . .
I must strike the match
And light the wick.
Then out You dance;
Sputtering, joyful, and beckoning
Then calm and calming.
You who waited within
Come to fuse us together.

II

Candle of my people,
In this dim and quiet light,
Telling tales of history
As you burn in the night.

My mother and my mother's mothers
Lit you in the past.
And the energy of your flame
Has made tradition last.

Our daughters and our daughters' daughters
Will light you everywhere.
And the future and the past are linked
In our first Shabbat prayer.

III

Your center glows
A single flame appears
    light and warmth from your heart.
Reaching out to me
Signaling that time of peace.

Five Poems by Jewish Women

T his sampling of poems written by women over the last two centuries
in celebration of Shabbat is drawn from the collection *Women
Speak to God: The Prayers and Poems of Jewish Women*, edited by Marcia
Cohn Spiegel and Deborah Lipton Kremsdorf.

Prayer for Sabbath

CHANA KATZ

1817, Holland

Translated from the Yiddish by Bertha Held

and Mahlia Lynn Schubert

In the early nineteenth century Chana Katz described, in simply rhymed
couplets, the joys of the Sabbath and her faith that Sabbath observance
would lead to the coming of the Messiah.

> Dear God I sing my praise to You,
> Creator of all things, old and new.
>
> And gratefully we all give thanks
> That You made us Your chosen people.

How proud we are, our God is You.
Creator of heaven, the earth we view.

Good food, sweet drink from which we live
With all the pleasures and joys You give.

And whoever the beloved Sabbath keeps pure,
Will be deserving of husband and children,
Respect and riches will come to her.

So I keep holy Sabbath with its obligations,
With all the good food, the sweets and the spices,
And what is prepared, let it be what entices.

This dear holy Sabbath, like a Garden of Eden,
Let us please deserve it also in heaven.

And beloved Messiah shall lead us by the right hand,
And bring us into that holy land.

Daughters of Israel

PENINA MOÏSE

1841, United States

Charleston, South Carolina, is justly proud of Penina Moïse, who composed the first American hymnal. Some of the poems in it can still be found in Reform Jewish prayer books.

Daughters of Israel, arise!
   The Sabbath-morn to greet,
Send songs and praises to the skies
   Then frankincense more sweet.

Take heed, lest ye the drift mistake
　　Of heaven's hallowed hours,
And from those dreams too late awake,
　　That show you but life's flowers.

Leave not the spirit unarrayed,
　　To deck the mortal frame;
With gems of grace let woman aid
　　Charms that from nature came.

With jewels of a gentle mind,
　　More precious far than gold,
Brightened by love, by faith refined,
　　And set in chastest mould.

Wife! mother! sister! on ye all
　　A tender task devolves;
Child, husband, brother, on ye call
　　To nerve the best resolves.

Your hands must gird the buckler on,
　　The moral weapons cleanse,
By which that battle may be won,
　　That in self-conquest ends.

Sabbath Eve

JESSIE SAMPTER

1937, United States and Israel

Influenced by Henrietta Szold, Jessie Sampter left the comforts of the United States to pioneer in Palestine, where she taught Yemenite Jews and published two fine books of verse.

Sarah, the Princess, in her door
Stands basking in the lowered sun;
The Sabbath light is on her face
Of many labors done.

Her brow is lined with graven lines,
A kerchief whitely round it tied;
Mother of mothers, tall and strong,
Broad-hipped and tender-eyed!

The tenements that teem with youth
Resound with children of her kin;
But she stands silent, Sabbath-eyed,
Her quiet soul within.

Her sons are like the rocks of earth,
So strong and terrible and mild,
Because she taught them ancient prayers
Too fearful for a child.

Light a Candle

ZELDA

1967, Israel

Translated from the Hebrew by Marcia Falk

Although she is a traditionally observant Jewish woman, Zelda's poetry has wide popularity in Israel among both secular and religious Jews.

Light a candle.
Drink wine.
Softly the Sabbath has plucked
the sinking sun.
Slowly the Sabbath descends,
the rose of heaven in her hand.

How can the Sabbath
plant a huge and shining flower
in a blind and narrow heart?
How can the Sabbath
plant the bud of angels
in a heart of raving flesh?

Can the rose of eternity grow
in an age enslaved
to destruction,
an age enslaved
to death?

Light a candle!
Drink wine!
Slowly the Sabbath descends
and in her hand
the flower,
and in her hand
the sinking sun.

Shechinah

CHANA BELL

1977, Los Angeles

Chana Bell introduces the image of the *Shechinah*, the feminine aspect of
God, in her poem of welcome to the Sabbath.

Perched on our shoulders
a colorful butterfly
you whisper
into pores
shabbat's sweetness

we breathe you in
breathe the week out
take in roundness
letting go of sharp angles

we breathe in the *neshama yiteira*
the soul of the world to come
in awe
we sway   not march

As we kindle shabbat candles
you glide into our dark corners
warming us
dissolving our dense bodies
into light

Challah

RON WOLFSON

C hallah is the most tangible part of Shabbat. It is real. It is not a symbolic expression or a transformation of time and cognition. It is bread, basic. You can even bake it yourself. Of all the parts of the Shabbat Seder, challah is the most real. It is the one Shabbat symbol you get by taking a ticket at the bakery; the one that comes out of the oven, the freezer, or the microwave.

The Judaism we know emerged from the farm. The most basic rhythms and insights of Jewish celebrations weren't intellectual: they came from people who worked the soil. They were profoundly simple. When each harvest was ready, the people came together. Success was celebrated, food was shared with those in need, and a unity of purpose was solidified. This was the practice of the three pilgrimage festivals: Sukkot, Pesach, and Shavuot. Farmers worked from just after dawn till just before dusk. A brief, simple meal was eaten, and darkness brought sleep. Once a week, dusk brought the time to kindle lights and to celebrate a day of rest—this was Shabbat. Then, the warm loaf of bread freshly baked from the oven was the direct result of a week's worth of work in the field. It brought a very specific lesson.

The Torah carefully regulated the farm. As farmers, Jews were never allowed to imagine that they fully owned their land or anything it produced. Always, there were the tithes. Portions of everything raised and everything grown had to be shared. Part went as an offering to God—an acknowledgment that without divine help, nothing would grow or mature. Part went to the Temple, manifesting in every individual act of work a common connection to the national vision of the future and the communal relationship with God. And part was left for the widow, the poor, the orphan, and the stranger. Ownership (even ownership of only a little) brought the responsibility to share with those in need that which God allowed us to produce.

For the biblical farmer, the warm loaf of bread on Shabbat eve wasn't challah. For that farmer, the challah had already been taken. Like every other step in the cultivation of food, a tithe had to be taken when dough was made. In baking the bread from grain raised in their own field, the biblical family took a portion of the dough as a "gift to the Lord" (Num. 15:19–20). This dough was given to the priests who worked in the Temple and was called the "challah portion." Later on, the loaves themselves were called challot. In the dim light of a Shabbat lamp, the taste of warm new bread brought the satisfaction of accomplishment and a practical reminder of a covenantal partnership.

If it is possible to talk about a best-loved Shabbat symbol, it would have to be challah. People rip into it with joy. They excavate caves in it, removing the soft center and leaving the crust. Others take great delight in slicing it into neat, even slices. Challah is a hands-on experience. This simple egg bread—braided, round or square, homemade or on standing bakery order, with its raisins or sesame seeds—is the catalyst that breaks the formality of the Shabbat Seder service and lets the meal begin.

A Family Sabbath:
Dreams and Reality

SUE LEVI ELWELL

Come in peace, angelic messengers of peace.
("Shalom Aleikhem," Sabbath song based on BT *Shabbat* 119b)

I long for a Friday when I rise, help my children off to school, shop, cook, and ready myself and my house for Shabbat (Sabbath). In my dreams, I pick up one daughter from school and welcome her home to a house filled with the smells of carrots, onions, and fresh noodle pudding. She sets the table, running her hand lovingly over my grandmother's embroidered cloth, humming to herself as she sets out the Kiddush cup (special cup or goblet used when reciting the blessing over wine on sacred occasions), the challah (braided egg bread), the candlesticks. She remembers that once as a small child she chided me for setting the Shabbat table in the kitchen instead of the dining room. "The angels need to see the white tablecloth and the candles burning," she warned. "They won't come if we sit in the kitchen." She laughs, the twelve-year-old delighting in her five-year-old self.

As the day wanes, my older daughter comes home from the bakery where she works after school, carrying challot under her arm. The girls tease one another, arguing about who will take the first shower. One lingers in the kitchen while I stir the soup, and we talk about the friends who are about to arrive, as the matzah balls nod to one another in the steaming broth. In my dreams, this happens every week.

In real life, Shabbat with my daughters is a rare pleasure. When we are together, our dance is one of approach and retreat. My Shabbat is not theirs. We do not agree on who should share our table, on what to eat, on which tunes to sing or prayers to say. Each daughter has her own complaints: "I already made Shabbat in school today," or "If you think that this is going to insure that I'll be Jewish when I can choose for myself, you're wrong." I try to remember: How was this different before I became a rabbi and had to work on too many Shabbatot? I am now absent on many Friday nights, making Shabbat for other families while longing for my own home, my own table, my own children at my side. How was this different before the divorce? We were more careful then, more afraid of loud voices and disagreements, always aware of the delicate balance we maintained. They were smaller then, more compliant, less opinionated, and less bruised by the world.

Our lives, our Shabbatot have changed. And as I sit at the head of our table, I think of the women throughout Jewish history who have presided at Shabbat tables by default or by design, women who have guided children as contentious as mine into a Shabbat of nourishing food and healing song. I think of the many women who juggle their passion for teaching Judaism with their love for their families. I think of women like me who have realized our dreams in Shabbatot that exist in real time, with real families.

Even without freshly baked kugel (noodle pudding) or guests we all agree upon, Shabbat arrives. The table is set with a white cloth, and the candles are placed in their holders. She *does* remember the challah, and we begin to sing. And then, between the Kiddush and Motzi (blessings recited over wine and bread, respectively), each of my daughters grudgingly grants me a moment, and I whisper my blessing into their ears. Then, the angels once again surround our table.

Shabbat as Fantasy

DOV PERETZ ELKINS

When someone keeps Shabbat, it is as though that
person has fulfilled the entire Torah. (Midrash, *Pesikta*)

I n Judaism holiness and morality, ritual and ethics, are inextricably intertwined. The ultimate goal of Judaism is to train and educate Jews to
be compassionate, sensitive, caring *menschen*—people with a heart. The
best example I know of how Judaism is a system of holiness and morality
bound together is Shabbat. I want you to cooperate with me in a novel
experiment.

I want you to use your imagination, as I speak, to visualize the scene I
paint for you. If you will do this for me, then my words will have a much
better chance of reaching you. If I were a practitioner of some esoteric
cult, you might be reluctant to participate in a psychological experiment,
but I assure you that this is not a figment of your imagination. I do not
want you to give up all your worldly possessions and come live in my
ashram. I merely want you to feel very deeply what I have to say, and keep
it with you in your memory and in your heart, and discuss it with your
family and friends, and let it simmer in your soul for some time. I hope
you will visualize a picture with the potential to bring you better health,
more serenity, a more closely knit family, deeper emotional security, lots
of beauty in the way of art, music, and poetry, and a feeling of being closer
to God. All that at once. It's worth giving it a try, isn't it?

The Journey

Picture yourself in a small European shtetl, a little village totally inhabited
by your fellow Jews, some time in the nineteenth century. It's Thursday af-

ternoon, and all week, since last Saturday night, you've been waiting for this time to come closer, closer to Shabbat. You go to the market to shop for Shabbat dinner and bring home the very best foods available. Since chicken is a great delicacy for you, that's the main course. You buy all of the other delectable foods you relish for your loving family and bring them home.

The next morning, Friday, if you are the wife, you begin to clean the house (as women did in Eastern Europe), and if you are the husband, you are chopping wood for the Shabbat fire, or picking the most beautiful flowers for the Shabbat table, or helping with the cleaning around the house for the special guest, the Shabbat bride, who will soon be coming.

Now it's late Friday afternoon, and everyone has bathed. The table is set beautifully, as befits a Sabbath-observing family. Silver goblets embellish the table, brimfull of delicious sweet crimson wine, and the freshly baked challahs are golden, warm, and soft. The mood is serene and hushed. An unusual and special quiet descends on the home, an inner peacefulness and joy. The past six days have been filled with hard work, much accomplishment, frantic business; and now the world is slowing down on its axis, and spinning a bit more gently and gradually.

As the sun begins to fade in the sky, its red ball of fire is sinking behind the leaves and branches of the trees, and the sky is a mixture of gray, blue, and orange, with a few puffs of white clouds dotting the horizon. Without the warm rays of the sun beaming through the window of your home, it's getting colder, and the family snuggles together to provide warmth. Mother approaches the beautiful golden candelabrum, handed down to her from her mother and grandmother, which has room for five candles, one for each member of the family. Just as she is about to light the Shabbat candles, Papa enters the house with a guest—a stranger in town. For after all, what is Shabbat without a guest at the table? He is an itinerant merchant who found himself far from home on Shabbat. So he went to the local shul, and when he started to leave at the end of services, several men approached him to invite him to come home with them for dinner. Papa, you were the first to reach him, and he accepted your invitation.

For the next few moments of our story, let me read to you a personal account in a poem, by Philip Raskin, called "Kindling the Sabbath Light."

> From memory's spring flows a vision tonight;
> My mother is kindling and blessing the light.
> The light of queen Sabbath, the heavenly flame

That one day in seven quells hunger and shame.
My mother is praying, and screening her face.
Too bashful to gaze at the Sabbath light's grace.
She murmurs devoutly: "Almighty, be blessed
For sending Thy angel of joy and of rest.
And may, as the candles of Sabbath divine,
The eyes of my son in Thy Law ever shine. . ."
Of childhood, fair childhood, the years are long fled;
Youth's candles are quenched, and my mother is dead.
And yet ev'ry Friday, when twilight arrives,
The face of my mother within me revives;
A prayer on her lips: "O Almighty, be blessed
For sending us Sabbath, the angel of rest."
And some hidden feelings I cannot control
A Sabbath light kindles deep, deep in my soul.

(from *Songs of a Wanderer,* 1917)

Continuing our Shabbat imagery now, Papa then blesses the children, with his hands resting gently and lovingly on their heads, and plants a soft kiss on their cheeks when he is finished. Next he reads the loving poem of praise to his *eshet chayil,* his woman of valor—whose worth is far above rubies and who exceeds all other women in her qualities of generosity and piety.

Papa then chants the Kiddush, in which he praises God for sanctifying the Shabbat, a day of rest recalling God's own rest after the six days of creation, and reminding us of God's command that every person be as liberated as the people who left Egyptian slavery. Only a free person can enjoy a Shabbat; a slave cannot appreciate the meaning of rest, or of freedom or Shabbat. The challah has been covered, so that the innocent challah would not be offended by seeing that the wine was blessed first. Papa removes the cover and picks up the two shiny home-baked loaves, the double portion reminding the family of the double measure of joy they are to celebrate on the Sabbath, and thanks God with the Motzi for the privilege of having such sumptuous food on the table, at least this once during the week.

After dinner the family revels in singing some Shabbat *z'mirot* (Sabbath hymns) together, as they linger at the table in great leisure. There is nowhere to go, no appointments to rush to. They have only to satisfy their physical appetites for food, drink, song, and relaxation. When Mama and

Papa finally go to bed, they have a double mitzvah for having sexual relations that night, for it is a great mitzvah to enjoy each other's physical and spiritual love on Shabbat. Shabbat is a mitzvah, and sex is a mitzvah, but sex on Shabbat is literally an embarrassment of riches.

Our reverie is now complete, and you may awaken, if you wish. Or, if you prefer, if you are really totally immersed in the scene in which you joined me in your mind's eye, then you may remain there, because the picture in your head is indeed worth a thousand words.

Seudat Mitzvah

RON WOLFSON

F ast food is a mentality. It rapidly becomes a way of life. Endless fif-
teen-and thirty-second commercial spots have trained us to eat to the
beat of a drum–machine (with dancers gyrating and spinning in our mental background). Afterward, we dump the paper in the trash container
and stack our tray. At home, the eating pattern is often equally rushed.
After all what else can you do on a TV tray?

Dining is a whole different activity. Think cloth napkins and everything
slows down. From television, we've learned to dance our way from win-
ning the big game to fast eating. Dining takes dressing up, going to a special setting, and changing the rhythm. While good food is important, the
essence of fine dining is conversation, communication, and connection. A
real dinner isn't merely a moment of human grazing, it is an event, an occasion, an experience. It's not the formality, the lavishness, the two forks
and three spoons that make a difference. These are merely props that help
to cue the time-signature. Dining is when we go beyond "grabbing a bite"
(or even "taking" a lunch) to breaking bread together. A quick meal is a
pause, a momentary replenishment, a few shared remarks. Dining is when
there is time to talk, to savor, to spend a period of significant time together around the table.

The talmudic rabbis introduced the concept of a *seudat mitzvah*, a ritual meal that accompanies the performance of a mitzvah. Every caterer
will confirm that it is the dinner that makes the bar/bat mitzvah, the wedding, the *simha* (happy occasion) special. There is something about the
collective focus of a table and the shared experience of eating that almost

automatically allows people to create their own good time. Yet, the rabbinic concept of *seudat mitzvah* was not stressed merely to produce nice affairs. It started with their view of mitzvot.

Mitzvot are more than commandments. They are opportunities, potential moments of linkage. The performance of a mitzvah can take a Jew far beyond mere compliance with Jewish law. When done with intention and conscious direction, simple actions (often focused through a blessing) can become religious encounters. On one level, the Jew is obligated to perform certain acts because of a legal covenant made with God, accepting the Torah and its way of life. On a second level, the mitzvah becomes a personal way of experiencing a whole national historical tradition. Standing at the bima publicly reading the Torah for the first time is an act that has the potential to create a profound experience of membership and continuity for the bar/bat mitzvah child. The glow of the Hanukkah menorah really can inspire a family that it is worth struggling to preserve the difference and uniqueness of Jewish life. Mitzvot provide us with the opportunity to make Jewish values, Jewish lessons, and Jewish experiences part of our life-rhythm.

Mitzvot aren't fast-food experiences. They work best with reflection. The twofold message of Shabbat—the wonder of creation and the joy of liberation—takes reflection. The Rabbis knew that reflection takes a catalyst, time for the experiential to mix with the symbolic. That's the essence of a *seudat mitzvah* (a mitzvah meal). The ritual serves as a metronome for the dinner, while the dinner process allows the symbols to become personal, interactive—part of the family's experience of being a family. Family traditions, with their private jokes and impromptu rituals, are the building blocks that actualize the Jewish tradition. The Shabbat Seder and *seudat Shabbat* work together. They are interwoven. The Shabbat Seder is not a meal preceded by a short service, nor a service followed by dining. Rather, the Rabbis evolved it as a whole table evening; a celebration that lets us dance to a different drum–machine.

The Home Where Warmth Rules over Technology

JONATHAN SACKS

The ideal Jewish home is a superbly situated ambassadorial-style residence comprising six bedrooms, seven bathrooms (three *milchik*, three *fleishik*, one *parev*), set in undisturbed countryside only five minutes from the nearest *shtibl* (near enough for easy Shabbos access, far enough away for you not to be awakened when they are short of a minyan), architect-designed Pesach kitchen with turbo-driven double dishwashers, luxury jacuzzi/*mikva* complex, self-contained bubbe annex, and wired throughout to state-of-the-art Shabbos-observing microchip technology?

Perhaps not. Ideal homes, Jewishly speaking, don't come constructed out of real estate agents' hype or float from the pages of glossy dream-magazines. An ideal home is . . . well, *haimish*—warm and welcoming.

The outward march of Jewish suburbia has long carried with it its changing symbols: in the early postwar years, the interconnecting drawing room—Does this have religious significance? builders used to ask—then the double garage, and slowly but surely the swimming pool/sauna.

In New York's Boro Park, a Jewish home used to be defined as one which had chandeliers in the bathroom. In Los Angeles they speak in awed tones of the modern couple who, instead of the old-fashioned mezzuza on every door, installed a master mezzuza on the roof.

Yet in all this spiraling upward mobility something, surely, is lost. A Jewish home is measured not in property values but in human values. As a hasidic rabbi once said: a home is like a bed on a cold night. First you warm it, then it warms you. *Haimish*.

Here then is my impromptu checklist for an ideal Jewish home:

It's a place where you don't need a written invitation to drop in, where if three visitors call (as they did once on Abraham) they aren't asked, What are you collecting for? Hospitality, said the rabbis, is greater than welcoming the Divine Presence. They also said the Hebrew letter which means home (*beit/bayit*) is open on one side to show that a home must always be open to the unexpected guest.

It's a place where the mezzuzot on the doors don't take second place to the stripped pine of the doors themselves. The Torah is alive to the nonverbal language of furnishing a home. A house can say, "I am Jewish but I am pretending not to be." Or it can wear the signs of its identity—the candlesticks, the framed *ketubah*, the sepia-tinted pictures of grandparents—with a certain unself-conscious pride.

It's a place where certain sounds are heard: singing on Shabbat, children telling parents what they learned in this week's Hebrew lessons, a husband telling a wife on Friday evening: *Eshet chayil mi yimtzah*. More than anything else, a Jewish home is sensed in its sounds.

And its smells. Shabbat announces its arrival through the nose. Chicken soup? Cholent? It varies from culture to culture, Ashkenazi, Sephardi, East European, Oriental, perhaps from family to family. One can almost imagine an olfactory Sherlock Holmes, blindfolded, brought into the house on Friday afternoon sniffing the air and able to say with precision, "A kugel from Kovno; a borsht from Bratslav."

Food is part of a Jewish home, in its special way. It says: What we eat is not a function of appetite alone. But the Torah was generous. It chose to sanctify rather than frustrate desire. In eating, through *kashrut* and the blessings over food; in sexuality, through *mikva* and the code of husband–wife relations, it takes us away through a route of affirmation rather than denial. Rav said—in a talmudic aphorism that never ceases to amaze—that in the world to come we will be judged for every legitimate pleasure we denied ourselves.

A Jewish home has its rhythm of time. Like a well-structured symphony, you can feel the coming allegro or adagio long before it arrives. Before Pesach, the flurry of cleaning and cooking; before Purim, getting the children's costumes ready; before Sukkot, the sound of hammer hitting nail or thumb; before Shabbat, the rush to beat the Jewish Parkinson's Law which says that getting ready takes just longer than the time available for it. Time is patterned, in a Jewish home, by something other than the TV guide.

A Jewish home is: a place where you say *mazel tov* if someone breaks a plate instead of pretending not to notice. A place where husbands help—on good, ancient, rabbinic insistence—in the preparations. Where the Kiddush wine—that perverse mixture of port and cough syrup—still tastes better than the discreetly supervised Château Bois de Saint-Jean. Where children share a common language with parents. Where no guest feels that his footprints are an affront. Where what is most valuable can't be stolen.

Somewhere there is a house outwardly indistinguishable from all the others in its neighborhood. What makes it special is that the family who lives there has taken it on themselves to invite home every new or lonely or unattached person they meet in shul on Shabbat morning. Perhaps there are many such homes, direct descendants of Abraham's and Sarah's. *Haimish.*

Once a week, in such a house, one can almost feel the Divine Presence, welcomed in, made to feel part of the family. That is my ideal Jewish home.

Shabbat on Middle Mountain

GAVRIEL AND
PAMELA GOLDMAN

I t was the fourth night of our ten-day camping adventure in the wilds of West Virginia. We were the only people at the primitive campsite of Stuart's Park and had pitched our tents under a canopy of towering rhododendrons. As we ate the meal we had cooked over a campfire, we examined the casts of animal tracks we had made earlier in the day, part of a game we called "tracking kosher animals." That day we had tracked turkey and deer and made casts of bear, muskrat, and raccoon tracks.

The sky was changing from dark blue to deep purple and finally to starry blackness. It was the perfect occasion to read the evening blessing, Hamaariv Aravim.

Blessed are You, Lord our God, King of the Universe, who by His word brings on evening . . . changing the times, varying the seasons and arranging the stars in their places in the sky.

To rediscover the beauty of and meaning in Judaism was a primary goal of the physically and emotionally challenging trip we'd undertaken with our children, Ashirah, 13; Miriam, 10; Shulamit, 7; and Aryeh, 4. We hoped living Jewishly in the midst of nature would lead us to new insights. We were not disappointed.

We knew our Orthodox lifestyle would present challenges. We had to plan meals carefully, knowing we would not find kosher food in rural West Virginia.

Our decision to spend Shabbat at the Middle Mountain Cabins would also present interesting difficulties. As it turned out, that experience proved to be the spiritual pinnacle of our adventure.

The cabins are halfway up the mountain, an isolated region of the Laurel Fork South Wilderness. They were built in the 1930s to house the rangers who worked the backwoods fire-watch towers. Though a propane gas stove and refrigerator were added recently, the cabins are still without electricity and indoor plumbing.

FS 14, the old logging route that took us to the cabins, was an unpaved dirt road barely wider than a single lane. Chunks of fallen rock were strewn across the road and deep ruts marked the passage of logging trucks. We averaged ten miles per hour and prayed no cars would come down from the other direction.

When we finally arrived, our tensions dissolved. There beside a mountain runoff stood three delightful cabins. In front was a hand pump for water; a small pond glittered among the trees. Surrounding us was a magnificent pine forest extending into the distance on softly contoured hillsides.

The insides of the cabins were as clean and comfortable as the outsides were quaint and beautiful. Each included a large stone fireplace and a king-size bed or bunks, a table and comfortable chairs, all made from pine logs and wooden nails. We found minitreasures—woodcarvings, old bottle openers called "church keys," photographs from the 1940s, and probably the only jar of nonkosher herring in the country, complete with a recipe for "fried salt herring."

We put a chicken cholent on the stove to cook overnight for our Shabbat lunch. For our Friday-night meal we prepared freshly caught bass, baked potatoes, soup, and sliced vegetables. Dessert would be granola bars and tea made from the sassafras root we'd dug. At last we turned our attention to our lighting needs. We hung our gas lantern over the picnic table and placed a small candle lantern in each cabin and one beside the outhouse.

When everything was ready for Shabbat, we made an old-fashioned seesaw from a log stump and railroad tie. We wanted to make something other families could enjoy. As a finishing touch, we engraved "By the Goldmans" on the tie and carved a Star of David. Our last act before Shabbat was to lock our wristwatches in the van. We would live—for the next little while—in accordance with our inner biological and spiritual clocks.

We sang Kiddush around a Shabbat table as regal as any. As we ate we could hear the spring peepers and crickets chirping by the pond, the cries of small prey being snatched by hunting owls, and the footsteps of nearby deer crunching leaves. We experienced the natural world through our senses with immediacy and acuteness.

The scent of the pine forest blended into the smell of the Shabbat candles. The words of our blessings and songs melded into the sounds of the forest. We experienced the feeling of being a part of creation, in harmony with the world around us.

We davened in the woods, now and again spotting a deer between the trees. We used the sun and stars to govern our Shabbat awareness and observance. We became conscious of the ongoing struggle for survival in the natural world. And we were able to take the time to marvel at the infinite order and purpose and meaning in nature.

We watched a hawk drop a snake from high in the sky to kill it before eating it or taking it back to its young. We discovered the bleached bones of a deer long dead. We saw how useful even dead trees were, trees which had blown over in high winds or been toppled by lightning. We recognized the truth of the midrash that states that even the lowest creature was created with purpose.

We were granted one final experience late Shabbat afternoon that touched our souls and will live in our memories. Ashirah captured the experience in a short story she calls "The Lion and the Deer."

> We were sitting outside when we noticed a deer coming out of the trees. The deer was watching us. Everyone was quiet. Even though we had seen a lot of deer, each time was as special as the first. My four-year-old brother, Aryeh (which means "lion" in Hebrew), wanted to go over to touch the deer. He got up and began to walk toward it. We cringed, expecting the deer to bolt. But she didn't. She looked at Aryeh for a moment and began to graze.
>
> Aryeh bent down to pick grass for the deer and while his back was turned, the deer began to walk toward him! It seemed like the deer wanted to go to him but was too scared. When Aryeh stood up, the deer just watched as he walked closer to offer the grass he had picked.
>
> They stood looking at each other only three feet apart! The lion and deer, each too afraid to go closer, yet each attracted by shared curiosity.
>
> Eventually the deer left. Aryeh insisted on leaving the grass and a cup of water. None of us thought the deer would drink the water because there was a pond right there. We let him leave the cup so

he would feel good. Later that night my mother and father heard a sound behind the cabins. It was the deer drinking the water. We have a picture of it. Needless to say, Aryeh was very happy the next morning when he saw the cup empty. The memory of that very special encounter between the lion and the deer will stay with us forever.

That night the Havdala candle cast its flickering light across the table and onto our faces. Living in a world of instant-on light makes it difficult to feel the joy of the Havdala candle. Standing in the midst of miles and miles of forest darkness, the feeling of joy and hope generated by the candle was overwhelming. We said the blessings in unison, our words echoing off the hillsides.

Blessed are You, Lord our God, who makes a distinction between kodesh *(the holy) and* hol *(the ordinary); between light and darkness; between Israel and other people; between the seventh day and the other six days of creation.*

We knew at that moment that our trip had been a lesson in seeing the distinction between *kodesh* and *hol.* At first, we thought the distinction was the difference between living in the fast lane of urban life and existing moment by moment in the natural world. Life in the fast lane is rushing to get places. Existing in nature is seeing, feeling, hearing, and smelling God's handiwork.

The real beauty invested in the natural world is found in its infinite levels of purpose. We realized *kedusha* (holiness) had nothing to do with the esthetics of form but rather was related to purpose. Quite simply, that which is done in accordance with God's purpose is *kodesh,* that which is not is *hol.*

By this definition it was easy to understand why being in nature felt so spiritually rewarding. All parts of nature continually fulfill the purpose of the creation. Trees grow toward the sun. Water flows downhill. Grapes ripen at their appointed time. And nature performs its designated purpose with a level of *kavana* (intention and focus) that we can never hope to achieve.

On the other hand, nature has no choice. But human beings have *behira,* freedom of choice—the ultimate level of God's trust. By freely choosing to perform mitzvot, to live purposeful lives fulfilling the will of the Creator, we distinguish ourselves from the rest of the natural world.

Ironically, that Shabbat we also came to recognize our separateness from the natural world: when an animal is thirsty, it drinks, and when it's tired, it sleeps. When we were thirsty, however, we made a *brakha* before satisfying our desires; and before going to sleep after a long day of hiking, we said the Shema. It was in these pauses that the meaning of our Jewishness was to be discovered. That Shabbat we realized nature does not rest. Nature has no experience parallel to Shabbat. Shabbat is unnatural; it is the ultimate pause.

When Shabbat ended, we felt we had never experienced so strongly the sublimity of the distinction "between the seventh day and the other six days of creation." Never before had we recognized so clearly the difference between *kodesh* and *hol*—and never before had we appreciated so fully the characteristics of each.

· IV ·

SHABBAT
IN MODERN
THOUGHT

Tending to Our Cosmic Oasis

ISMAR SCHORSCH

We must dare to reexamine our longstanding preference for history over nature. The celebration of "historical monotheism" (Salo Baron) is a legacy of nineteenth-century Christian–Jewish polemics, a fierce attempt by Jewish thinkers to distance Judaism from the world of paganism. But the disclaimer has its downside by casting Judaism into an adversarial relationship with the natural world. Nature is faulted for the primitiveness and decadence of pagan religion, and the modern Jew is saddled with a reading of his tradition that is one-dimensional. Judaism has been made to dull our sensitivity to the awe-inspiring power of nature. Preoccupied with the ghosts of paganism, it appears indifferent and unresponsive to the supreme challenge of our age: humanity's degradation of the environment. Our planet is under siege and we as Jews are transfixed in silence.

What a monumental disservice to Judaism and humankind! For, properly understood, Judaism pulsates with reverence for God's handiwork. The human species may embody the highest form of consciousness in the universe but hardly merits the limitless power of an absolute monarch. Humanity's unique ability to unravel the secrets of nature does not make us the equal of its creator. In the tart words of William Blake, the unrepentant critic of Newton and the Enlightenment: "He who sees the infinite in all things sees God. He who sees the Ratio only sees himself only." Judaism is a religious tapestry designed to sharpen our eye for the divine, in nature as well as in history, and thus is laced with universal motifs relevant to our contemporary crisis.

Let me cite but three suggestive examples. First, the three pilgrimage festivals, despite the historicizing overlay and the long exilic experience, never lost their agricultural roots. No matter how urban Jewish life became, these ancient harvest festivals have echoed liturgically and ritually with an undertone of anxiety. The fertility of nature is the most basic condition of human survival. Graphically, the Mishnah conveys this sense of collective dependence:

> Four times a year the world is judged: at Passover on the grain, at the Festival of Weeks on the fruit of the trees . . . and on the Festival of Huts humankind is judged in terms of water.
>
> (*Rosh Hashanah* 1)

What has become so shockingly clear of late is that our own reckless assault on the environment—whether stemming from indescribable poverty or ever more industrialization—is part of the sentence. The rhythm of the natural year undulates through the Jewish calendar, which in turn yields an annual rendition of Judaism's utopian vision of balance and harmony—"In that day, will I make a covenant for them with the beasts of the field, the birds of the air, and the creeping things of the ground. I will banish bow, sword, and war from the land and let them lie down in safety" (Hos. 2:20).

My second example is less obvious but more potent. The weekly message of Shabbat rings with environmental import, if we but dare to understand it on its own terms. Instead, our wont is to render it in the liberating, anthropocentric spirit of Jesus: "The Sabbath was made for the sake of man and not man for the Sabbath." But to my mind, this profound and uniquely biblical institution is not intended to ennoble the human race but to humble it. With its incessant strictures against work, Shabbat reminds us of our earthly status as tenant and not overlord. To rest is to acknowledge our limitations. One day out of seven we cease to exercise our power to tinker and transform. Willful inactivity is a statement of subservience to a power greater than our own. On the meaning of Shabbat, Samson Raphael Hirsch, the hardliner, spoke more tellingly than his liberal counterparts:

> On each Sabbath day, the world, so to speak, is restored to God, and thus man proclaims, both to himself and to his surroundings, that he enjoys only a borrowed authority. . . . Even the smallest

work done on the Sabbath is a denial of the fact that God is the Creator and Master of the World. (*Horeb* 56)

The design of Shabbat to rein in our lust for grandeur and gratification, then, addresses the environmental issue head on. For the first time, a species has the power to render this planet uninhabitable, either cataclysmically or incrementally. Precisely at this juncture, the archaic texts of the Hebrew Bible confront us with a vision of responsibility. We are not free to act indifferently or selfishly. Our mission is to tend to this cosmic oasis, to perpetuate an islet of consciousness in a seemingly mindless universe. More immediately, how salutary for the environment if one day a week we turned off the engines to walk rather than drive, to cultivate our inner lives, to relate to family and friends. How much cleaner the air is in Jerusalem on Shabbat!

Underlying Shabbat, and for that matter much of Judaism, is the insistence on divine kingship, my third and final example. The concept is one of the root ideas of Judaism, enunciated in the quotidian *berakhah* as in the exalted liturgy of the High Holy Days. Judaism is a religion of constraints, with an unvarnished view of human nature. It rests squarely on the portrait of mortal human as sketched in chapter two of Genesis rather than on that of the superhuman in chapter one. Whereas Adam I is a paragon without want or weakness, commissioned to conquer the Earth and free of all restraints, Adam II is frail and flawed. Incapable of abiding by the single stricture imposed upon him, he is lonely, weak, and passive. To till and tend his garden, no more. That is his assignment. For the Bible, the tumultuous course of human events is driven by the errant nature of Adam II and not by the perfection of Adam I, which lingers on as an ever elusive vision beyond human grasp.

Errant and powerful, like the awesome potential of a gifted natural athlete, human nature needs to be focused, disciplined, and trained. The awareness of God's dominion, a proprietorship anchored in creation, is the ultimate constraint erected by Judaism to stay the hand of self-destruction. The ecological nightmare of our own making cries out for the reinculcation of this reverential mindset. In the words of Rainer Maria Rilke: "Who speaks of victory? To endure is all."

Shabbat

MICHAEL LERNER

S habbat is the quintessential Jewish observance and one of the most important contributions the Jews have to offer to the larger world. It is a pleasure and a joy, yet its message is deep and abidingly important. I had almost no clue of this when I grew up in a Conservative synagogue where Shabbat simply meant a Friday-night service. All the rhetoric about pleasure seemed to reduce to a good spread of food at the Oneg Shabbat or Kiddush that followed services. Most of the people went home, turned on their televisions to catch a late-night show. A smaller group did bother to come to shul the next morning, but many of them went shopping afterward, or to some sports event, or were attending to parts of leftover work, or paying bills, getting the car or home repaired, mowing the lawn, or doing other chores. Needless to say, I had no idea of the traditional experience of Shabbat as twenty-five hours of withdrawal from the way we normally lead our lives, immersion in a joyous and celebratory ritual whose rhythms challenge our world's logic of domination and consumption. When I encountered Shabbat as performed by people who were seriously into it, it was like going from the jingle on a television commercial to a great symphony.

Shabbat is the moment in which Jews withdraw from the human activities involved in mastering and controlling the world, and focus instead on responding to the grandeur of the universe with awe, wonder, and radical amazement. As the psalm for Shabbat proclaims, "I rejoice in Your works, O God, I will exalt in the works of Your hands!"

All week long we are involved in getting and spending, in acting on the world to make it turn out the way we want. On Shabbat we cease from that whirlwind of activity. We change the mode from active to receptive. We embrace Mother Earth with joy and celebration, we sing songs to the sun and the moon and the stars. As we express our delight at God's creation, we are overwhelmed with the immense preciousness of Being.

In celebrating the world, we stand in reverence at the Source of all being. The Creator is beyond all our categories. Language allows us to reidentify the repeatable and publicly observable aspects of reality. But God is beyond all language, the Source of all Being. No wonder, then, that language is of such little avail.

As Abraham Joshua Heschel used to point out, there are two attitudes through which we can approach the world: one in which we seek to accumulate information in order to dominate, the other in which we deepen our appreciation in order to respond. "As civilization advances, the sense of wonder almost necessarily declines. . . . Mankind will not perish for want of information, but only for want of appreciation. The beginning of our happiness lies in the understanding that life without wonder is not worth living."[1] Shabbat is the moment each week fully dedicated to responding with appreciation. It is, Heschel once said to me, greeting the world not with the tools we have made but with the soul with which we are born: not like a hunter who seeks prey but like a lover to reciprocate love.

Shabbat is for appreciation, for receptivity, for wonder.

It is twenty-five hours dedicated to being open to the world, responding, celebrating. In some respects Shabbat affirms a part of religious experience that is not uniquely Jewish. Other religions also have religious celebrations of the grandeur of the universe and the magnificence of creation.

But Shabbat is also something else, the weekly celebration of the possibility of emancipation from oppression and domination: *zeycher le'tziyat mitzrayim.*

Shabbat is both the result and celebration of the first national liberation struggle. Ruling elites throughout most of recorded history have sought unlimited power to expropriate the labor of others. When there is no limit, when people are forced to work till they drop or drop dead, we have a condition of slavery. Shabbat is the first historical imposition of a limit on the ability of ruling elites to exploit labor. It is the embodiment of the first time when the people who work were able to say no to a ruling elite and make it stick.

The notion that working people could do this, that they had rights that limited the power of the bosses, was a new notion in history. The Jews built their religion around it.

Shabbat wasn't a day of rest only for those who could afford it. "Six days shalt thou work, and the seventh day is a Sabbath to your God. On it, you shall do no work, neither you, nor your family members, nor your animals, nor anyone who works for you, nor the stranger who is within your gates."

Shabbat is the first completely democratic sharing of rest. It was the Jews who won this, and as the Jewish way of organizing the week spread, it became the gift of the Jewish people to the rest of the world. It was only in the twentieth century that this gift was extended to a second day, creating a weekend. And when that happened, it was through social movements that had disproportionately large Jewish participation in their leadership and activists.

Shabbat is a nonreformist reform. It provides a space and a concept through which people are encouraged to get more power.

Shabbat is the real-world testimonial to the fact that the world can be transformed from what is to what ought to be, and God is the Force in the universe that made that possible.

People often ask the question, "Is there any society in which people are actually living according to the utopian ideals that you espouse?" The answer is, "Wherever people observe Shabbat, they are proving that the utopian ideals are really possible."

"But it's only one day in seven," you might say.

That's also its genius. Shabbat becomes an assessment of what is possible in a world of oppression. Rejecting the position that every step along the way toward a liberated world is useless because it is so limited, Shabbat testifies to the power of achieving partial gains in the struggle. It is a taste of the world to come, but a taste that gives them incentive to fight for more. That's why Jewish tradition encourages us to prolong Shabbat and to take the spirit of Shabbat into the rest of the week with us. It may take us the whole Shabbat just to get rid of the pressures of the week enough so that we can begin to taste a different rhythm by its end.

When Mao Zedong was fighting to liberate China from feudalism, he did so by liberating bits of land in which the Communists could begin to actualize their vision of the future. The experience energized the cadres, whose taste of the possible gave them strength to fight to change the actual. Shabbat works that same way. So Shabbat promotes a consciousness that detaches us from commodities, encourages us to focus on the world not from the standpoint of how we fit into it, but as creatures who sing to God its praises.

The weekly choice to dedicate one day *not* to the shopping mall, *not* to the television or telephone or computer, *not* to the consciousness of the market, opens the possibility for sacred time in which the call of God can be heard. It stands in contradiction to the logic of the competitive marketplace and to all other forms of oppression. In giving us this taste of what a future world could feel like, it becomes liberated time, the vanguard of the struggle to liberate all time from the sophisticated forms of domination of consciousness.

Social-Change Movements Need Shabbat

One of the great weaknesses of contemporary social-change movements is their one-dimensionality. People get together for the purpose of trying to change the world, but rarely do they recognize their own needs for emotional, ethical, and spiritual nourishment.

When these universal needs are not addressed in a progressive context, they may be addressed in a conservative context. The very people who may attend a political meeting one day find themselves at a more conservative church or synagogue the next day, and they hear discouraging messages. Little serious attention has been paid to providing a spiritual framework that may help sustain political work.

We need a variety of political contexts in which people can participate, some designed to maximize safety, and others to maximize connection.

If secular political movements were to dedicate one twenty-five-hour period a week to celebrating the grandeur and mystery of the universe and to recalling and honoring the struggles for liberation of past generations, and to resting, that would be a major step toward providing the kind of nourishment their members need to sustain themselves. Imagine if people from all different faiths as well as secular people were to meet for a joint celebration and potluck once a week, share music, stories, dance, and play—and if they were to dedicate some of this time to public ceremonies of gratitude for the world and for the Force within it that makes for the possibility of liberation. Imagine if they were even to adopt Shabbat restrictions: no work, no money, no shopping, no involvement in shaping, building, creating, or destroying things.

The development of the most transformative visions requires getting out of the narrow rhythm of goal-directed energies. When your whole body and mind are swinging to that rhythm, the pace is so speeded up and the anxiety level so high that you can focus only on the short term. There's plenty of time for that, all week long, every evening, and on Sunday. But imagine one day a week when a different kind of political energy prevails, one concerned with envisaging the future we really want, reconnecting us with our transformative visions of the possible, and allowing us to *feel* those possibilities. That can be done only when the rhythm of the work week has dimmed, and a different, more transformative energy enters our souls. When Shabbat works we are open to that energy; a more transformative, relaxed, and quiet excitement makes it possible for us to recognize a whole different part of our being. A progressive social-change movement that understood the importance of such an experience would have a profound impact on the world.

How to Make Shabbat

All week long we sell our labor to those who own and control the institutions of the world of work. Time itself is organized according to the needs of production and consumption. Even when we are not working, we often use our time to acquire or plan how to acquire.

Shabbat is a different rhythm, a rhythm of calm, peace, rest, joy, pleasure, song, wonder, amazement, celebration.

A religious family often begins planning for Shabbat early in the week, inviting guests for Friday-night dinner or Sunday lunch. *Hach'nasat orchim*, bringing guests to your table, is one of the many joys of Shabbat and runs counter to the isolating nuclearization of family life in our world.

Cooking for Shabbat meals often starts on Thursday night. Since cooking and purchasing food (or anything else) is forbidden on Shabbat, everything is prepared in advance (though making salads or other dishes that do not require cooking is permitted). It's a tradition to put special energy into preparing delicious food, cleaning oneself and one's household, putting out special dishes and tablecloths and flowers, surrounding the home with beauty. People often don't get home in time to do all the preparations, and even if they've been working ahead, a last surge of energy often has a rushed and frenetic feeling, mirroring the world of work. Over the course of the next many hours, that pace is going to change radically. Monitor it—because the degree to which you move beyond that to a more centered, calm, and quiet place is the measure of how profoundly you have allowed yourself to enter into Shabbat.

Shabbat begins eighteen minutes before sundown on Friday night with the lighting of Shabbat candles and the traditional blessings. It is customary for families to bless their children and for members of a religious community to offer blessings to one another. Then, off to the community to connect with friends and family.

In smaller Jewish-renewal communities it is typical for people to gather together in groups of twenty to fifty to sing and pray the Shabbat evening service. Unlike the austere settings of so many temples, the Jewish-renewal gatherings are often in living rooms, sometimes followed by a potluck dinner. As people get together, they greet one another with hugs and embraces and expressions of pleasure. The group will hum or sing a few songs to get everyone settled in and to allow time for the children to join the mood or to be settled at their own child-oriented service elsewhere in the home.

A good way to begin the Friday-night service is with a guided meditation that leads people through the events of the week, encouraging us to remember all that has happened and to allow each of the problems and struggles to be put aside for the next twenty-five hours. The meditation then focuses on relaxation and on recalling the aspects of the world that we want to celebrate in the coming day.

The Welcoming of Sabbath and the Evening Service are chockfull of moving passages that provide a special entree into the holiness of the day.

First, there is the awakening of all our senses and of our yearning for full connection with all that we could be and will eventually be. "*Yedid Nefesh*, the precious One of my soul, draw me, Your servant, to Your will." Singing as though to a highly sexualized other, Israel calls upon God to reveal Her/Himself, to spread Her/His canopy of peace over us, so that we can be strengthened and participate in eternal joy. Come, my beloved, to greet the Shabbat. Long enough have we dwelled in the valley of tears—God will make it possible for the ancient city to be rebuilt on its ancient site, those who have devoured us will be devoured, and God will rejoice over us as a bridegroom and bride rejoice together.

There is an unmistakable sexual charge to Friday evening, shaped in part by the recognition that after services the two main things that are on the religious agenda are a delicious meal and sex. It's wonderful to allow these anticipations to mix with the sensuous religious texts and to savor in anticipation a coming sensual delight. Far from demeaning spirituality, sex and food are critical elements of a Jewish spirituality. Pleasure is good!

Next, there is the evening service. We greet the transformation from light to darkness to light. Many Jewish-renewal communities go outside at this point, to look at the stars, to witness the evening twilight, to stand in its glow, and to repeat our thanksgiving at the wonder of nature. Suddenly moved from background to foreground, no longer treated as "the eternal just there" but instead as a daily miracle to which we have grown stale, we respond to the magnitude of our world. Here we are, one small group of people out of the four billion alive at this moment, on a small planet revolving around a small star, peering out onto an evening sky filled with thousands of such stars, some of which may no longer be in existence even as we gaze upon their light, we are suddenly aware of our small place in the magnitude and grandeur of creation. We become deeply aware of how we take for granted the daily movements from light to darkness and darkness to light. Our spiritual smallness is not meant as belittling or to set us up to be better servants to an all-powerful God, but rather to set a realistic context for seeing ourselves, and our nobility and adequacy, as one tiny speck of the totality, and our own lives as one momentary speck in the tiny pebble we call the planet Earth.

From here our consciousness moves to the joy of getting all this. The recognition that we are subject to commandments about how to live, the sheer joy of having such commandments, and the opportunity to study Torah and to do them—and to function as a religious community testifying to God's presence—fill our souls, for they are our life and the length of our days.

And then, the proclamation of faith: Hear, O Israel, the Lord our God, the Lord is One. And the message: to love this Power that makes for the possibility of transformation with all our hearts, our souls, our might. And to teach this to our children and to proclaim it in the public arena as well as in private. To recognize that the physical universe will work only if we create a just society. And to remember that our own liberation from Egypt is a present reality. Through quiet space, and then through joint singing, to proclaim that the world will be transformed and that when that transformation has taken place, on that day God will be unified and be one.

Together in community, or back in one's family space, a blessing over the wine is recited, because wine gladdens our hearts. Washing of hands with a blessing, and then the blessing over the bread, usually two challot (twisted loaves). And on to a sumptuous meal, together with *zmirot* (special Shabbat songs). It is customary to study some text together or for one of the guests or participants to prepare a teaching, often from some aspect of the week's Torah portion, but possibly from any aspect of the tradition or relevant spiritual teachings.

After the meal, the traditional blessing—Birkat Hamazon, sung communally. Because the blessings sometimes take on a rote quality, it has become traditional in some Jewish-renewal communities to stop in the middle of this ten-minute blessing and to have each person insert his or her own words of blessing to God for the food, for the land, for the goodness that we have experienced, and/or to add petitions that the All-Merciful One will grant us some special blessing that is then described.

I've found that by the time one gets to the Shabbat teaching at the table, the songs, and the blessing after the meal, a first serious level of relaxation enters consciousness. The body is beginning to get the notion that it doesn't have another immediate task in front of it. The joy of singing together, the playful little phrases and melodies of the Birkat Hamazon are beginning to condition the body to believe that it may have some real rest in front of it. And real sensuous pleasure.

In Orthodox circles, it's a religious obligation for man and wife to have sexual relations on Shabbat when that is physically possible (physical ailments or disabilities excuse, but physical absence does not—couples are under religious injunction to find a way, if at all possible, not to be separated on Shabbat, even if that means coming home from a long trip). Jewish-renewal circles tend to extend the mitzvah of sex to unmarried couples who are already engaged in sexual relations.

Friday night is a real pleasure. But one does not have a taste of the experience of Shabbat unless one keeps its energy going for the entire twenty-five hours. Given the stresses of the world of work, it often isn't until Shabbat afternoon that our bodies fully relax enough to really begin to benefit from the restfulness that Shabbat offers.

The next morning people get up to thank God for the morning, for bodies that are still functioning, for consciousness that returns to full awareness, for a physical world that gives us solidity under our feet and removes the tiredness from our bones.

Jewish-renewal communities have developed a variety of different Shabbat-morning services. Some tend to follow the traditional prayer book and to include a full reading of the Torah portion (the Torah having been divided into a different section for each week of the year). Others have put their primary focus on celebrating the body and nature, and then moving to a focused study of the Torah portion, sometimes with a group of people putting on a play to act out some of the issues raised, sometimes with an individual preparing a commentary, sometimes with a free-for-all general discussion of what the Torah portion means, sometimes with a more formal teacher giving a more scholarly talk.

Some communities combine this with a discussion of the issues of the larger world. Jewish renewal does not accept the notion that the week's political events are somehow irrelevant or a distraction from Shabbat services. While specific political organizing strategies tend to be avoided because of the anxiety that would be provoked by having to debate them out, more theoretical analyses of contemporary situations are encouraged. The two things that are never ruled out of a Jewish-renewal community are God and politics. Not, of course, the politics of which particular candidate to endorse or support, but the politics that involves discussing the contemporary world and evaluating the latest developments in it from the standpoint of Torah or God-based insights and concerns.

Jewish-renewal events in the morning can be very high and very meditative. Nevertheless, there remains in the body the rhythm of the week, so that there is often a frenzy to the Shabbat-morning experience, even among communities that consciously know that it ought to be otherwise. But since in fact the body does not face the kinds of tasks it has had all week, it slowly begins to recognize that something else may be in store for it.

It's traditional to return home then and have another festive meal—a sumptuous lunch, together with singing, blessings before and after the meal, and study of the weekly Torah reading at the table.

Shabbat afternoon is dedicated to pleasure. Singing, hanging out with friends, food, sex, reading (as long as it's not connected to work or to some obligatory task— it must be aimed at pleasure, though the pleasure of learning or grappling with complex topics is certainly part of this). It's not unusual for people to take long walks to reexperience their ties to the natural world, to organize a picnic or a gathering of friends to discuss some shared issue in intellectual, cultural, political, or spiritual life, or to meet with friends for singing or shmoozing. For others who have a week full of interactions with others, Shabbat is a moment of escape from social responsibilities, so the afternoon is used in solitary meditation, reading, walks, or even just plain sleeping.

The traditional restrictions on Shabbat (no cooking, cleaning, gardening, turning electricity on or off, riding in cars or subways, traveling long distances, writing, smoking, talking on the phone, spending money, paying bills, tearing, or any of the thirty-nine kinds of work that were needed to complete the original Temple Sanctuary in the desert) flow from one central theoretical idea: human beings should not be acting on the world to make their impact on it, but rather should be dedicating one day to spirituality, that is, to dealing with the world not from the standpoint of manipulation and control, but from the standpoint of rejoicing, celebration, awe, wonder, and radical amazement. So every act of transformation of the world from one state of being to another is avoided. For twenty-five hours, just pure receptivity to what is there, joy, celebration, awe, and wonder.

I've found that it's harder to observe Shabbat when you are trying to take a bit or a piece of it—a two-hour stretch on Friday night, for instance—and stick it into a busy life. You really can't get a feel for what it's like. It's a meditative practice, one that takes time for you to move from one state of consciousness preparatory to the next, and you really can't skip stages. You haven't had the experience until you've tried doing it for the full twenty-five hours, and doing it for a year or two minimum. Eventually you train your consciousness to slow down, so that Shabbat energy starts to hit you even in the first few hours. Eventually it brings some of the greatest pleasure and greatest inner peace and relaxation you could ever hope to experience—but only for those who are willing to allow themselves to get into it, do it in the full way. That's why the rigid boundaries, the restrictions on what you can do, are essential. But you haven't yet had the Shabbat experience if all you're aware of is what you *can't* do. For many people it can take a good eighteen hours of Shabbat before the body starts to give itself messages that suggest that it may be safe to let down a few more barriers to being fully present—and that's after months of getting into it. At first the anxiety produced by "trying" to do Shabbat "correctly" is going to outweigh the possible joy and relaxation energy that comes when one allows oneself to relax into the Shabbat rhythm. When you start to experience it as a liberation and a pleasure, as a special treat, then you are actually having the relevant experience, and then you are in a position to understand why Jews have often said with full enthusiasm that Shabbat is one proof that God loves us—because we never would have been able to devise such a wonderful experience without divine inspiration.

Some Jewish-renewal groups get together late Saturday afternoon for study or discussion of a Jewish text, to share visions with one another about the world to come and their hopes for it and how one might get there. To sing, to share a third Shabbat meal, or just to shmooze. I've been to groups that always integrate a good half-hour of shared visions about how the world could and should be changed, or have a speaker sharing some such vision. But this is not a meeting—there are no votes to be taken or debates to be won; it's envisioning for the sake of the vision. When we are encouraged to go very deeply into this, to not let any "they won't let us do it that way" kind of statements block our ability to conceptualize how we really want the world to be, then this vision-sharing can be very empowering. But on Shabbat it is best when interspersed with songs, dancing, *bentsch*ing.

One custom I recommend for these late–Saturday-afternoon gatherings: the exchange of humorous stories. I've seen Shabbat gatherings in which people take their turns as wanna-be stand-up comedians, others at which some of the most humorous literature of our and other traditions is read aloud, still others at which people construct humorous skits based on the weekly Torah portion. Shabbat is for fun, and a humor-oriented Shabbat afternoon full of rowdiness and playfulness can give a Jewish-renewal group a zap of energy to make sure that not everything is deep, soulful, and serious.

No wonder, then, that Jews typically become quieter, more pensive, even wistful or sad as Shabbat departs. It's typical for friends or families to gather together with wine, spicebox, and multiflamed candles and do the Havdalah (separation) ceremony at night after the appearance of three stars in the sky. Stories are told of the "days to come," the messianic period when our fullest visions of what human life could be like will be realized. The task is to bring that Shabbat energy into the rest of the week, and with it to become reinfused with the commitment to the healing and repair that our planet so badly needs.

How Did We Lose Shabbat?

If Shabbat is so wonderful, how come so many Jews stopped observing it early in the twentieth century?

There are several factors. First, it's a lot less fun when people don't have the barest level of material needs met. If you're hungry—and many Jews have been—Shabbat, and for that matter all kinds of spiritual practices, feel less fulfilling. Still, a hungry community would probably observe Shabbat. But it becomes less fulfilling if, second, you have a class structure in which some people have money and more than enough food, and others have little or none. If those who have are observing Shabbat and making it their observance, the others feel left out. Some may feel resentful of those who have more and deflect the anger onto Shabbat. Others may feel put down, implicitly "less than," because they have less opportunity to take pleasure in Shabbat and may feel that those who do ought to be sharing more of what they do have. So they feel that the synagogue and the community really have been appropriated by these others, the ones who get called to Torah, who have the most influence over selecting the rabbi, who seem to be defining community practices. And so Shabbat seems less real, less about the celebration of working people who have managed to win a victory, more the celebration of the self-satisfied. And that makes Shabbat lose some of its taste. Third, as the level of oppression of Jews increased, the level of joy decreased, and many of the official definers of Shabbat put more energy into defining the boundaries than into celebrating the joy. Fourth, many people abandoned Shabbat when they immigrated to the United States and then faced the choice of either not getting any work at all or working on Shabbat. Without the supportive structures of a Jewish community able to provide adequate economic help, many "chose" to abandon Shabbat and justified it to themselves by telling themselves they weren't really giving up so much (which, as point three indicates, may have been how some actually came to experience it).

The last point is important for understanding why some religious people have argued for legal restrictions to impose a day of rest. Without those restrictions, the capitalist market forces people to "choose" to work. The dynamics of the marketplace work like this: one store stays open on Shabbat, and then it makes more money because it gets all the sales from those who hadn't found time to do their shopping during the rest of the week. With its more money, it can afford to lower prices on individual items, because it is selling more goods than its competitors. This gives them a market advantage that may soon drive competitors out of business. So the competitors must stay open on Shabbat also, so that no one gets an unfair market advantage. But this has the effect of forcing people to violate Shabbat, since they will be employed by these firms only if some of them are willing to work on Shabbat. This creates the case for a legal forced closing—because then no one gets the advantage, and hence everyone gets the benefit of the holiday.

The problem with legally mandated closing is that religious coercion, once it begins, can easily get out of hand. Not only does this pose an unacceptable risk to our individual freedoms, but, as Israeli society shows, it can lead to the widespread discrediting of all the truths in religion, because people feel that they are being forced to observe things they don't want to observe. Yet the converse is equally true, though not widely understood: the way in which the capitalist market compels people to abandon spiritual space for material well-being. It's only when this is more deeply understood that a community can begin to contain market forces. And at that point, Shabbat should not be enforced through the intervention of government, with its coercive powers, but through the consensus of a community that refuses to patronize stores or businesspeople who violate its ethical or spiritual norms. But this kind of tactic certainly ought not be tried in a period in which the majority or even significant minorities *want* to do business on Shabbat, not only because it would be wrong to coerce them, but because the entire spiritual community that tries to observe Shabbat would be undermined by the presence within it of people who feel coerced into it. Spirituality requires choice. This goes for imposition on teenagers or children as well. Better to create safe spaces for children or teenagers who don't want to be part of Shabbat (community centers, playgrounds, schools, movie theaters, athletic facilities, dance halls) than to forcibly integrate them where they don't want to be. The rebellion against coercion is part of the God energy within our children, and it should be treasured and nurtured, not suppressed or resented. Shabbat can work only as a choice and as a gift, never as an imposition and a demand. Let them see your joy in doing it and the joy of others in your community, and let them understand it as a special treat, not as a requirement for proving that they are obedient or really care about you as parents.

While those who become part of the Jewish-renewal community will voluntarily accept the boundaries of Shabbat, people should always feel free to join or to leave the community or to negotiate their own degree of participation. In the course of a life, one may have moments when one is deeply engaged in Jewish renewal, other moments in which Jewish renewal is peripheral or when one is simply not involved—and that must always be a free choice on the part of each individual, or the whole community will suffer.

The tragic irony of contemporary Jewish life: Only a small part of our community actually allows itself the pleasure of this twenty-five–hour weekly meditation and joyous celebration. Without this experience, no wonder they imagine religious life as a ponderous obligation rather than a miraculous and healing gift.

NOTES

1. Abraham Joshua Heschel, *Man Is Not Alone: A Philosophy of Religion* (Philadelphia: Jewish Publication Society, 1951), 37.

The Meaning of the Sabbath

ERICH FROMM

To the modern mind, there is not much of a problem in the Sabbath institution. The idea that man should rest from his work one day every week sounds to us like a self-evident, social-hygienic measure intended to give man the physical and spiritual rest and relaxation he needs in order not to be swallowed up by his daily work. No doubt, this explanation is true as far as it goes—but it does not answer some questions which arise if we pay closer attention to the Sabbath law of the Bible and particularly to the Sabbath ritual as it developed in the postbiblical tradition.

A more detailed analysis of the symbolic meaning of the Sabbath ritual will show that we are dealing not with obsessional overstrictness but with a concept of work and rest which is different from our modern concept.

To begin with, the essential point—the concept of work underlying the biblical and the later talmudic concept—is not simply that of physical effort but can be defined thus: *"Work" is any interference by man, be it constructive or destructive, with the physical world. "Rest" is a state of peace between man and nature.* Man must leave nature untouched, not change it in any way, neither by building nor by destroying anything: even the smallest change made by man in the natural process is a violation of "rest." The Sabbath is the day of peace between man and nature; work is any kind of disturbance of the man–nature equilibrium. On the basis of this general definition, we can understand the Sabbath ritual. Indeed, any heavy work like plowing or building is work in this as well as in our modern sense. But lighting a match and pulling up a grass blade, while not requiring effort, are symbols of human interference with the natural process, are a breach of peace between man and nature. On the basis of this principle, we understand also the talmudic prohibition of carrying something of even little weight on one's person. In fact, the carrying of something as such is not forbidden. I can carry a heavy load within my house or my estate without violating the Sabbath ritual. But I must not carry even a handkerchief from one domain to the other, for instance, from the private domain of the house to the public domain of the street. This law is an extension of the idea of peace from the natural to the social realm. Just as man must not interfere with or change the natural equilibrium, he must refrain from changing the social order. That means not only not to do business but also the avoidance of that most primitive form of transference of property, namely, its local transference from one domain to the other.

The Sabbath symbolizes a state of complete harmony between man and nature and between man and man. By not working—that is to say, by not participating in the process of natural and social change—man is free from the chains of nature and from the chains of time, although only for one day a week.

The full significance of this idea can be understood only in the context of the biblical philosophy of the relationship between man and nature. Before Adam's "fall"—that is, before man had reason—he lived in complete harmony with nature; the first act of disobedience, which is also the beginning of human freedom, "opens his eyes," he knows how to judge good and evil, he has become aware of himself and of his fellows, the same and yet unique, tied together by bonds of love and yet alone. Human history has begun. He is cursed by God for his disobedience. What is the curse? Enmity and struggle are proclaimed between man and animals. ("And I will put enmity between thee [the serpent] and the woman, and between thy seed and her seed; it shall bruise thy head, and thou shalt bruise his heel"), between man and the soil ("cursed is the ground for thy sake; in sorrow shalt thou eat of it all the days of thy life; thorns also and thistles shall it bring forth to thee; and thou shalt eat the herb of the field; in the sweat of thy face shalt thou eat bread, til thou return unto the ground"), between man and woman ("And thy desire shall be to thy husband, and he shall rule over thee"), between woman and her own natural function ("in sorrow thou shalt bring forth children"). The original, preindividualist harmony was replaced by conflict and struggle.

What then is—in the prophetic view—the goal of man? To live in peace and harmony again with his fellow men, with animals, with the soil. The new harmony is different from that of paradise. It can be obtained only if man develops fully in order to become truly human, if he knows the truth and does justice, if he develops his power of reason to a point which frees him from the bondage of man and from the bondage of irrational passions. The prophetic descriptions abound with symbols of this idea. The earth is unboundedly fruitful again, swords will be changed into plowshares, lion and lamb will live together in peace, there will be no war any more, women will bear children in truth and in love. This new harmony, the achievement of which is the goal of the historical process, is symbolized by the figure of the Messiah.

On this basis we can understand fully the meaning of the Sabbath ritual. The Sabbath is the anticipation of the messianic time, just as the messianic period is called the time of "continuous Sabbath." In fact, the Sabbath is not only the symbolic anticipation of the messianic time but is considered its real precursor. As the Talmud puts it, "If all of Israel observed the Sabbath fully only once, the Messiah would be here."

Resting, not working, then has a meaning different from the modern meaning of relaxation. In the state of rest, man anticipates the state of human freedom that will be fulfilled eventually. The relationship of man and nature and of man and man is one of harmony, of peace, of noninterference. Work is a symbol of conflict and disharmony; rest is an expression of dignity, peace, and freedom.

In the light of this understanding some of the previously raised questions find an answer. The Sabbath ritual has such a central place in the biblical religion because it is more than a "day of rest" in the modern sense; it is a symbol of salvation and freedom. This is also the meaning of God's rest; this rest is not necessary for God because he is tired, but it expresses the idea that great as creation is, greater and crowning creation is peace; God's work is a condescension; he must really "rest," not because he is tired but because he is free and fully God only when he has ceased to work. So is man fully man only when he does not work, when he is at peace with nature and his fellow man; that is why the Sabbath commandment is at one time motivated by God's rest and at the other by liberation from Egypt. Both mean the same and interpret each other; "rest" is freedom.

Shabbat

ARTHUR WASKOW

In the biblical traditions, there are two strands of thought about Shabbat (rest from work). One of these strands sees Shabbat as a reflection of cosmic rhythms of time, embedded in creation. The other sees Shabbat as an affirmation of human freedom, justice, and equality.

These strands are intertwined in the Bible. The second is probably a midrash on the first that arose in a period when social conflict between the rich and poor was intense, and the desire to see Shabbat as an act of social justice was strong.

The first strand, that of cosmos and creation, dominates the books of Genesis and Exodus. The second is more characteristic of Deuteronomy and the prophets Jeremiah, Ezekiel, and 2 Isaiah, which are probably connected with a period of internal social conflict. The two are most effectively intertwined in Leviticus 25.

The "cosmos" strand begins with the biblical story of creation (Gen. 2:1–4). God ceases (*shavat*) on the seventh day from the work of creating, blesses the seventh day, and "calls" it holy. This "calling" speaks to the depths of reality, but not yet to human ears. Not until the generation of the Exodus do human beings learn that Shabbat is necessary.

The first communication of Shabbat to human beings occurs in the midst of one of the tales of the rebellious generation in the wilderness (Exod. 16). God sent manna to feed the Israelites. On the sixth day, twice as much manna appeared, and unlike the manna which the Israelites had earlier tried to hoard overnight, this twofold portion did not rot on the seventh day. Even so, some Israelites went out on the seventh day to look for more manna—but none had fallen. Not until then did Moses explain these unusual happenings as the consequence of God's giving the people a Shabbat. "Let no one leave his place on the seventh day," says Moses. So the people learned to "rest," "pause," or "remain inactive."

The Shabbat portrayed here follows directly from God's creation of reality—from, one might say, the nourishing breast of reality, which feeds and pauses, gives and withholds. It is only after this direct experience of the Shabbat reality that the people learn of Shabbat as a central and crucial element in their lives—as one of the ten formal proclamations that come from God at Sinai. Of the Ten Commandments, the Shabbat is the longest and most detailed. "Remember" *(zakhor)* the day of Shabbat, says the version preserved in Exodus 20. It proclaims six days of work and prescribes rest on the seventh day for adults, children, slaves, cattle, and strangers "within your gates"—all this because God had rested after working to create the world.

Thus Exodus sees the seventh-day Shabbat as a cosmic event, placed by God within the rhythms of the universe. It emerges from within those rhythms themselves and impinges upon the human consciousness, becoming a symbol and an enactment of that cosmic and creative rhythm.

Mishkan

The "cosmic" strand of Shabbat connects it closely with the Sanctuary that represents a microcosm, a miniature version of the universe in which God dwells. When Moses ascends Mount Sinai, he hears from God a detailed description of how to build a portable shrine, a *mishkan* (literally: "bearer of the Presence") that the people are to carry through the wilderness. This description is completed (Exod. 31:12–17) with a repetition of the command to keep Shabbat, on pain of death.

Shabbat is to be for the Israelites a symbol of their covenant with God—the God who made heaven and earth in six days, and then on the seventh day *"shavat vayinafash,"* "paused and caught a breath," or "rested to become spiritually refreshed." The text itself seems to suggest that, just as God made Shabbat after constructing the world—and perhaps could only complete and fully hallow the building by an act of not-building—so the people Israel, constructing the microworld of the *mishkan*, must hallow the process of building by pausing for Shabbat.

In transmitting to the people the command to build the *mishkan,* Moses begins with a warning to observe the Shabbat (Exod. 35:2–3). He adds a specific prohibition respecting work: "You shall kindle no fire throughout your settlements on the day of Shabbat."

Although the "cosmos" vision of Shabbat dominates the Book of Exodus, there is also a hint there of Shabbat as an act of social justice, liberation, and equality. Exodus 23:12 commands rest from work on every seventh day "so that your ox and your ass may rest and that your bondman and the stranger may catch their breath." This command is closely connected with the command to make every seventh year a year of *shemitah,* when the land shall be free of cultivation and the poor shall have free access to its freely growing produce (Exod. 23:10). And perhaps a penumbral power of Shabbat appears in the requirement (Exod. 21:2) that those who have had to sell themselves into indentured servitude must be freed in the seventh year of their service.

Leviticus

It is in Leviticus that the concept of Shabbat is connected with the longer rhythms of natural time. It is here that the seventh month and the seventh year, as well as the seventh day, are made "Shabbat." Leviticus (23:23, 32, 39) requires that the first, tenth, fifteenth, and twenty-second days of the seventh month (corresponding to the festivals we now know as Rosh Hashanah, Yom Kippur, Sukkot, and Shemini Atzeret) are each to be observed as Shabbaton, and of these Yom Kippur is described even more intensely as "Shabbat Shabbaton."

Leviticus 25 caps this expanding spiral of rhythmic time by providing that in every seventh year, the land itself shall observe a Shabbat. It shall have a *shemitah* (rest, release, or liberation) so as to be free of cultivation or organized harvesting. And in the fiftieth year—after seven "Shabbats" of sabbatical years (forty-nine years), the land is to rest yet again, and each piece of it is to be returned to its original owner. For "the land is Mine," says God (Lev. 25:23).

These Levitical provisions reinforce the sense that Shabbat is embedded by the Creator in the cosmic rhythms of time and must be honored by the people in order to recognize and keep covenant with the Creator. Just as the earth in its daily rotation around the sun marks Shabbat at the seventh turning, so the moon marks Shabbat in its seventh renewing, and the earth again in its seventh annual revolution around the sun.

Two provisions of Leviticus 25, however, weave into this cosmic rhythm of Shabbat the liberating and justice-making aspect of Shabbat.

One of these is the provision for the restoration of equality in landholding. This is to be accomplished every fifty years by restoring to those who have become poor their family's equal share in the land. In addition, Leviticus 25 provides that in this Jubilee year all slaves shall simultaneously be freed.

The liberating aspect of Shabbat becomes its central element in the Deuteronomic version of the Sinaitic decalogue (Deut. 5). Here, Shabbat is grounded not in the creation, but in the liberation from slavery in Egypt, and its rationale is given as the release of slaves as well as masters from their work.

Deuteronomy (15:1) also strengthens this political–historical aspect of Shabbat by providing that in the seventh year—the year of freeing the land from cultivation—all debts shall be annulled. And Deuteronomy strengthens the provision for the seventh-year release of individual servants by providing that their liberation shall include severance pay in the form of grain, oil, and animals of the flock.

In the crisis that befalls the people of Israel beginning just before the destruction of the First Temple and extending through the Babylonian Exile and the Return, this sense of Shabbat as a redemptive social force is powerfully expressed by Jeremiah, Ezekiel, and 2 Isaiah.

Jeremiah

Jeremiah (17:21–25) calls for merchants to pause from their carrying of commercial burdens through the gates of Jerusalem[1]—and promises that if they do, the Davidic kings will be carried freely, in triumph, through those same gates. As a consequence of their creating Shabbat on the seventh day, a greater Shabbat will be created for them.

Conversely, Jeremiah (34) invokes the Jubilee tradition of the *deror*, liberation, of all slaves—and calls for it to be carried out. When the masters first agree and then revoke their *deror*, Jeremiah proclaims a *deror* to war and famine. As 2 Chronicles (36:21) reports, Jeremiah's prophecy was fulfilled: For the times of Shabbat the people did not let the land keep, "the land paid back its Shabbat; as long as it lay desolate it kept Shabbat, till seventy years were fulfilled."

Ezekiel (20:12–24; 22; 23:28) connects desecration of Shabbat with child sacrifice, bribery leading to the condemnation of the innocent, the taking of interest, and the oppression of the poor. These betrayals, and especially the betrayal of Shabbat, brought on the Exile. For Ezekiel, a most powerful image of redemption is that a renewed priesthood will hallow Shabbat in a new way by bringing a new sacrifice that vividly symbolizes the rhythm of workdays and rest: six lambs and a ram.

For 2 Isaiah (58), making Shabbat a delight is intimately intertwined with feeding the poor and freeing the prisoner. How is Shabbat to be made delightful? By halting the pursuit of normal business so as to honor the God who loves the poor.

This passage, later assigned by the rabbis to be read on Yom Kippur— itself the Shabbat Shabbaton—may originally have been spoken by 2 Isaiah on a Yom Kippur. Since each Jubilee was to begin on Yom Kippur, it may even have been a call to make this Shabbat Shabbaton into a still greater and more delightful Shabbat by enacting the Jubilee. Indeed, in chapter 61, Isaiah specifically calls for "the year of YHWH's desire"—a year when the oppressed shall hear good tidings and the captives shall be freed—probably a Jubilee.

Deuteronomy, Leviticus, and the Prophets felt no contradiction between the theme of liberation and justice and the theme of cosmos and creation. Cosmic creation and social re-creation were seen as analogous, even isomorphic. Rest, Shabbat, was seen as the action (or inaction) that expressed both. And Shabbat was closely related to the concepts of *shemitah* and *deror*, "release" and "liberation."

Social Justice Is Rest

What are moderns to make of so tight a connection between the cosmic–natural and the historical–political, two areas of life we usually hold separate? What moderns call "social justice" is, in this biblical outlook, treated as a form of *rest*—as social repose or social renewal. Institutional structures of domination and control are themselves seen as a kind of work.

To *rest* means to return to a state of nature—which is seen as loving. It is when the earth grows peacefully as it wishes, without economic coercion, and the human community grows peacefully in "natural" clans and families, without institutional coercion. In this state of repose, the land and the community are directly in touch with each other—the land freely feeds the people without intervention by owners, masters, employers, or creditors.

This is Shabbat. It re-creates the Shabbat of the beginning, the Shabbat that seals the creation, because at that Shabbat all was free, loving, and in the state of plenitude, sharing, and repose. To act in this way is most fully to honor and imitate the Creator. And indeed for the Creator to act again in this way—as in the Liberation from Egypt and from every slavery—is most fully to repeat the act of creation.

Shabbat comes from its cosmic place to dwell among the people Israel as the first step in redemption of the human race from the curse of endless toil that ends the delight of Eden: "In the sweat of your brow shall you eat bread," say God to Adam. Between Adam and *adamah*, between human and humus, "*all* the days of your life" there shall be agony and conflict (Gen. 3:17–19). But in the moment of liberation from slavery, there rises up from its hidden cosmic place *one* day that will not be toil and agony; *one* day of rest, of Eden. To begin with, only one day—and only for one people. But it is because Shabbat echoes the fullness of Eden that it also beckons us toward the messianic days when *all* days will be fully Shabbat for all peoples.

From this perspective, it is no accident that just as in Eden the war between humans and the Earth is precipitated by an act of *eating*, so in the wilderness the advent of Shabbat comes with an act of eating. For *eating*—in strife or in peace—is the crucial nexus between humans and the Earth.

Mishnah

In the next great crisis of the people Israel—the period of cultural and military conquest by Hellenism and dispersion from the land of Israel— there occurred yet another redefinition of Shabbat. The agrarian Shabbat of the *shemitah* and Jubilee years was diminished in force. The seventh-day Shabbat was made more "portable," and the prohibitions of work were made detailed and urban.

By the time of the codification of the Mishnah (about 200 C.E.), abstentions from work and the definition of "rest" had been greatly broadened. The Mishnah's discussions of the boundaries of permissible work suggest some interesting underlying ideas.

The opening discussion in the Mishnah on Shabbat makes a seemingly odd assertion: that an act considered work if one person did it, and therefore prohibited on Shabbat, is not work if it is begun by one person and completed by another. The underlying thought may be that "work" is the full accomplishment of a willed act by a single willing soul. Perhaps an act that is only initiated or only concluded by a single person is what today we would call "play," and this is permissible on Shabbat.

For six chapters, the Mishnah examines and settles such specifics as whether cloth may be dyed before Shabbat if the colors will continue setting after Shabbat begins. Only in the seventh chapter does the Mishnah turn to more *Shabbosdik* questions of general principle. Among these principles is the statement of the "forty minus one" labors that are forbidden on Shabbat—cast in a near-poetic or liturgical form:

> Main labors: forty minus one.
> Sowing, ploughing, reaping, binding;
> Threshing, winnowing, combing, grinding; . . .
> Here they are—
> Main labors: forty minus one.

Talmud

The Gemara (redacted ca. 500 C.E.) affirms that these "forty minus one" main labors are known from Torah (Babylonian Talmud *Shabbat* 49b), but it is at first not certain why this is so. It concludes that they correspond to the forms of labor necessary to build the traveling shrine or *mishkan* in the wilderness, presumably because the broad commands for resting on Shabbat were included with the command to build the *mishkan* (Exod. 35). God rested from making the cosmos, hence the people rest from making the microcosm (the *mishkan*); they rested from making the microcosm, hence we rest from "remaking" the cosmos. The holiest act of work—even and *especially* the holiest act—is fulfilled only by stopping to recognize and celebrate its completeness.

In addition, the rabbis prohibited other activities (called *shevut*), which include such acts as blowing the shofar or throwing an object from one private domain to another. The rabbis enjoined the people to avoid situations that would make Shabbat violations more likely—handling tools, for example, out of fear that if they are close at hand, someone may forget it is Shabbat and use them.

The rabbis also gave Shabbat a special air of celebration through special meals, the lighting of candles and the drinking of wine at the beginning and at the end of the day, wearing festive clothes, and walking slowly rather than hurrying. Among all Jewish communities, it was understood that the whole community was responsible to make sure that all families had the food, wine, shelter, and companionship to celebrate Shabbat with joy. Through this practice, Shabbat became a time to affirm and act out—for only a moment, and therefore imperfectly—the social equality of all Jews.

Utter Release

This direct experience of Shabbat as a moment of utter release *from* the burdens of work, commerce, and poverty and *into* the realm of song, joy, sharing, prayer, and Torah study—this direct experience lay beneath the rabbis' comment that Shabbat was a foretaste of the Messianic Age. If all Israel kept Shabbat properly just one time (or, said some, twice in a row), the Messianic Age would begin.

These connections between Shabbat and the days of the Messiah—the days that would be *"yom shekulo Shabbat,"* fully Shabbat—are an index to the seriousness with which Jewish tradition has taken Shabbat as a theological category. Shabbat, and only Shabbat, connected the three supernal moments of history: the creation of the world, the revelation of the Torah at Sinai, and the messianic redemption. The entrance of Shabbat into human experience will be fulfilled when the world can fully celebrate Shabbat.

We have sketched three moments of crisis in Jewish history in which there seems to have been some sense of reformulation of Shabbat. We now seem ot be in another such crisis moment. We live in generations that are struggling to reformulate Judaism under the pressure of modernity.

Fromm

In these circumstances, such thinkers as Erich Fromm[2] and Abraham Joshua Heschel[3] have again reformulated Shabbat. In an era of technological triumph, writing in the immediate aftermath of the Nazi Holocaust and the first use of nuclear weapons, they see Shabbat as an affirmation of values beyond technology. Says Fromm, *"Work" is any interference by man, be it constructive or destructive, with the physical world. "Rest" is a state of peace between man and nature.*[4] In this way, Fromm interprets the seemingly obsessive rabbinic prohibitions of even the lightest, least effortful changes of the ownership or place of objects in the world. Shabbat becomes for him an actual (though brief) transformation of the human path into a real experience of messianic harmony and peace.

Heschel

For Heschel, Shabbat is an affirmation that holiness is borne more by the flow and rhythm of time than by objects in space. He, too, sees Shabbat as a challenge to "technical civilization," obsessed with the conquest of space and the improvement of objects:

> To set apart one day a week for freedom, a day on which we would not use the instruments which have been so easily turned into weapons of destruction, a day of detachment from the vulgar, of in-dependence of external obligations, a day on which we stop wor-shiping the idols of technical civilization, a day on which we use no money, a day of armistice in the economic struggle with our fellow men and the forces of nature—is there any institution that holds out a greater hope for man's progress than the Sabbath?[5]

It is notable that both Fromm and Heschel suggest that the practice of Shabbat, in some form, may be of profound importance to the whole human race—not to the Jewish people alone—in redeeming the world from the threat of untrammeled technology.

The current crisis of modernity and technology may be connected with another crisis, the remaking of relationships between women and men. And the connection may extend into the world of Shabbat. The tradi-tional forms of practice of Shabbat face new questions in light of the full participation by women in all aspects of Jewish life. The traditional prac-tice of Shabbat neither required nor encouraged women who were doing the "work" of nurturing a family and raising children to "rest" from that work. Rather, traditional Judaism saw precisely such nurturance and com-munion as "rest," rather than work. While Shabbat freed men to do this resting, it did not free women.

Under the new conditions of relationship between women and men, the full celebration of Shabbat may require that on that day there be even a fuller sharing of nurturance and community, even a more conscious shattering of separate roles of women and men. As Shabbat entered the conscious practice of the people Israel as a first step in reversing the curse upon Adam that he must toil in the sweat of his brow to wrest bread from the hostile earth, so it may also become a first step in reversing the curse upon Eve: that she must be ruled over by her husband and must suffer child-bearing as painful labor.

From these complementary "postmodern" perspectives, there might emerge a reexamination not only of the Shabbat of the seventh day, but of the Shabbat of the seventh year and fiftieth year. For the human species as a whole, can "the land" be seen as "the Earth"? What would be the implications of pausing every seventh year from technological research and development to reevaluate its meaning and direction? What would it mean to proclaim a "shabbat" upon the development of new weapons?

The advent of such questions within the Jewish community may signal another moment in the reformulation of Shabbat. If the Deuteronomic period saw the theme of social justice and liberation as an unfolding of the "cosmos" theme of Shabbat, we may see ourselves as taking the process of unfolding another spiral turn. We are moving from concerns over human justice and liberation toward reaffirming the creation and pausing from "production" in order to preserve the creation itself (and with it, human freedom and justice).

At the end of an epoch in which the human race gained enormous knowledge and great mastery, Shabbat remains the emblem and practice of mystery. If we do not know what to do next, instead of trying to conquer our ignorance, we may more fruitfully—and truthfully—celebrate Shabbat as our way of making known that we do *not* know: that there is in the world not merely ignorance, but mystery.

NOTES

1. Jeremiah's criticism was probably directed at the commerce, not at riding a horse or donkey on Shabbat. In 2 Kings 4:23, we have evidence that in Elisha's day, about 250 years before, it was normal to ride a donkey on Shabbat in order to visit a "man of God."

2. *The Forgotten Language,* 241 ff. *You Shall Be as Gods,* 152–57.

3. *The Sabbath.*

4. *You Shall Be as Gods,* 154. Italics in original.

5. *The Sabbath,* 28.

Thinking Shabbat

LAWRENCE KUSHNER

A nd God saw all that God had made and behold it was very good . . . *Va-yeculu ha-shamayim v'ha-aretz.* The heaven and the earth were finished . . ." (Gen. 1:31–2:1).

At last the world-work was done and it was good. It was very good. A beautiful place. But being done and very good are not the same as perfect.

God had decided, you see, as a final creative act to make men and women. And we are not perfect. We are the unstable element, the restless ones. Too hungry for our own good, covetous, oversexed, neurotic, and conflicted. But we are part of creation, so therefore, on account of us, creation is incomplete, unstable, and imperfect.

"And on the seventh day God rested, *Va-yinafash*" (Exod. 31:17), which Arthur Waskow translates not as "and was refreshed" but as "and God said, 'Whew!'" Now if God can do something as imperfect as setting you and me up in business in the world–garden and then rest, surely we can be excused from our six-day-a-week compulsive fantasies of perfection and rest as well. To help, I offer three metaphors which I have found useful in my attempts to reclaim Shabbat. The first begins on Passover.

My grandfather, *alav ha-shalom,* a German Reform Jew, used to make Pesach as follows. We would religiously remove leaven or *hometz* (which we defined as bread and cereal) from our home and stash it in an off-limits cupboard. Though we were conscientious, we were also human and oversights did occur. I remember once, a few days into Passover, how we found a box of "The Breakfast of Champions" that one of us boys, months earlier, must have taken to an unlikely place and forgotten about.

"Look, Grandpa, some *hometz* we missed. What should we do?" "What *hometz?*" he said, staring right at the cereal box. "This one here," I said. "I don't see it," he replied. And I understood.

You do the very best you can. But when the deadline comes, whether or not you are done, you announce that you are done. Traditional Passover Haggadot still preserve this strange yet indispensable proclamation of freedom from compulsion by concluding the search for leaven before Seder with the Aramaic formula, "*Kol hamira,* all leaven in my possession, whether or not I have seen it, disposed of it, or know about it—doesn't exist. It is ownerless property, *k'afra d'ara,* like dust of the earth."

Work is to Shabbat like *hometz* is to Pesach. Come twilight on Friday afternoon I announce: All my jobs, tasks, and work, whether they are done or not, I hereby declare are done. I reject their claim on me. I deny their existence. We recite the first paragraph of the second chapter of Genesis, just before we make Kiddush at home. It begins: "*Va-yeculu,* the heaven and the earth were finished . . ." which tractate *Shabbat* (119b) deliberately mistranslates not as the passive "*Va-yeculu* and they [the heaven and the earth] were finished" but in the active voice "*Va-yecalu* and they [God and humanity] finished." Partners in creation. Partners also in saying, "We finished."

Heschel taught us that the Sabbath is a sanctuary in time, and I would suggest that the reason, at least in part, is because ordinary time has come to an end. Life goes on but without the clocks. For not only have we closed the books on the past week, we don't care about next week either. On Shabbat there can be no future; only an eternal present. And that is the second point.

Without a future, everything we do and the reasons for everything we do can only be here and now. If the world-work is at last done, then you cannot do anything toward making it better later because there is no later. Shabbat is a daylong spiritual fiction by which we are permitted to stop planning, preparing, investing, conniving, evaluating, fixing, manipulating, arranging, staging, and all the other things we do, not for the sake of doing them, but with an ulterior motive for the sake of some future accomplishment.

Most of us can forget the past and its imperfections with some practice, but to cut ourselves loose from planning and evaluating and fixing things for the future is unimaginable. We rest so we can go back to work.

We play so that we can go back to work. We love so that we can go back to work. One ulterior motive after another. Living in the future.

We are either tied through our uncompleted tasks to the past or compulsively drawn through our need to complete them into the future. We stubbornly convince ourselves that all we need to find tranquility is to haul a little bit of past into the present or take just a little bit of the present and arrange it for the future. On Shabbat we do not have to go anywhere. We are already there.

We need a way to describe liberal Jews who are serious about Shabbat. *Shomer* Shabbat, Keeper of Shabbat, based as it is on the language of the actual commandment in Deuteronomy, could be ideal. Unfortunately it has been appropriated and defined, meticulously and oppressively, by someone else. So we return to the text of the Fourth Commandment and realize that it is said twice, once in Deuteronomy and again in Exodus. In Deuteronomy (5:11) we are told "*Shamor,*" keep the Sabbath. But in Exodus (2:7) the verb is different; we are told "*Zachor,*" remember the Sabbath. Perhaps it is for us to create a new standard of Shabbat behavior called "*Zachor* Shabbat." One who is "*Zocher* Shabbat" would remember throughout the day's duration that it was Shabbat. (Not so easy as it first sounds.) We say to one another, Do anything you want—as long as you will remember it is Shabbat, and that will insure that whatever you do will be *lichvod ha-Shabbat,* for the honor of Shabbat.

The Serenity of the Shabbat Walk

AMY EILBERG

As some of you know, this past month has marked a significant change in my Jewish life. Through a series of rather unpleasant circumstances, my family needed to leave the home which we had rented at a comfortable walking distance from the shul. It emerged that there was no reasonable housing that met our needs within walking distance of Har Zion. I was keenly aware that it had been eighteen years since I had made the commitment not to drive on Shabbat. However, at this point in my life, it became clear that, at least temporarily, I would choose a home for my family that would require me to ride to shul on Shabbat.

Some of you, kindly, have asked what it has been like for me, these first weeks of using a car on Shabbat, if only for the limited purpose of coming to and from Shabbat services. I can best answer this way. The first Friday night in our new house, I kissed my daughter and husband goodbye, heading for shul, and closed the door behind me before I realized that I had left the house without my keys! Change is always difficult.

Now that I have had some weeks to adapt to the change, I find myself reflecting on it somewhat differently than that first, very strange Shabbat that I found myself in the car. I still sense the strangeness of it for me. I still fantasize about being stopped, for some reason, by a police officer on my way to shul, and trying to get him to understand why I don't have my license and registration: "You see, officer, today is my Sabbath, and I don't involve myself with the world of commerce, and so I don't carry my wallet . . ." I still occasionally review the process by which I concluded that, despite my commitment to halacha, my commitment to my family in this case made the move to Ardmore imperative and justified.

But now a new set of questions has emerged. They are questions that are new to me in terms of the particulars of driving, but they are shared by every Jew who cares about sanctifying a day in the midst of the rush of contemporary life. Now that I use a car to get to shul on Shabbat, one more distinction between Shabbat and weekdays has fallen away. Now, how do I make sure to keep Shabbat special? How do I avoid more atrophy, more slippage, more loss of my personal commitment to keep one day out of seven separate, sanctified, immune to the pressures and concerns of the week? How do I take advantage of technology on the one hand, and at the same time celebrate Shabbat as the day of distancing from the world-conquering, world-manipulating mode of the work week? How do I turn the ignition key, drive past the Shop 'N Bag, become annoyed at the inconsiderate driver ahead of me, and still maintain Shabbat as a day of holiness, of appreciation for the God-given wonders in my life, of protected time for my family and for my own spiritual aspirations? How do I be sure not to lose what has been so precious to me over the years: the certainty that one day will be sacred, set aside, inviolate in the midst of a life that constantly intrudes on the need for quiet, for shared time, for personal peace?

These questions are new for me in terms of my use of my car on Shabbat. And then again, they are the questions with which all of us must wrestle, in our own way, in our time—questions about how we make Shabbat holy and real in our life and the lives of our families. It is the question of how I personalize Judaism's imperatives, how I make the most of my tradition's wisdom about a day of rest, how I integrate that wisdom into my life in a way that is both true to tradition and enriching for my life.

Perhaps it was meant to be that I would need to make the decision to experiment with driving on Shabbat. Perhaps I needed this change to shake me out of my lethargy, to force me to reconsider issues that had been dormant in me for too long. Perhaps it was time that I gave Shabbat another look, to make sure that I was making the most of its gift, learning everything that I could from it, and reaping the benefit of its promise of peace and sanctity.

Reclaiming Shabbat

ARNOLD JACOB WOLF

Reform Jews of an earlier generation were more disciplined than is commonly believed. My grandmother, for example, a characteristic Reform Jew of the turn of the century, never sewed, marketed, or did housework on Saturday. Her family went to services every week on Friday night or sometimes on Shabbat morning. Reform Jews had a real halachic standard in those days: they obeyed what they believed to be God's will.

That Halachah, to be sure, was not identical with the *Shulchan Aruch,* a code followed by many Orthodox Jews. And my family did not routinely ask ritual questions of their rabbis, though during periods of mourning or crisis they might have asked *she'elot* of a traditional kind. The Reform body of law was much smaller than the traditional one and was based much more on what was thought to be biblical rather than rabbinic. My grandmother, for example, did not obey the late rabbinic strictures against listening to the radio and riding in a car on Shabbat. I'm sure she never even heard of them and wouldn't have believed anyone who told her such activities were forbidden. Her tradition was the tradition. Any Jew less observant was too lax, anyone more observant was a fanatic.

Not Ritual Anarchists

The old Reform law was strict about ethical matters: business dealings, marital loyalty, telling a lie. But it was also very concerned with certain so-called ritual matters: matzah on Pesach, fasting on Yom Kippur, doing something regular on Shabbat, even reciting the Motzi before meals. It is just not true that Reform Jews were ritual anarchists or ethical free-thinkers. Their duties, though fewer than those of the Orthodox, were upheld as matters of life and death for Judaism.

In recent decades, Reform has vastly increased the scope of its religious practice. Fifty years ago, Reform Jews knew nothing about Havdalah and little about *kashrut*. Today the list of Jewish options is much larger, and that can only be seen as a gain for Reform. How, otherwise, could we know what we personally should or should not do?

But there is also a loss. What was once (at least for some Reform Jews) a small but strict code has become a wide array of acceptable alternatives. The new freedom and the range are impressive, but we have lost something crucial in the area of discipline. I am reminded of the *New Yorker* cartoon about a progressive school where one of the youngsters asks plaintively: "Teacher, do we have to do what we want to do?" Judaism is, I believe, not just choice; it is also duty. Judaism is not ceremonial, free-floating, subjective. It is law and obligation, and it is objectively binding. Shabbat is not our own invention, but one of the Ten Commandments; it is not a nice idea, but what God wants us to do.

God-given Duty

Can Reform Jews once again accept Shabbat as a God-given duty? Well, some of them used to and they didn't think doing so abridged their freedom to be themselves. Shabbat was, perhaps, not well served by a Friday-night service with its center in a long, theoretical sermon. We have now moved toward Shabbat dinners, music, sharing, and communal study of sacred texts. These are much better ways to observe the Sabbath, but they are not yet Halachah. To them I would add not smoking, not driving an automobile except to services, not reading our mail, and, perhaps, not answering the telephone. In these matters, Halachah merges with deep psychological needs: In order to find ourselves in a technological world, we must abandon some technology and rediscover our premodern selves. We must choose to be commanded again, remembering that God, not human desire, is at the center of Shabbat.

Jewish Work and Rest

The "work" that is forbidden by Jewish law on the Sabbath is not measured in the expenditure of energy. It takes real effort to pray, to study, to walk to synagogue. They are "rest" but not restful. Forbidden "work" is acquisition, aggrandizement, altering the world. On Shabbat we are obliged to be, to reflect, to love and make love, to eat, to enjoy. We may not be able to observe all the commandments connected with Shabbat (I, for one, can't), but we are not free wholly to abstain.

The Sabbath as Theology

We Reform Jews must learn much more about the Sabbath as theology and as law.

Nothing Jewish is irrelevant or impossible in advance. When we learn more, we may learn about a Shabbat that is both harder and easier than the one we have. It is not in Heaven; it is not beyond the sea. Shabbat is in our mouths and in our hearts. It is part of the divine agenda but also wholly human and humane. Shabbat is a taste of eternity. Without Shabbat we may be lost. In its rediscovery we may yet be found.

The Sabbath as Protest

W. GUNTHER PLAUT

Rest from Unrest

I
f the Sabbath is to have any significance it must confront one of modern man's greatest curses, his internal and external unrest. This unrest arises from the fact that today he leads a life without goals and, as a consequence, that he is involved in competition without end.

Life without goals

Formerly, both the physical and spiritual goals of man were clear. He needed to survive physically and do everything and anything that would help him achieve this goal. He tried to survive in nature's as well as in society's jungle. He had to fight the devils of sickness and starvation and whatever else was his lot. If only he could survive he had achieved life's major physical goal. Spiritually, the matter was even simpler. With Jew, Christian, and Mohammedan, living the good life or the life of faith was sure to bring some form of salvation: Paradise, Heaven, or Life in the presence of God. It was happiness postponed, but as a goal it remained quite clear.

In today's Western society, purely physical survival is no longer the clearly defined physical goal (although for a good portion of mankind it still is, and therefore their Sabbath needs would be entirely different from ours). For us, to keep from starvation is no longer the problem. Rather, if I may so put it, the problem is that we no longer know what the problem is. We no longer know what life's physical goal might be or even if there is one altogether. Further, except for those who truly believe in salvation in the old sense, few men are sure what life's spiritual goals are. So they talk of happiness or use similar empty phrases to cover their aimlessness.

I often ask young people who come to me to discuss their marriage plans just what their goals are. The two outstanding answers are "happiness" and "security" (the latter is the preferred answer of women). But when I press my visitors further and ask what they mean and how they aim to achieve these goals, they become very vague. The fact is that, like their parents, they have no clear goals, a lack of which from the outset is a built-in cause of marital unrest.

Added to the general conundrum is the ever-increasing infantilization of our culture. The child wants his satisfactions now and not later. The "now" dimension has become the overriding aspect of our youth culture and has increased their sense of unrest (which in turn affects their elders), because the moment now is experienced another now is at hand. Thus now becomes never, and never is the feeding place of restlessness.

I therefore view the Sabbath as potentially an enormous relief from, and a protest against, these basic causes of unrest. Once a week it provides us with an opportunity to address ourselves to the who-ness rather than the what-ness of life, to persons rather than things, to creation and our part in it, to society and its needs, to ourselves as individuals and yet as social beings. That is what Pieper called "the inner source of leisure," the setting of goals which are both realistic and within one's reach, yet also beyond one's self.

I rarely find a better place for such redirection than a religious service, whose major function ought to be not just the repetition of well-worn formulae but the celebration of human goals, setting them within the context of creation. If nothing happens to us during this or any Sabbath experience except an enlarging of our vision, we will have gained a new perspective of life's meaning and will have diminished our sense of unrest. That will be Sabbath rest, in the sense required by our time.

Competition without end

Endless competition is a specific form of goallessness. Formerly there was probably not as much economic competition as there is today, but however much there was had a clearly defined objective. For most people it was to gain a livelihood. In today's Western civilization, that is simply no longer enough.

Nowadays, everything is competitive, but the end is never quite defined. Our culture asks us to acquire and acquire ever more, but we are never told when we will have enough. Women are urged to beautify themselves, for the sake not only of other women but also of other men, but are never told to what end such competition is entered into.

I view the Sabbath as a surcease from and a protest against all forms of competition, even when they come in attractive packages marked "self-advancement" or "self-improvement." I view the Sabbath in this respect as a "useless" day. Our forefathers had a keen understanding of the fact that sleep on the Sabbath day was a form of coming closer to God. We must once again understand that doing nothing, being silent and open to the world, letting things happen inside can be as important as, and sometimes more important than, what we commonly call the useful.

I am often asked why we have more than the necessary number of Torah scrolls in the synagogue. Actually, only one single scroll is needed; two and on rare occasions three are useful in the sense that when various passages are required to be read at the same service the congregation need not wait until the single scroll is rolled back and forth. But many congregations have ten, fifteen, twenty, or even more scrolls in the Ark (more than they can possibly use) and these scrolls are considered the prize possessions of the synagogue. That to me is a marvelous example that the House of God is essentially not useful. Besides, it does stand empty a great deal of the week, its facilities are not always used, nor are the activities that take place there useful in the ordinary sense.

Formerly, a person who did not work was considered useless; what we need now is a *purposive uselessness,* an activity (or nonactivity!) which is important in that it becomes an essential protest against that basic unrest which comes from competition without end.

In the Jewish context I would therefore suggest that on the Sabbath one ought to abstain from everything which on one level or another is considered usefully competitive. For instance, going to the hairdresser's on the Sabbath is in my view a form of sexual or social competition and ought to be left to other days. Equally, going to classes at night to advance oneself usefully would fall into the same category of Sabbath prohibition. Let there be some special time during the week when we do for the sake of doing, when we love the trivial and in fact simply love, when we do for others rather than for ourselves and thus provide a counterbalance for the weight of endless competition that burdens our every day.

The Sanctification of Freedom

The Sabbath gives us a quantity of free time and thereby a quality potential of freedom time, when a man can be himself and in some area do for himself and for others what in the workaday world he cannot. Such Sabbath observance is a sanctification of freedom.

Part of the hopelessness of our age is our sense of imprisonment. This comes not merely from the increasing complexity of society and our experience of marginality, but from the ever- growing importance of machines and the advance of automation. Everyone can add to the stories that illustrate this experience. For example, this exclamation by an adult: "See that beautiful flower! It looks as perfect as if it were artificial!" Or the marvel of a child who upon seeing a pianist says: "Look, Daddy, he is playing with his own hands!" Automation not only removes men further and further from their work, but also from the opportunity of making decisions. And a man who makes no decisions is ultimately a man who is bereft of a basic freedom.

It is for this reason that, on the whole, spectator sports and other spectacles which now fill much of men's free time too often represent missed opportunities. True, when we sit and watch we may celebrate the uselessness of the day. But is this the only way to escape the time machine, or can we put something else in its place? There ought to be occasions when free time becomes sanctified freedom time.

In contemplating these matters, I have come to wonder why baseball, formerly America's favorite spectator sport, has lately fallen from grace. Is it because it is too slow for today's taste? Perhaps, but there may be another, subtler reason. Over the decades the record book has become such a major factor in the game that it has begun to overwhelm spectator and player alike. What a man does is at once measured against the performances of the book; his own individual effort in the framework of the game is frequently dwarfed by the record of the ages. And somehow, somewhere, deep down in the public's mind there may be some doubt that their own needs of escaping from the machine and its pressures are sufficiently served by this constant recourse to statistics.

It is perhaps this very fact which attracts so many to the game of golf, both in the doing and in the watching. For here a man competes ultimately not for the money (that is reserved to the few professionals) and not even primarily against others, but essentially against himself and his own potential. Thereby he opens up a measure of freedom which may give him some relief of the soul—despite the ulcers and other frustrations which the game may otherwise produce. (Of course, I am not unaware that people might come to any game or program "with many different attitudes and approaches. And what might look like the same activity because it has a similar format might have an entirely different value with respect to whether the person is increasing his or her personal freedom through the experience.")[1]

The words "sanctification of freedom" imply yet another dimension. It has to do with that hope which attempts to make possible what is apparently impossible. There is a special kind of freedom which enables us to strive for the perfection of the essentially imperfect and thereby to enter the dimension of the Divine into a segment of human time. Abraham J. Heschel speaks of Judaism as

> a religion of time aiming at a sanctification of time. Unlike the spaceminded man whose time is unvaried, iterative, homogeneous, to whom all hours are alike, qualityless, empty shells, the Bible senses the diversified character of time. There are no two hours alike. Every hour is unique and the only one given at the moment, exclusive and endlessly precious. Judaism teaches us to be attached to holiness and time; to be attached to sacred events, to learn how to consecrate sanctuaries and emerge from the magnificent stream of the year. The Sabbaths are our great cathedrals. . . . Jewish ritual may be characterized as the art of significant form in time, as architecture of time.[2]

To the religious person God is the source of holiness, and the Sabbath therefore a truly sanctified segment of hope which lights up the dark horizon of pessimism. It is not only useless time, but nonrational time, for in the final analysis hope like faith is nonrational (to be distinguished from irrational).

A fascinating number of parallels suggest themselves, especially from the world of psychology.

The English psychologist R. D. Laing, for instance, has suggested that man's true liberation might have to come from a temporary retreat into schizophrenia. That is to say, with the world being what it is, one must experience unreality in order to both understand and master reality. In order to be oneself one must, so to speak, learn to get outside oneself. In his book *The Divided Self,*[3] Laing suggests a retreat into simulated insanity as the extreme means of liberation, to propel us out of the box in which we are imprisoned. I am in no position to comment on these latest theories, but it occurs to me that since ancient times religious people have often been closely linked to what were considered the crazy and the insane—only we used more pleasing words such as vision and mystic trance for otherwise dubious experiences.

However, we do not have to go to extremes of religious apprehension to understand that the religious man who escapes from the machine does indeed escape from the normal. The man who attains freedom on any level in our day is, in effect, abnormal when measured against the normalcy of automation. Because it encourages this kind of nonrational escape, the Sabbath may therefore be described as an opportunity for "religious schizophrenia," a pious *meshuggas* which R. D. Laing would find a source of real hope. I use this terminology only to indicate again how closely the concerns of religion may be related to those of psychology and how closely the prescriptions resemble one another.

In pursuing yet another avenue of psychological inquiry, one can consider all religious ritual a kind of sacred play or game, a retreat into the "as-ifness" of our soul. Johann Huizinga describes three qualities which religion and play have in common: both strive seriously for perfection; both have specially assigned spaces with their own rules and sanctions; and both religion and play rely on symbols, pageantry, vestments, and special languages.

Both religion and play, we might add, are important retreats from the realness of the machine and the pressure of the everyday, and are on their level avenues of hope—whatever that hope may be: either to win a game, or to score, or perchance to win salvation. To put it yet in a different way, prayer may be regarded as a form of sacred recreation—and saying this does not demean either prayer or recreation. Frequently, study belongs to the same category. Judaism has always encouraged study in every form and on every level. Study for its own sake and not for the sake of self-advancement is basically an exercise in "as-ifness," a sacred kind of game where thought takes wings and imagination replaces automation.

For where hope exists, decision exists; and where decision exists, there is freedom. And freedom comes in many packages. It comes alone or in groups, it comes in effort and doing, or it comes in openness and in silence. It comes in retreat from men as protest against the oppression of man and machine. It may fill a day or only a portion of it. However much or little, it is a precious time to sanctify freedom. And for him who knows this day to be beloved of God, it is indeed a very special day with special opportunities. To celebrate it, let a man do those things which liberate him from the ordinary and give him areas of free decision, of doing for himself and for others those things he wills to do rather than those which he must do; where he indulges in recreation both sacred and other which will help him to escape from the oppression of our civilization.

The Protest

I titled this essay "The Sabbath as Protest"—but it is not only the Sabbath which does the protesting; it is also that which it represents, namely, the religious venture of man. For religion itself at its best is a protest. It is the unusual that denies the ordinary; it is standing still and sitting down; it is doing something and nothing; it is hoping and being. The Sabbath can be the paradigm of this understanding of the religious quest.

Two French psychologists, André Virel and Roger Frétigny, talk about four states of human consciousness: imaginative, active, reflexive, and contemplative.⁴ The two middle states (activity and reflexive response) characterize our automated society; the two other (imagination and contemplation) are the redeeming features which make life livable. These are the qualities to which the Sabbath addresses itself, for imagination is a form of freedom, and contemplation is rest from unrest.

I have spoken from the vantage point of a Jew, but the problems and the opportunities are not Judaism's alone. Every man, and not just a Jew, needs rest from unrest, needs surcease from goallessness and endless competition, and in the face of automation needs to sanctify his free time as freedom time. In the process, work and leisure will have to get themselves new vestments so that the increasing quantities of free time which society will have in the years to come may become true freedom time for many—until that day when the protest will no longer be necessary and when the Sabbath will have become the antechamber to the Messianic Era. Until then, I fear, it will have to be a protest against what is, and a celebration of what may yet come to be.

NOTES

1. Kenneth Benne, *Conference on the New Leisure*, pt. 2, 74.
2. *Man Is Not Alone* (Philadelphia: Jewish Publication Society, 1951), 28–29.
3. R. D. Laing, *The Divided Self* (New York: Pantheon, 1970).
4. *Imagerie Mentale* (Paris, 1968).

The Sabbath:
Mystery against History

ALICIA SUSKIN OSTRIKER

Remember the Sabbath day, to keep it holy. (Exod. 20:8)

The mystery of the Sabbath . . . that unites itself through the mystery of the One . . . And as they unite above, so also do they unite below in the mystery of oneness.

(*Zohar*)

And besides, there is the Sabbath. And besides, there is the ladder God lets down from the aperture of heaven. Lets it cascade down, pulls it up, lets it down. And besides, there is the Sabbath. How could it be forgotten? Bliss, then. A stab in the ticking of the celestial mattress, a puncture so that the softest of down feathers keeps pouring out. And light keeps pouring out, from the wound of time, which heals at sunset but opens six days later, pours out like blood but isn't blood. Because God rested, we are permitted to escape time and to rest peacefully together in the shower of eternity. As above, so below. We, and our families, and our animals, and everyone who works, and the strangers among us. And the further we scatter ourselves, the more this peaceful concentrated light pours everywhere, among the nations. We catch it in the bowls of our hands. Bliss, then. It flies into the candles. It swims in glasses of wine. We chew it in bread. We bless everything.

And besides, there is the Sabbath. It ripples from Sinai, through space and time, until this very evening.

A Creative
Havdalah Service

WOMAN'S INSTITUTE FOR

CONTINUING JEWISH EDUCATION

*A*t the end of Shabbat we gather together once more to make Havdalah, the ceremony that separates the Shabbat we have just observed from the week we will soon begin.

The candle is lit and given to the youngest person present. Lights are off.

Reader: Behold, before us, around us, and within us shines the glorious Light of Shabbat joy.

All: With a flame we ushered in Shabbat, and we hope that this reflection of her glory will entice her to linger a moment longer with us.

Reader: At the beginning of this day we hurried to meet the Shabbat bride; our souls were full of yearning and our hearts were beating with expectancy.

All: Our yearning has been fulfilled with Shabbat love and our beating hearts calmed with Shabbat peace.

Reader: We were weary from a week of dealing with the day-to-day cares of earning a living and keeping a home.

All: We have found refuge from the worldly concerns of commerce and the mundane affairs of the house.

Reader: We have invested the hours of Shabbat well: in study of Torah, in peaceful contemplation of our blessings, and in loving contact with our family and friends.

All: Together we have had a glimpse of that heavenly time which is called *yom shekulo Shabbat*, a time that is all Shabbat.

Reader: Blessed is the Giver of peace, with peace shall the world be delivered.

All: Blessed are all who strive for peace, may their dreams soon be fulfilled.

Reader: Blessed is the Name to whom I call in my fear. You are my Strength and my Safety.

All: Blessed are all who stand guard against fear, may they soon find relief from their burden.

Reader: Blessed is the Source of all life, the Well-spring of all mercy.

All: Blessed are all mothers and fathers, and blessed are the children.

Reader raises the wine cup.

Reader: This is the wine of joy, fruit of the vine, gift of the Munificent One, who smiled upon our mothers as they hurried to their wells at the end of Havdalah. Our mothers believed that if they were swift enough, they might draw up water which still held a lingering Shabbat blessing.

On a festival day add:

And with this cup we joyfully thank You, who provides reason for joy, for the gift of this *yom tov*. May the special blessings of this_____spill over into the coming week and increase its goodness.

בָּרוּךְ אַתָּה, יְיָ אֱלֹהֵינוּ, מֶלֶךְ הָעוֹלָם, בּוֹרֵא פְּרִי הַגָּפֶן.

All: *Baruch Ata, Adonai Eloheinu, melech haolam, borei peri hagafen.*

Blessed are You, Eternal our God, Sovereign of the Universe, Creator of the fruit of the vine.

The wine is passed. The reader raises the spice box.

Reader: Comes the Bride, and her smell is sweet. We open our nostrils to her fragrance because the Torah says, "Then the Sovereign God formed man of the dust of the ground, and breathed into his nostrils the breath of life; and man became a living soul" (Gen. 2:7).

So it is during Shabbat that we draw a breath of life, gain a day of regrowth, and at the end of Shabbat we breathe one last breath of the scent of her passing.

בָּרוּךְ אַתָּה, יְיָ אֱלֹהֵינוּ, מֶלֶךְ הָעוֹלָם, בּוֹרֵא מִינֵי בְשָׂמִים.

All: *Baruch Ata, Adonai Eloheinu, melech haolam, borei minei besamim.*

Blessed are You, Eternal our God, Sovereign of the Universe, Creator of all the kinds of spices.

The spice box is passed. The candle is raised.

Reader: This is the light which the Creator gave to the universe, "To rule over the day and over the night, and to divide the light from the darkness," so that the children of Eve need not fear the darkness (Gen. 1:18). With this light we divide Shabbat from the rest of the week, and by its light we face the week without fear. It is for this reason that we reach out to the light, and we see within our grasp both the light and the darkness. Where the light divides the darkness is Havdalah.

בָּרוּךְ אַתָּה, יְיָ אֱלֹהֵינוּ, מֶלֶךְ הָעוֹלָם, בּוֹרֵא מְאוֹרֵי הָאֵשׁ.

All: *Baruch Ata, Adonai Eloheinu, melech haolam, borei meorei haeish.*

Blessed are You, Eternal God, Sovereign of the Universe, Creator of the light of fire.

Reader: The Torah says, "So that you will know that I am God in the center of the world . . . I will make a division between My people and thy people" (Exod. 8:18, 19). When we divide ourselves from the ungodly, we make Havdalah.

All: When we choose to do the will of the Lawgiver, we make Havdalah.

Reader: When we divide our days into work and rest, rather than sloth and waste, we make Havdalah.

All: When we choose honor and duty, we make Havdalah.

Reader: When we divide our words from vanities, we make Havdalah.

All: When we choose to fill our ears with the words of Justice, we make Havdalah.

Reader: May it please the *Shechinah*, Giver of all wisdom, to show us the division between the holy and the profane. We pray that the Merciful One will lead us to choose that which is good, righteous, and holy.

בָּרוּךְ אַתָּה, יְיָ אֱלֹהֵינוּ, מֶלֶךְ הָעוֹלָם, הַמַּבְדִּיל בֵּין קֹדֶשׁ לְחוֹל, בֵּין אוֹר לְחֹשֶׁךְ, בֵּין יוֹם הַשְּׁבִיעִי לְשֵׁשֶׁת יְמֵי הַמַּעֲשֶׂה.

All: *Baruch Ata, Adonai Eloheinu, melech haolam, hamavdil bein kodesh lechol, bein or lechoshech, bein yom hashevii lesheishet yemei hamaaseh.*

Blessed are You, Eternal our God, Sovereign of the Universe, who separates sacred from profane, light from darkness, the seventh day of rest from the six days of labor.

בָּרוּךְ אַתָּה יְיָ, הַמַּבְדִּיל בֵּין קֹדֶשׁ לְחוֹל.

Baruch Ata, Adonai Eloheinu, hamavdil bein kodesh lechol.

Blessed are You, Eternal our God, who separates the sacred from the profane.

The candle is extinguished. Lights are turned on.

Reader: The light of Shabbat is gone. We have divided Shabbat from us for another week, yet even as we look longingly back at the day ended, so do we look forward to the joys and pleasures of the week to come. We know that this week will culminate in Shabbat, and that a day will come when we kindle the light of the Shabbat for which there is no Havdalah.

Suggestions for
Further Reading

1. General Reading on Shabbat

Arzt, Max. *Joy and Remembrance: Commentary on the Sabbath Eve Liturgy.* Bridgeport, CT: Hartmore House, 1979. The late Rabbi Max Arzt was one of America's most beloved rabbis. After serving for many years on the pulpit, he became vice chancellor of the Jewish Theological Seminary. While there he published his first book on Jewish liturgy, *Justice and Mercy,* on the *Machzor* (High Holy Day prayer book). *Joy and Remembrance* was published posthumously from his notes, offering readers commentaries on, talmudic sources about, and personal, devotional interpretations of many of the prayers from the Friday-night service.

Dresner, Samuel H. *The Sabbath.* New York: United Synagogue Book Service/Burning Bush Press, 1970. This ninety-four-page handbook written for lay people is an excellent introduction to the entire concept of Shabbat.

Ginsburg, Elliot K. *The Sabbath in the Classical Kabbalah.* Albany: SUNY Press, 1989. This volume is a critical study of the mystical celebration of Shabbat in the classical period of the Kabbalah, from the late twelfth to the early sixteenth centuries.

_____. *Sod Ha-Shabbat: The Mystery of the Sabbath.* Albany: SUNY Press, 1989. A companion volume to *The Sabbath in the Classical Kabbalah,* this important text is a focused, systematic study of the mystical view of Shabbat prior to the Safed Renaissance.

Goldman, Solomon. *A Guide to the Sabbath.* London: Jewish Chronicle Publications, 1961. This small book, written by a British rabbi, is part of the six-volume set on the holidays published by *The Jewish Chronicle.* It contains ten short, scholarly yet popular chapters on Shabbat as a precious gift, as a day of holiness, as a day of humor and delight, and as a day of rest. There are also chapters on Shabbat in rabbinic Judaism, in the home, and in the synagogue. Problems of Shabbat observance are also covered. The last chapter is called "A Foretaste of Redemption." Brief but excellent.

Greenberg, Irving. *The Jewish Way: Living the Holidays.* New York: Summit Books, 1988. This superb book contains chapters on all Jewish holy days.

Chapter 5 is called "The Dream and How to Live It: Shabbat."

Greenberg, Sidney. *A Treasury of Shabbat Inspiration.* New York: United Synagogue of Conservative Judaism: Commission on Jewish Education, 1995. A very useful anthology of brief quotations about Shabbat presented by topic. Authors include A. J. Heschel, Leo Baeck, Harry Golden, David Hartman, Neil Gillman, and Hannah Senesh.

Grunfeld, Dayan I. *The Sabbath.* New York: Feldheim, 1960. A short book by one of England's leading Orthodox scholars. Good compilation of Orthodox law and philosophy on the subject of Shabbat.

Heschel, Abraham Joshua. *The Sabbath.* (1951) New York: Farrar, Straus & Giroux, 1996. A short, poetic account of what Shabbat meant to the pious Jews of Eastern Europe before the *Shoah.* Much significant material and ideas for modern Jews—especially the hasidic tales and the notion of Shabbat as a "palace in time."

Kaplan, Aryeh. *Sabbath: Day of Eternity.* New York: National Council of Synagogue Youth, 1982. The late Rabbi Aryeh Kaplan was a *baal teshuvah,* a latecomer to traditional Judaism. His brilliant mind enabled him to master traditional rabbinic, midrashic, and medieval sources very quickly, and his output was prolific. This small book is a very carefully reasoned defense of the traditional observance of Shabbat. It includes a fair gleaning of rabbinic explanations of various Shabbat concepts and practices. Anything by Aryeh Kaplan is, in my opinion, worth reading, whether one agrees with him or not.

Kaplan, Mordecai M. *The Meaning of God in Modern Jewish Religion.* New York: Reconstructionist Foundation, 1947. (See especially chap. 2, "God as the Power That Makes for Salvation.") Rabbi Mordecai Kaplan, late Professor of Theology at the Jewish Theological Seminary, was the founder of Reconstructionism, a new approach to Jewish life. This book is Kaplan's attempt to reinterpret each Jewish holy day and festival in terms of twentieth-century theology. He defines Shabbat as the day on which the importance of the person as a creative animal is recognized. An excellent introduction to Reconstructionist theology and, for those theologically oriented, a satisfying reinterpretation of how Shabbat can function for us today.

Millgram, Abraham Ezra. *The Day of Delight.* Philadelphia: Jewish Publication Society, 1965. One volume in a large series published by the Jewish Publication Society on Jewish holidays. This classic anthology of almost five hundred pages contains something for everyone. Sections include "The Sabbath in Practice," "Stories for Children," "Poems," "The Sabbath in the Synagogue," "The Oneg Shabbat," "Law of the Sabbath," "The Sabbath in Literature, Art, and Music," "The Sabbath in History," and a significant music supplement of one hundred pages.

Peli, Pinchas H. *Shabbat Shalom: A Renewed Encounter with the Sabbath.* Washington, DC: B'nai B'rith Books, 1988. Paperback ed.: *The Jewish Sabbath.* New York: Schocken Books, 1991. A recent work of theological and homiletic interpretation by one of Israel's leading adult-education experts and popular writers. Deals with the liturgical, historical, and philosophical aspects of Shabbat. Excellent.

Segal, Samuel M. *The Sabbath Book: A Treasury of Jewish Sabbath Thought through the Centuries.* New York: Thomas Yoseloff, 1957. A very good presentation of many aspects of Shabbat. Topics include Friday-night celebration, Shabbat day, Shabbat afternoon and evening, Shabbat legends, Shabbat in Jewish theology, Shabbat in the Kabbalah.

Siegel, Richard, Michael Strassfeld, and Sharon Strassfeld. *The Jewish Catalog.* Philadelphia: Jewish Publication Society, 1974. This wonderful how-to handbook has been a best-seller since it was published fifteen years ago and has a splendid chapter on

Shabbat, written under the guidance of the mystical philosophy of Rabbi Zalman Schachter-Shalomi of Philadelphia. It describes the "flow" of Shabbat, the changes of moods from Friday afternoon until Saturday night up until Havdalah. A very special description of what Shabbat can be for the deeply aware person.

Strassfeld, Michael. *A Shabbat Haggadah: For Celebration and Study.* New York: Institute of Human Relations Press/American Jewish Committee, 1981. This is an unusual little book by one of the authors of *The Jewish Catalog.* The book is divided into two sections. Part 1 is about the Erev Shabbat celebration, from candlelighting to Birkat Hamazon. Part 2 contains twelve units, each of which has a short reading from some well-known author (e.g., I. L. Peretz, Moses Maimonides, Abraham Joshua Heschel, Bernard Malamud, S. Y. Agnon). Each unit is followed by questions for discussion and questions for children.

Wolfson, Ron. *The Shabbat Seder.* Woodstock, VT: Jewish Lights Publishing, 1996. (Originally published by the Federation of Jewish Men's Clubs, 1985.) This student textbook describes the ten steps in learning how to observe Friday night at home. It contains abundant study material on the history, Halachah, ritual, background, and meaning of all the steps in making Friday night a beautiful family experience, from cleaning the house to lighting the candles, blessing the children to reciting the Kiddush, Hamotzi, and Birkat Hamazon. Comes with a small book to use at the Friday-night table and an audiocassette.

Wouk, Herman. *This Is My God.* Garden City, NY: Doubleday, 1959. An older book, but still a classic. Wouk's memoir is also an excellent introduction to Judaism. Take a look at chapter 4, "The Sabbath." Wouk's description of what Shabbat has meant to him personally and professionally is very moving.

Zborowski, Mark, and Elizabeth Herzog. *Life Is with People: The Culture of the Shtetl.* New York: Schocken Books, 1996. This is an excellent description of life in the European shtetl. It covers life-cycle events, holiday observance, and home life. Provides a lovely description of the meaning that Shabbat had for our ancestors.

2. On Shabbat in the Liturgy

Arzt, Max. *Joy and Remembrance: Commentary on the Sabbath Eve Liturgy.* Bridgeport, CT: Hartmore House, 1979. (See description above.)

Donin, Hayim Halevy. *To Pray as a Jew: A Guide to the Prayer Book and the Synagogue Service.* New York: Basic Books, 1980. The late Rabbi Donin, a graduate of the Isaac Elchanan Theological Seminary of Yeshiva University, served a congregation in Detroit before he retired and made *aliyah* to Israel. His book is very popular and is easy and comfortable to read. Some special chapters on Shabbat include "The Amidah for the Sabbath and Festivals," "Welcoming the Sabbath: Kabbalat Shabbat," and "Home Prayers for Sabbath and Festivals."

Elbogen, Ismar. *Jewish Liturgy: A Comprehensive History.* Philadelphia: Jewish Publication Society, 1993. This scholarly and comprehensive study of Jewish liturgy is considered the major work of Professor Elbogen, who was born in Germany in 1874 and died in America (where he immigrated in 1938) in 1943. The book was published in German in 1913 and until this new English translation appeared was available only in German and Hebrew. Rabbi Ismar Schorsch wrote of Professor Elbogen that he was "a great scholar of genuine religious passion [who] elegantly bridged the chasm between the study and the synagogue." While the entire book contains interesting material about the Shabbat liturgy, chapter 2, "Prayers for

Special Days," contains several sections devoted exclusively to the prayers, rituals, and ceremonies of Shabbat.

Garfiel, Evelyn. *The Service of the Heart: A Guide to the Jewish Prayer Book.* New York: Thomas Yoseloff, 1958. This popular guide to the Siddur includes five brief and interesting chapters on Shabbat (chaps. 11–15). Dr. Garfiel follows the systematic theology of her late husband, Professor Max Kaddushin of the Jewish Theological Seminary.

Goldstein, Rose. *A Time to Pray: A Personal Approach to the Jewish Prayer Book.* Bridgeport, CT: Hartmore House, 1972. Rose Goldstein, the late wife of Rabbi David A. Goldstein of Har Zion Temple in Penn Valley, Pennsylvania, taught classes on the Siddur to hundreds of women in her congregation's sisterhood and in the Women's League for Conservative Judaism. Rose Goldstein was a pious and learned woman who writes in the first person, describing the meaning and usefulness that the prayers have brought to her own spiritual life.

Hammer, Reuven. *Entering Jewish Prayer: A Guide to Personal Devotion and the Worship Service.* New York: Schocken Books, 1994. Rabbi Reuven Hammer is a modern Conservative rabbi who served congregations in America and then made *aliyah* to Israel. He now lives and teaches in Jerusalem. He is a fine educator and clear writer, who brings scholarly insight, clear interpretations, and complete descriptions of the Jewish liturgy. Chapter 11 gives a more complete description of the Shabbat liturgy, but other chapters describe very well many of the prayers that are included in both Shabbat and daily prayers.

Idelsohn, A. Z. *Jewish Liturgy and Its Development.* New York: HUC-JIR Sacred Music Press, 1932. An older scholarly work on the entire cycle of Jewish liturgy. The reader can learn much from the entire book, which includes prayers that are repeated daily and on Shabbat. There are two special chapters on Shabbat: "Sabbath Services" and "Sabbath Meditations and Songs (*zemiroth*) for the Home."

Jacobson, B. S. *The Sabbath Service: An Exposition and Analysis of Its Structure, Contents, Language, and Ideas.* Tel Aviv: Sinai Publishers, 1981. The late B. S. Jacobson had written a multivolume work on Jewish liturgy. This volume, the first of the series, is dedicated to the entire liturgy of Shabbat, from candlelighting, Kabbalat Shabbat, and Maariv on Friday night, through the entire Shabbat-morning service, up to Mincha and Havdalah. It is an indispensable resource for those who wish to delve deeply into the history and meaning of the Shabbat prayers.

Millgram, Abraham. *Jewish Worship.* Philadelphia: Jewish Publication Society, 1971. Rabbi Abraham Millgram was director of the Commission on Jewish Education of the United Synagogue of America until his retirement. He has been living in Jerusalem since 1963. This mammoth work of immense scholarship is well documented and written with scholarship and love. Chapter 7 deals with Shabbat liturgy, which is discussed in great detail with a special focus on its historical development.

Raphael, Chaim, ed. *The Sabbath Evening Service: With a New Translation and Commentary.* West Orange, NJ: Behrman House, 1985. A well-known British historian and writer, Chaim Raphael has enriched Jewish culture with many books about Jewish life and tradition. This commentary is simple, yet elegant, eloquent, and inspiring.

Rosenberg, Arnold S. *Jewish Liturgy as a Spiritual System.* Northvale, NJ: Jason Aronson, 1997. This book delves into the spiritual and poetic meanings of each prayer and ritual of the Jewish liturgy. There are lovely explanations of various Shabbat prayers and customs, including several well-documented and annotated meanings of Friday-night candles, Kiddush, challah, etc. It also offers midrashic meanings for all the regular evening, morning, and afternoon prayers in the Shabbat and general liturgy.

Schach, Stephen R. *The Structure of the Siddur.* Northvale, NJ: Jason Aronson, 1996. For those who like to understand the building blocks of the Shabbat liturgy through the use of charts, schematics, and carefully executed diagrams, graphs, and outlines, this book will provide the reader with a clear and well-organized understanding of the Shabbat prayers and the rest of the Siddur.

Sherman, Nosson, ed. *The Siddur: Translation, Commentary, and Overviews.* New York: Artscroll Mesorah Series, 1981. This collection is one of the commentaries in the well-known Artscroll series published by the Orthodox community. The short selections are chosen from a wide range of traditional commentators and medieval authorities. One of the special values of this collection is that full source references are provided for each quotation, so that the reader can become familiar with the names of the early giants of rabbinic and midrashic works. This commentary aims to inspire as well as inform.

3. For Young People and Families

Brin, Ruth F. *The Shabbat Catalog.* Hoboken, NJ: Ktav, 1978. An excellent collection for the home and the classroom. It includes eight stories for children, a series of dialogue/discussions for parents and children ages six to thirteen on creation, prayer, and Havdalah. Another section offers ideas for arts-and-crafts projects, games, and activities, such as making an embroidered challah cover, candlemaking, a Saturday-afternoon nature walk, and more. There is a ten-page unit on favorite Shabbat songs, with music, and another ten pages of recipes. Finally there is a section of Sabbath blessings and ceremonies, including a beautiful new "Wife's Reply to Ayshet Chayil," composed by the editor, Ruth F. Brin, who is also a talented poet and writer.

Garfinkel, Stephen, ed. *Slow Down and Live: A Guide to Shabbat Observance and Enjoyment.* New York: United Synagogue Youth, 1982. (Program guide.) This 125-page book, published by United Synagogue Youth for its membership, contains nine chapters divided into four major sections: (1) Themes and Concepts; (2) Sources and Resources; (3) Programs and Projects; (4) Ritual and Practice, including a practical guide to rituals, ceremonies, and songs. A well-rounded collection.

Isaacs, Ronald. *The Jewish Family Game Book: For the Sabbath and Festivals.* Hoboken, NJ: Ktav, 1989. This excellent little book of just over one hundred pages contains a varied collection of family games: twelve or so with Shabbat themes and another forty-five or so for the rest of the Jewish holidays. Very worthwhile for *shabbatonim* (weekend retreats), classroom, and especially for the Friday-night dinner table.

Jacobs, Louis. *The Book of Jewish Practice.* West Orange, NJ: Behrman House, 1987. This is an 8½ x 11 high school textbook, which includes chapters on Jewish life-cycle milestones and holidays. Chapter 11 covers the Sabbath. In the short space of seven pages, Dr. Jacobs, a leading Conservative rabbi and scholar in London, presents the highlights of Shabbat theology and practice.

4. For Children

(Gratitude is expressed to Susan Traub, Ralph Simon, and Roslyn Vanderbilt for their help in compiling this section.)

Abrams, Leah. *Because We Love Shabbat.* Cassette and book of music. Owings Mills, MD: Tara Publications, 1978. Songs, stories, and activities for young children and their families.

Aronin, Ben. *The Secret of the Sabbath Fish.* Philadelphia: Jewish Publication Society, 1978.

Bearman, Jane. *Good Shabbos.* New York: Union of American Hebrew Congregations, 1950.

Cardozo, Arlene Rossen. *Jewish Family Celebrations: The Sabbath, Festivals, and Ceremonials.* New York: St. Martin's Press, 1982.

Cedarbaum, Sophia. *The Sabbath: A Day of Delight.* New York: Union of American Hebrew Congregations, 1976. Young Danny and Debbie take readers along as they prepare for the very special day. Prayers and songs, foods, and traditions are presented in a lively way.

Chaikin, Miriam. *The Seventh Day: The Story of the Jewish Sabbath.* New York: Doubleday, 1980. When read aloud at family gatherings, the biblical cadence of the text and the stunning woodcut illustrations serve to enrich the celebration.

Charles, Freda. *The Mystery of the Missing Challah.* Middle Village, NY: Jonathan David, 1959. A charming mainstay picture book. Eight little sisters cooperate in the cleaning and cooking for Shabbat—but, alas, where is the all-important challah?

Cohen, Floreva G. *Before Shabbat Begins.* New York: New York Board of Jewish Education, 1985.

_____. *My Special Friend.* New York: New York Board of Jewish Education, 1986. Doren and his friend Jonathan (a special-needs child) participate in a Shabbat service.

Cone, Molly. *The Jewish Sabbath.* New York: Thomas Crowell Co., 1966. Shabbat is presented with clarity and warmth of language. Moving legends are retold about traditions that have been celebrated since biblical times.

Drucker, Malka. *Shabbat: A Peaceful Island.* New York: Holiday House, 1983. A comprehensive discussion of Shabbat for a wide audience. Information on customs, rituals, and historical events is included.

Emerman, Ellen. *Is It Shabbat Yet?* New York: HaCha Distributions, 1960. Malkie and her mommy joyfully prepare for and enjoy Shabbat.

Feinberg, Miriam. United Synagogue of America, Commission on Jewish Education, 1991. When Shabbat comes, a little house grows to accommodate the many guests.

Freehof, Lillian S. *Star Light Stories: Holiday and Sabbath Tales.* New York: Bloch Publishing, 1952.

Ganz, Yaffa. *Savta Simcha and the Incredible Shabbos Bag.* New York: Feldheim, 1980. Like a Jewish Mary Poppins, this lovable and zany woman brings the warmth of Shabbat sharing into the lives of all she meets.

Garvey, Robert. *Good Shabbos Everybody.* New York: United Synagogue, 1951. Little Mimmy's excitement mounts as she helps her mother prepare for the Sabbath before her father walks in the door.

Gellman, Ellie. *Shai's Shabbat Walk*. Rockville, MD: Kar-Ben Copies, 1985.

Gottlieb, Yaffa. *A Thousand Guests for Shabbos*. New York: Torah Aura Publications, 1984. Who is welcome at the Shabbat table of Abner Quim? A youth imagines in zany fashion the kind of Shabbat he will keep when he is grown.

Groner, Judy, and Madeline Wikler. *Shabbat Shalom*. Rockville, MD: Kar-Ben Copies, 1988. A wordless boardbook conveys the joy of celebrating Shabbat.

Hirsh, Marilyn. *Joseph Who Loved the Sabbath*. New York: Viking, 1986. An energetic retelling of a Jewish folktale for all ages. Joseph's hard work and observance of Shabbat bring him unexpected joy and good fortune.

Kahn, Katherine Janus. *Shabbat Fun for Little Hands*. Rockville, MD: Kar-Ben Copies, 1992. A simple activity book including games and projects for Shabbat.

Klaperman, Libby M. *Adam and the First Sabbath*. New York: Behrman House, 1953.

Klein, Joyce. *The Shabbat Book: A Weekly Guide for the Whole Family*. Scopus Films, 1994. A child-oriented summary of each week's *parashah*.

Kobre, Faige. *A Sense of Shabbat*. Los Angeles: Torah Aura Productions, 1989. A lovely introduction to the special tastes, sights, and smells of Shabbat.

Kress, Camille. *Tot Shabbat*. New York: UAHC Press, 1997. Attractively illustrated boardbook shares the sensory experience of a family's preparation for Shabbat.

Leah, Devorah. *Lost Erev Shabbos in the Zoo*. New York: Judaica Press, 1983. In large colorful pictures, a brother and sister find their way from the zoo to home, just in time to welcome the Sabbath.

Lipson, Ruth. *Shabbos Is Coming*. New York: Feldheim Publishers, 1985.

Lubavich Women's Organization. *A Candle of My Own*. New York: Lubavich Women's Organization, 1979. A collection of girls' thoughts on lighting Shabbat candles.

Manuskin. *Starlight and Candles: The Joys of the Sabbath*. New York: Simon and Schuster for Young Readers, 1995. Jake and Rosy help to celebrate Shabbat, their favorite day.

Miller, Deborah. *Poppy Seeds Too*. Rockville, MD: Kar-Ben Copies, 1982. What doesn't go into this challah? A witty rhyme makes this a fun story to share with little ones.

Rosman, Steven. *The Bird of Paradise and Other Sabbath Stories*. New York: UAHC Press, 1994. A collection of Jewish stories—both original and adaptations based on the weekly portions of the Torah.

Saypol, Judith. *Come, Let Us Welcome Shabbat*. Rockville, MD: Kar-Ben Copies, 1984. An attractive oversize paperback that introduces the young family to the customs of Shabbat.

Scharfstein, Sol. *Shabbat Pop-Up Book*. Hoboken, NJ: Ktav, 1986.

_____. *See, Smell, and Touch Shabbat*. Hoboken, NJ: Ktav, 1986.

Schlein, Miriam. *Shabbat*. West Orange, NJ: Behrman House, 1983.

Schur, Maxine Rose. *A Jewish Sabbath in Ethiopia*. New York: Dial Books for Young Readers, 1994. A young Ethiopian boy and his family make preparations for Shabbat.

Schwartz, Amy. *Mrs. Moskowitz and the Sabbath Candlesticks*. Philadelphia: Jewish Publication Society, 1983. When Mrs. Moskowitz moves from her home to an apartment, she is filled with family memories. When old candlesticks are unpacked and polished, the magic begins for children of any age.

Schwartz, Howard, and Barbara Rush. *The Sabbath Lion: A Jewish Folktale from Algeria*. New York: HarperCollins, 1992. A young boy, with the protection of a lion, keeps the Sabbath on a journey across the desert.

Schweigger-Dmi'el, Itzhak. *Hanna's Sabbath Dress*. New York: Simon and Schuster, 1996. When Hanna helps an old man and her Sabbath dress gets dirty, she is afraid her mother will be upset.

Sidi, Smadar Shir. *Sabbath A–Z*. New York: Adama Books, 1989. The many aspects of Shabbat, described through the Hebrew alphabet.

Simon, Norma. *Every Friday Night*. New York: United Synagogue, 1961. With brief, poetic text, Simon's book emphasizes how young children celebrate Shabbat.

Snyder, Carol. *God Must Like Cookies, Too*. Philadelphia: Jewish Publication Society, 1993. A young girl and her grandmother attend Friday-night services together.

Sol, Robert. *A Wonderful Shabbos*. Hoboken, NJ: Ktav, 1961.

Swartz, Daniel. *Bim and Bom: A Shabbat Tale*. Rockville, MD: Kar-Ben Copies, 1996. Bim and her brother Bom work all week and then joyfully meet to celebrate Shabbat together.

Topek, Susan Remick. *A Holiday for Noah*. Rockville, MD: Kar-Ben Copies, 1990. Noah loves Shabbat—a special "challah" day in school.

Weilerstein, Sadie Rose. *Dick: The Horse That Kept the Sabbath*. New York: Bloch Publishing Co., 1955.

_____. *Molly and the Sabbath Queen*. West Orange, NJ: Behrman House, 1949.

Wikler, Madeline, and Judy Groner. *Shabbat Shalom*. Rockville, MD: Kar-Ben Copies, 1988.

Zim, Sol. *The Joy of Shabbos Songbook: Original Hasidic Melodies*. Owings Mills, MD: Tara Publications, 1978.

_____. *More Joy of Shabbos Songbook: Original Hasidic Melodies*. Owings Mills, MD: Tara Publications, 1984.

Zwerin, Raymond. *Shabbat Can Be*. New York: UAHC Press, 1979. This large, brightly illustrated picture book presents the idea that Shabbat can be many things, all of which hold joy and delight.

5. Curricular Materials

Grishaver, Joel Lurie. *Shabbat*. From the "Building Jewish Life" series. Los Angeles: Torah Aura Productions, 1990. These materials support a partnership between the Jewish classroom and the Jewish home. *Shabbat* includes background, activities, stories, and prayers in short chapters on Preparing for Shabbat, Welcoming Shabbat, Shabbat Day, and Ending Shabbat. The text conveys the values and wisdom Shabbat holds for modern life. (Ages 5–8)

Herman, Dorothy C. *The Joy of Shabbat*. Miami: CAJE Publications, 1989. A curriculum designed to involve students and parents in a meaningful Shabbat experience of learning, sharing a Shabbat dinner, and worshiping together. Includes experiences in Bible, music, art, prayer, and cooking. Each lesson is detailed so that even the novice teacher would feel comfortable.

Ross, Lillian. *Shabbat: The Fourth Commandment*. Miami: CAJE, 1989. This manual is designed to reflect the primacy of Shabbat in the life of the Jewish people. It includes materials on Shabbat's history and background, as well as items on the link between Shabbat and creation, the *havurah*, and worship. There are teaching strategies for all levels, from primary through upper grades, and its emphasis is on diverse classroom techniques. Included are games, songs, crafts, dances, and other activities.

Shabbat Placemat. Miami: CAJE, 1989. Illustrated games.

"The Sabbath." *Keeping Posted* (November 1981) 27:2. A special eight-page additional section in the "Leader's Edition" is included.